THEY SHALL
TAKE UP
SERPENTS

GRANT
WACKER

⟩ THEY SHALL
TAKE UP
SERPENTS

PSYCHOLOGY OF
THE SOUTHERN SNAKE-HANDLING CULT

Weston La Barre
With a New Introduction by the Author

SCHOCKEN BOOKS · NEW YORK

FOR

Dr. George Caverno Ham

THE BEST HUNTING PARTNER

A FELLOW EVER HAD

First SCHOCKEN PAPERBACK edition 1969

Third Printing, 1976

Published by arrangement with the University of Minnesota Press
Copyright © 1962 by the University of Minnesota
Introduction Copyright © 1969 by Weston La Barre
Library of Congress Catalog Card No. 71-91547
Manufactured in the United States of America

THANKS are due the following for permission to use copyrighted materials:
Steed Rollins of the *Durham Morning Herald* (quotations on pages 26–27,
38); John R. Barry, *Durham Sun* (quotation on page 153 and photographs); J. S. Riley, *Bristol Herald Courier* (quotation on page 45); Ben
Karpman, *Archives of Criminal Psychodynamics* (quotations on pages
143–146 from Walter Bromberg's "The Psychopathic Personality Concept
Re-Evaluated," and Carlos J. Dalmau's "Psychopathy and Psychopathic
Behavior: A Psychoanalytic Approach"); William Alanson White Psychiatric Foundation, Inc., and *Psychiatry* (quotation on page 153 from Talcott Parsons' "Certain Primary Sources and Patterns of Aggression in the
Social Structure of the Western World"); and Dr. William Sargant and
the Royal Society of Medicine (pictures published in the *Proceedings of
the Royal Society of Medicine*).

Table of Contents

Introduction to the Paperback Edition   vii

The Cult

1 THE PRESENT AND RECENT PAST   3
2 ORIGINS AND EARLY HISTORY   11
3 PUBLICITY AND PERSECUTION   24
4 THE INTERSTATE CONVENTION   34
5 LATER HISTORY AND SPREAD   44

The Symbolism

6 SNAKE CULTS IN AFRICA   53
7 CLASSIC NEAR EAST CULTS   65
8 RELIGION AND PSYCHIATRY   88

The People

9   BIOGRAPHY OF A CULT LEADER   113
10 PSYCHOLOGY OF A SNAKE CULTIST   126
11 PSYCHOPATHY AND CULTURE   140
12 BAREFOOT AND THE POOR WHITES   163
    ACKNOWLEDGMENTS   179
    NOTES   183
    INDEX   199

photographs between pages 36 and 37

Introduction to the Paperback Edition

IN TIMES OF acute unrest and upheaval like our own, we may well seek, as compass and guide, some knowledge and understanding of historic parallels to our mood, whether in the past or among other peoples. The numbed anomie, the helpless puzzlement and directionless acedia of our day resemble nothing so much as the "Hellenistic despair" and "failure of nerve" in the late-classic Greeks. Indeed the endless Viet-Nam War, as destructive to democratic process at home as it is to decency abroad, parallels uncannily the conscienceless adventure under the psychopathic Alcibiades overseas to Sicily, that unstaunchable wound to morale in the slow decay of Athens during the long Peloponnesian War. And, given a massive difference in scale and in technological efficiency, sickening slaughter in the tiny tributary island of Melos left Athenians with as little pride and trust in their own probity as reflective Americans can feel now after Hiroshima and Viet-Nam. The Washington letters of I. F. Stone depict the same misuse and abuse of naked power with the same cool insight and clear moral perception that infuse the mixed pity, contempt, cold indignation and dismay of the greatest historian of them all, Athenian Thucydides, when he saw his great city stumbling into chaos and moral death.

Again, swift technological change in our society is alike in kind, psychologically, to the acculturative stress and culture shock felt by primitive societies when they are overwhelmed by the juggernaut of change. We now fear what we ourselves do. The dread of invasion by men from Mars is, quite clinically, a phobia, a projected paranoid fear directly akin to our own imperialist "conquest of space" with barely disguised military-nationalist motives, at a time when many would prefer bread to the circuses provided us. Now as in the past, men wander on a darkling plain where ignorant armies clash by night. It is a time ripe for vast and violent, mindless and blindly anti-adaptive social movements, of which Goldwaterism and Wallace-ism have given us sufficient foretaste.

In earlier America, know-nothing religious reactionism often came out of rural upstate New York. Still later, the concentration there of retired old rural people, hoarding their life savings and anxiously awaiting the blank enigma of death, have made exploitative crisis cults endemic in southern California. Still more recently, the forgotten people of backwoods Appalachia, last stronghold of country innocence and archaic religiosity, have debouched onto the industrialized Piedmont of coastal states in the New South. It was among these latter displaced and naïve bucolic folk, undergoing profound culture shock and bewilderingly rapid social change, that there rose in the late 1940's and the early 1950's the zany and dangerous snake-handling cult of our present study.*

The plan of this book is simple and three-fold. First I have described the ethnography and the historic spread of the snake-handling cult. Secondly, the cultural "prehistory" of the modern movement is shown, in the only anthropologically sound

* Snake handling still barely survives, at this writing, near Big Stone Gap in Virginia and at Scrabble Creek in West Virginia. See my interpretative article on "The Snake-Handling Sect of the Southeast," in Edgar Thompson and Samuel Hill (eds.), *The Bible Belt in Continuity and Change,* in press, 1969. The ethnography is summarized in "The Snake-Handling Cult of the American Southeast," in Ward Goodenough (ed.), *Explorations in Cultural Anthropology: Essays in Honor of George Peter Murdock* (New York: McGraw-Hill, 1964, pp. 309-333). A fine documentary movie on the "Holy Ghost People" was filmed at the Scrabble Creek snake-handling meetings in 1967 by Peter Adair with Dr. Nathan Gerrard as consultant, produced by Blair Boyd and distributed by Contemporary Films & McGraw-Hill, Publishers.

way, in the Old World symbolisms of the snake in biblical and nearby lands that have preceded historically, and in direct cultural continuity, this fundamentalist cult of the Bible Belt. And, finally, I have tried to bring home the psychological immediacy of belief and practice through a careful clinical study of the biography of a prominent snake-handling minister of the cult. History and meaning in society, culture, and individual are thus successively told.

Snake handling is a typical "crisis cult" such as I have multiply exampled in my book on *The Ghost Dance* (in press) —and with a little moral imagination and intellectual self-discernment the sophisticated reader may see in it some edifying parallels to his own existentialist predicament. One may feel pity and compassion, as one must in every contemplation of bewildered men, and yet know where one stands ethically and intellectually himself. And even in the midst of threatening disaster, one may at least still strive to understand.

WESTON LA BARRE

April, 1969

} *THE CULT*

CHAPTER 1

The Present and Recent Past

IT IS a hot night toward the end of July in a southern textile-mill town. In the middleclass part of town people sit on their porches drinking cokes or iced lemonade, quietly sweating and fanning themselves in a desultory fashion in the breathless air. From time to time someone remarks again, unhopefully, about the one topic — the relentless heat and the length of time the tobacco land has been without rain. A block away a jalopy full of highschool children careens around a corner, going nowhere much too fast in the hot night. Except for such occasional louder noises there are only the low murmur of voices from the darkened porches up and down the street, the slow rasp somewhere of a porch swing, the unreasonably cheerful steady orchestra of crickets, and the inter-mittent angrier protests of a cicada. Westward — must be several counties out toward the mountains — there is soundless heat light-ning, but that is sure enough too far away to do this dry Piedmont section any good.

But down by the tracks of the Southern Railroad there are other signs of human life. On the corner diagonally across from the back end of the Sears Roebuck store, across the street from the Discount House, and down a bit from the Alcoholics Anonymous place, is the Zion Tabernacle. This is a plain one-room frame building, from which comes the warm-up singing of a church service just starting. The Tabernacle is a block behind Main Street, on the last street south before the railroad tracks, beyond which stretches "Haiti" (pronounced *Hay'-tye*), the local Negro section. Eastward are ware-houses, lumberyards, and nondescript businesses, and beyond that the white laboring-class section of town.

Many of the church members are already clapping, humming, and singing to guitar music. Most of them are whites who work in the cotton mill, in the tobacco plant, or for the Wright Machinery Company. The majority of the men wear their shirt sleeves folded loosely once upward above the wrist, but some wear shortsleeved sports shirts with their cheap cotton pants. The women have on standard ready-to-wear store dresses, of vivid cotton print or a quieter single color. Not counting the babies, the people present range from about seven to eighty years of age; children too old to be carried and those under seven have been left elsewhere, lest they be too great a bother to adults intent on their own emotional interests.

The minister begins his talk by stating that his first allegiance is to God. Holding up a white handkerchief striped with red and blue, he tells the following story: "I was on my way to visit a sick boy in Greensboro, and I was in such a hurry that I forgot my handker-chief. Because I felt that I would need one, I stopped along the way to buy it. When I reached my destination, Hettie, the Negro who usually prays with us — I like Hettie, don't you? — well, Hettie, she handed me a handkerchief. Now wasn't that phenomenal that Hettie should have thought that I needed a handkerchief? The other day when I took this handkerchief from my drawer, do you know what it reminded me of? Of this country; it's not what it used to be. More and more it's clamping down on religious freedom."

The minister continues: he thinks all people should have the right to worship as they wish. He plans to get as many names as possible in order to petition the state government to pass a religious freedom law. He would even go to the local Methodist divinity school and ask the students to sign this petition. One of these days, the fact that he had been denied religious freedom would be written up in the library at the state capitol. In years to come, people will be able to look back and see where religious rights were first being denied. He is glad that he lives in this country — it's still a nice place to live — but he owes his allegiance to no one nation, only to God.

The guitar-playing begins again, with the minister loudly leading the others into song. The verses are about the nature of heaven, "of a heaven where white, black, yellow, and brown can live and be happy together." At the end of the song, the minister adds that God loves all his children, no matter what color they are. The topic changes to his current problems with the police and a threatened jail sentence. He tells of the troubles his people are having in Tennessee and in Virginia, across the border in Georgia, and in North Carolina where they arrested a minister the previous winter. He speaks of two "brethern" up there who are already in jail for their religious beliefs. Some churches send their missionaries to foreign countries, but he is proud that his brethren would carry their mission to the prisoners. People may think that these incidents will divide the group, but instead it is bringing them closer and closer together.

The minister asks one of the men sitting on the platform to read from the Bible a passage ending, "And the man of righteousness will come with healing on his wings." The minister expands on the topic. Then two testimonies are announced, to be given by visitors from Chattahoochee. One, a pleasant-looking man of about thirty-five, says that he had had nervousness and trouble with his sleeping. But ever since last Sunday when the Reverend had prayed for him, all his troubles have disappeared. After him, his brother, in a high-pitched woman's voice, reports that he had had a cancer in his stomach and had hardly been eating anything. Since last Sunday, when the preached blessed him and prayed for him, he has been able to eat everything and has had no pain. If no one believes that, he says, they can ask Dr. Lassiter in Tallahassee or they can call Stone General Hospital.

The preacher takes over again, saying that several people who had heard about him through the widespread publicity he had been receiving in the local papers have been writing him about his healing powers. He continues, speaking rapidly. "Every man carries his death wish with him, but if we have faith in God, we can prolong that Death. I have one sister in a sanitorium, two sisters under the grave, a father who died of a goiter on his neck, and when I was young I had TB. But look at me now! Glory be to God! Praise

God! I don't believe the day will come when all men can be healed, because all men don't have faith. But I do believe that one of these days my hands will be able to heal. Maybe I won't be able to heal everyone. I can't heal people if they don't have faith. Even Jesus could not heal everyone. Faith is necessary! Glory be to God."

The next song is again about the life in heaven. About a fourth of those present join in with the words; others clap their hands and hum. The children especially seem to enjoy themselves, clapping and singing along very happily. The preacher says, "I once heard that I had to wait until I got to heaven until I had a happy life, but I can't wait that long! Heaven can be right now on this earth. I can live a happy life right now! Praise be to God." His manner of speaking is odd:* there are exaggerated intonations in the narrative, with unexpected rises and falls; but when he comes to phrases like "Praise the Lord," which one might expect would be uttered with some emphasis or emotion, he says these flatly, like punctuation, or like a hasty tic as he draws breath between sentences. The congregation puts far more feeling into these same phrases when they utter them.

More singing. The guitar music and singing gradually become louder. One man standing beside the woman guitarist shouts and sings even more loudly than the others present. Between fifteen and twenty women begin to have shaking reactions; it is hard to tell how many there are because the violence of the shaking differs in degree. At least ten women are jerking their heads and bodies around wildly. Of these, several stand up from the benches where

* Olmsted has characterized with elegance and discretion the "old timey" style of preaching. "Without often being violent in his manner, the speaker nearly all the time cried aloud at the utmost stretch of his voice, as if calling to some one a long distance off . . . The speaker, presently, was crying aloud, with a mournful, distressed, beseeching shriek, as if he was himself suffering torture . . . Those who refused to kneel, were addressed as standing on the brink of the infernal pit, into which the diabolical divinity was momentarily on the point of satisfying the necessities of his character by hurling them off . . . I can only judge from the fact that those I saw the next morning were so hoarse that they could scarcely speak, that the religious exercises they most enjoy are rather hard upon the lungs, whatever their effect may be upon the soul" (Frederick L. Olmsted, "A Journey in the Seaboard Slave States in the Years 1853–54" [2 vols., New York: Putnam] in H. Becker [ed.], *Societies Around the World*, New York: Holt, 1956, 555–567, pp. 561–562).

[6

most of the women sit. Several of them perform a vivacious dance which looks something like jitterbugging in the fast movements, but with more rapid and extreme jerkings of the body. Others stand with their heads and bodies shaking, their heads forward and their necks jerking. Two men also begin dancing around, one of them a very small and meek-looking man who drives a laundry truck on a route on the west side of town.

Suddenly the minister begins to speak in unknown tongues. Others answer him in the same style. This language is quite unlike the tobacco auctioneers' chant, which has a singing change of pitch especially at the beginning and end of the monotone rapid nonsense syllables. Speaking in tongues is better described as a loud chattering at breakneck speed. The dancing continues, now both on the platform and below it. In many the shaking reaction and other bodily movements seem beyond the control of the trance-eyed individuals experiencing them; most of the women in this state have their eyes closed and their mouths open, even when not vocalizing. One woman who appears especially dazed, though no longer jerking, is hardly able to find her way back to her seat.

The music having quieted down, a woman who had been shaking and dancing rises and says, "Praise the Lord! All these people here don't know what it is like to love the Lord, but there is nothing like it! If you love the Lord, you love everybody: blacks, whites, yellows, and even your enemies. I wish I could show you how to love the Lord, but it is something you'll have to find out for yourselves." As the service grows somewhat quieter, the preacher assures everyone of the importance of praying to God in a way meaningful to the individual.

He continues, saying that he had planned to bring a snake tonight, but had decided not to because the snake looked sick. He could bring only one at a time now so that the police would not get all their snakes. Next week he planned to go to the mountains for some new ones. He then asks if there is anyone who wants to handle snakes tonight. Only one woman lifts a hand. "See!" he continues, "We can have a good time without snakes. Someone once asked me if we worshiped the snake. No! We surely do not! The snake represents evil, the Devil. We just show that God, good, has power over the Devil. You know, I don't advise anyone to handle snakes! In fact, no one should unless he has the feeling and faith that makes him want to do so."

The preacher requests the guitarist to sing the "Sampson song." It is in lively ballad form and tells the story of Samson and Delilah. At the end of the song, the preacher tells a story about a young boy who revealed to his mother that because Samson had laid his head in Delilah's lap, he had lost all his power. "The mother thought that her son had told her an evil story, but it wasn't! The head is the part of the body that has made man a higher animal. We shouldn't trust our head in anyone's lap but God's! Glory be to God!" He then talks about marriage laws. He had once written the state attorney general asking him if, as a preacher, he could perform his own marriage. "The attorney general didn't think so, but I sure did. No, I didn't get married then — won't tell you why! But I still think that a man has the right to conduct his own marriage service!"

More music and song. An attractive woman leaves her seat to go to the center of the tabernacle where she kneels and prays. After a few minutes the minister says, "You should pray to God any way that you like. If you still don't feel free, pray any way that you can, until you do. It doesn't matter where we kneel. The trouble with most of us is that we don't pray enough when we're alone, but if anyone has the desire to kneel and pray now, go right ahead!"

Several other women follow the first one to the front of the church where they all pray together. The preacher leaves the platform to come among his listeners. "I want to shake everyone's hand! Everyone stand! I want to be friends with you all. If you feel that you have the need to pass on to the front and pray, you go right ahead! But if you just want me to pray for you, come and shake my hand!" Many people come forth, stretching to the center aisle to shake his hand. About twenty women have now joined the first kneeling woman, many of them sobbing and crying out, a few shaking. The song and music end. Gradually the women straggle back to their seats. One boy about fifteen, who had also knelt to pray and had apparently been crying, gets up and stands close to the preacher. Slowly everyone leaves, with much enthusiastic conversation, and the service is ended.

This is not like it was last month, before snake-handling was forbidden by the town authorities. Surely troubled times have fallen upon the people, for now they cannot practice the religion they believe the Bible enjoins upon them. At that earlier time, when the observer entered the Tabernacle there was already a mood of general excitement. Several people were fondling rattlesnakes and copperheads with apparent confidence. One deacon of the church twisted a snake around his head and arm and held the snake's head close to or just brushing his mouth. About twenty or thirty people were shaking violently. Many were dancing around, either alone or with others, some with persons of the same sex and others with persons of the opposite sex. Some were sobbing, shouting, and singing. A visiting minister did most of the preaching. He spoke dramatically, stressing the more spectacular aspects of the religion, such as faith cures and snake-handling. He loudly proclaimed that he believed every word in the Bible to be true. His sermon led into a healing ceremony which he, the local minister, and one of the latter's followers conducted in a somewhat unorganized manner.

As many men and women — but mostly women — came forward, the preachers and the other man grasped the heads of these communicants between the palms of their hands, repeated jumbled and at times incoherent words to them, and supported those who fell stiffly into their arms. With several women the local minister spent considerable time on the healing process. One young woman asked him to bless her foot, which had been giving her much trouble and pain. He asked her to remove her shoe. Then, while he held her foot in his hands and looked straight into her eyes, he encouraged her to have faith that her foot would be cured. He repeated his plea many times, emphasizing the importance of faith in the powers of God and in the many miracles that God could perform. After this, another woman, with a child in her arms, asked the preacher to bless and cure the child. Before he began, he asked the father to come forward, but only the mother was present. He then told her the importance of caring for the child and of showing the child the ways of the Lord. He pleaded with the mother to have faith in God and to do everything in her power to help her child get well. "With faith will come help," he said to her in a gentle and quiet but impressive voice.

Throughout the service the level of excitement was extremely high. The deacon's mother-in-law shouted, "This is the kind of thing we need more of!" A young woman in a dark suit-dress lay slightly twisted on her back upon the floor, the thumb of her half-opened right hand at her mouth, the left hand clasped at her turned-aside neck. The local preacher placed his left hand on her forehead, his right hand on her pubic region. Another woman lay flat on her back while he knelt on one knee and apparently massaged her throat. Still another, lying on her left side, he stroked on the shoulder with his left hand while he grasped the outside of her right thigh with his right hand. A plump girl in a black dress with a rhinestoned white collar, her eyes closed and mouth open in an expression half painful and half ecstatic, he held by both hands for a while; then she slid to the floor, her pelvis twisted downward, while the preacher held her right hand up in his left one and pressed her armpit with his right hand.

At one time there was a cluster of four middleaged men, two clasped in each other's arms, each weeping on the other's shoulder, while two other men stood, one behind and the other half behind, their left hands one atop the other on the shoulder of one of the embracing men. During part of the healing ceremony a young woman collapsed into the preacher's arms, where she remained stiff for several minutes. As she was coming out of her trance, the preacher began to speak of the wonders of a religion in which such phenomena could take place without there being the least intention of carnal desires. At least four men and four women handled snakes in this meeting. This time a young man accordionist supplied the musical accompaniment.

The service ended with shouting after the healing ceremony ceased.

CHAPTER 2

Origins and Early History

O N E hot day in the summer of 1909, in rural Grasshopper Valley, Tennessee, George Went Hensley, a short powerfully built man in his early thirties, was pondering in his mind a text from the Bible. The text was from Mark XVI, verses 17 and 18, which read as follows: *16 : 17 - 18*

And these signs shall follow them that believe: In my name shall they cast out devils; they shall speak with new tongues;

They shall take up serpents; and if they drink any deadly thing, it shall not hurt them; they shall lay hands on the sick, and they shall recover.

These words, spoken by Jesus after the Resurrection and immediately before the Ascension, were a command, Hensley felt, which he was bound to obey and to test out.* The more he thought about it, the more he felt he must put his faith to the test. So he climbed White Oak Mountain, which rims Grasshopper Valley on the east, and after some hunting found a large rattlesnake in a rocky gap. A few days later he began his evangelical work: in a religious meeting

---

* In all conscience, however, Higher Criticism must point out that both the Old and the New Testaments contain texts which might seem to argue *against* the handling of snakes. Ecclesiastes x, 11, states that "Surely the serpent will bite without enchantment; and a babbler is no better" — thus appearing to discourage both snake-handling and speaking in tongues. Even more to the point would seem the warning of St. Paul in I Corinthians x, 9, "Neither let us tempt Christ, as some of them also tempted, and were destroyed of serpents." As may be seen later, both statements were injunctions against ancient snake-handling.

at Sale Creek he cited these Bible texts and thrust the rattlesnake at the people for them to take up and thereby prove their faith.

In this sparsely settled region of Tennessee his converts were necessarily few, but in time they numbered as many as several score. They met in members' houses or in improvised brush shelters. They carried their Bibles and their snakes to meeting, chanted, spoke in tongues, prayed, and suffered ecstatic seizures. After nearly ten years of such meetings, one of the members, Garland Defriese, was bitten during a service by a large rattlesnake and fell to the ground, it is said with the rattler's fangs still fastened in his flesh. He recovered after a few weeks, but the incident aroused considerable commotion among the faithful, and the practice of snake-handling went into a state of suspended animation. But the more ardent of the cultists settled the theological problem involved by denouncing Defriese as a backslider.

Although snake-handling meetings stopped at Sale Creek in Grasshopper Valley, Hensley took his cult elsewhere with some success. He later became pastor of the East Pineville Church of God, and also introduced snake-handling at the Church of God at Pine Mountain, about seventeen miles from Harlan, Kentucky. In 1934, J. D. Browning, a ruddy-faced and pleasant-mannered man in early middle age, became pastor at Pine Mountain and shortly afterward re-introduced snake-handling. The Church of God perches on the steep wooded slope of Pine Mountain and was built by the volunteer labor of members on land donated by one of their number. It is an unpainted frame structure; inside are split log benches, the pulpit being merely a plain board on long legs placed at the edge of a platform stretching across one end of the building. The forty adult members are mostly poor farmers. Browning is an unordained minister and receives no pay; he farms fifty hillside acres nearby. He holds no monopoly, moreover, on the preaching: anyone in the congregation may stand up behind the pulpit and preach as the spirit moves him.

The Church of God of Pine Mountain is an independent fundamentalist "holy roller" church. Its communicants believe that the Holy Spirit confers supernatural gifts, such as the ability to speak in tongues and to heal by prayer, the laying on of hands, and anointing with oil. The sect forbids theater-going, dancing, smoking, drinking, immodest dress, and the cutting of women's hair. They call each other "saints" and the men kiss one another in greeting.[1] Browning thought in 1938 that his was the only church in which all the members handled snakes. Snakes, supplied by "unbelievers," were kept only about a month, because they grew sick if held in captivity any longer.

In the summer of 1938, a farmer named John Day, whose wife was a member of the cult, brought suit against three members of the Pine Mountain Church. He disliked snakes and objected to his wife's handling them. The three cultists were arrested for breach of the peace, but in the trial at Harlan they were all acquitted. The trial was reported by the Associated Press, whereupon the editor of *Pictures*, the rotogravure section of the St. Louis *Post-Dispatch*, sent Arthur Whitman, a staff photographer, and Keith Kerman, a reporter, to investigate the snake-handling religion further. Ker- *1942* man's report, although brief, is the earliest informed journalistic account of any consequence.[2] He described a meeting of about seventy-five men, women, and children at the Pine Mountain Church at which snakes were handled. Cymbals, tambourines, foot-stamping, and hand-clapping provided the rhythm for the worshipers who, men and women both, passed serpents from hand to hand while jerking violently all over their bodies. One man thrust a snake before a seated woman holding a baby; the woman smiled, and the baby gravely reached forward and touched the snake. A dark-haired timberman opened the mouth of one rattler to show its intact fangs to the visitors; another man showed the scars of at least three bites on his hand and arm.* Whitman's pictures accompanying Kerman's

* The commonest question that arises regarding ritual snake-handling is the surprisingly small number of fatalities. To lead readers to their own answer to this question, I cite Klauber, the undoubted authority on the rattlesnake. He considers (2:788) the eastern diamondback (*Crotalus adamanteus*) the most poisonous United States rattler in that it produces the highest percentage of deaths, because of its size and high venom delivery, though the venom is not a strong one for rattlers (the venom of elapine snakes in Asia, Africa, and Australia is more dangerous); perhaps its presence in more highly populated eastern agricultural regions may account for the larger number of bites reported. But the western diamondback is perhaps

text show an open-shirted, gallused, balding middleaged man with two rattlesnakes around his neck and a copperhead over his head; and, again, Sherman Lawson, a younger gallused man, his dark shirt open at the neck, holding the same snakes together in both hands over his head and crying out with a pleased smile as two older men look on approvingly. The snake-handling lasted about half an hour, but the service went on for an hour more. To the singing of such songs as "Jesus is Getting Us Ready for the Great Day," several female communicants, "Eyes shut, hands waving . . . moved their feet in a rhythmic step and wheeled slowly in backward circles. Frequently their bodies would jerk as if the spine were being snapped like a whip. Some of the men also performed this jerk." [3] Fire-handling by male saints was also performed: their hands, held in the flames of a kerosene torch and a miner's acetylene lamp, were blackened by smoke but otherwise appeared unhurt. [4] G. W. Hensley, the founder of the cult, was present at this meeting.

responsible for more serious bites than all other rattlers in the United States combined, because of its plentifulness in the large area of its range and its more powerful though smaller quantity of venom than the eastern diamond-back. Reassuringly, Klauber writes (2:907) that "the fatalities from this cause [rattlesnake bite] for the entire United States, with a population of over 160 million, seldom exceed 30 per year. Of every 100 people bitten by rattle-snakes, only about 3 will die." The chance of being bitten by a rattler in the United States, he calculates, is about 1 in 160,000; of being bitten fatally, fewer than 1 in 5,000,000. The moccasin is *not* more dangerous than the rattlesnake, despite its reputation, though its coldblooded prey is less susceptible than warmblooded prey (2:823); one authority states that the copperhead (closely related phylogenetically to the moccasin) rarely gives a fatal bite, because of its short fangs and meager venom supply.

I am convinced that, in all good faith, the snake cultists *never* "doctor" their specimens by defanging, milking the venom, sewing up the mouth, or the like. And despite Klauber's careful and sober remarks, surely the intentional and repeated handling of the reptiles must increase the statistical chances of one's being bitten and bitten fatally. Klauber (1:379) considers that some species of rattler may be "tamed" in the sense of becoming accustomed to gentle handling without striking, but sudden fright still makes them dangerous. Snake cultists, however, replace their snakes frequently (since snakes are unexpectedly delicate and fragile animals), so that training can scarcely be a major explanation for their not being bitten often, all the more so since the small and extremely simple brain of the snake would seem insusceptible of training by even the most patient and sentimental human. So far as responsiveness to the human voice or "charming" by music are concerned, the ancient Hebrews had already long ago correctly noted that all snakes are stone deaf (Psalms LVIII, 4) and hear no sounds whatever.

Indeed, the early sporadic appearances of the cult appear always to be associated with Hensley and his immediate followers. After he left Tennessee, following the accident to Garland Defriese, Hensley had kept the religion alive in Kentucky. More than forty years after the accident, in the late spring of 1943, an earlier convert of Hensley, a snake-handling preacher from Kentucky named Raymond Hays, came to Grasshopper Valley with a box of rattlesnakes and copperheads. He preached at a revival meeting to the people — many of whom remembered the practices of years back, which had gradually been abandoned after Defriese's accident. This revival meeting in the place where the snake-handling religion originated, is of historical importance to the survival and diffusion of the cult. The revival of faith was signalized by the building of a new church, "The Dolley Pond Church of God With Signs Following." [5] The name is taken from Mark XVI, 17, the King James Version, the version read by all the people in this region.

The leader of the snake cult in the mid-1940's was Tom Harden, a tall, slender, sharp-featured man of thirty, born in Grasshopper Valley, son of the Enoch Harden who had been a convert of Hensley some decades before. Young Harden went to school for barely a year and never learned to read and write until he "got the Holy Ghost" in 1938. He says that as soon as the power of the Lord came upon him, he took up the Book and read it and has been reading it ever since. He was taught snake-handling by the Reverend Hays, the visiting Kentucky revivalist who had brought snake-handling again to Grasshopper Valley. An ostensible threat to Harden's leadership served eventually only to confirm it. In one meeting he was bitten by a snake, and for four hours his life swayed in the balance while the communicants gathered around and fervently prayed over him. He recovered, thus confirming the Bible text and establishing his own faith. He attended the next meeting and there handled the same snake again. Since then he has again been bitten three times, but with evident spiritual immunity. "Twice I never hardly felt it," he says. "Once it felt like I'd hit the crazy bone in my elbow."

The Dolley Pond Church of God With Signs Following, where

Tom Harden led meetings, was the mother church of the snake-handling in the South. Originally the building was of rough lumber, unpainted, with the two-by-four studs exposed in the undecorated interior. At a later time of greater affluence, however, the exterior was covered with a tar-and-gravel paper which simulates two-tone bonded brickwork. The roof is now covered with a similar but differently patterned material. The floor is tramped earth. At one end of the shed inside is a rough wooden table or hurtle about a foot wide and four feet long, supported about four feet above the ground on two two-by-four timbers planted in the earth. During services this hurtle is covered with a cloth, on which is placed a Bible and a large glass kerosene lamp with a fat etched-glass chimney. The hurtle or pulpit is about three feet from the shed wall. Communicants can stand freely around it, following the backwoods Baptist pattern of extreme audience participation in services. On the wall behind the pulpit is the name of the church in neat block letters on a wooden sign, with Bible texts in smaller, cruder lettering. Benches for the women and a few folding chairs are in the room, mostly along the walls.

The men wear open-necked shirts (for no Bible text can be discovered which says Jesus or the apostles ever wore a necktie) and either pants with leather belts or bibbed and strapped overalls. The women wear plain-colored Mother Hubbards, or dresses of polka-dot, checked, or flowered cotton prints. These latter are home-made out of feedsacks, which feature these prints as a sales appeal to economical farm families, though some of the younger women wear store-boughten dresses of better cut, most often with simple white high V-shaped collars. Cosmetics, jewelry, and artificially curled hair are frowned upon as frivolous and worldly. Few of the older people can read or write, their school attendance being counted in weeks or months, and most of the younger people had their schooling cut short in seasons when their labor was needed in the fields. There is a typical rural uneasiness with or distrust of folks from towns or cities, which the Bible frequently says are fleshpots of sin and wickedness. This region, like much of the intransigently local-autonomous South, is a stronghold of bootleg corn liquor–making.

But, despite the evidence that Jesus drank wine, or at least con-
doned its use at weddings, there is a strong official prohibitionism
among church people. Nearly all the men work at farming or small-
scale sawmilling.

Taking medicine, either store-boughten or prescribed by a doctor, is considered a sure sign of lack of faith in God's ability to
cure the sick, as promised in Mark XVI, 18, the text on which the
church is founded. Some purists even proscribe eyeglasses, although
a visiting minister was observed to wear them in one meeting.
Drinking tea, coffee, or even soft drinks is also proscribed. A Coca-
Cola schism threatened when one deacon said that he had drunk a
coke one hot spell but had detected no lessening of his snake-
handling powers. The potential heresy was defeated, however, when
the preacher and some of the brethren challenged the deacon to
find a text in the Bible where it says that Coca-Cola-drinking is
permitted to the elect.

The sometimes picayune fanaticism of these rural folk must be
seen to be believed. An experienced and compassionate social
worker of my acquaintance tells of the time she met a bedraggled
mountain woman, near heat-exhaustion, on a street in the village
of Chapel Hill. She invited the woman into a nearby icecream parlor,
but the woman refused to enter because coke and other drinks were
sold there — and to women with powdered faces, painted mouths,
and curled hair! Finally, however, she accepted an icecream cone
from the social worker, but only on condition that the latter enter
this place of sin alone and bring it to her outside. Similarly, the
rural characters that emerge from the piney backwoods at tobacco-
auction time onto the streets of marketing cities like Durham and
Winston-Salem can shock, by their incontestable reality, even well-
traveled persons. Furthermore, both ethnographic and psychiatric
records convince the serious student that *Tobacco Road* is no artis-
tic caricature, but a faithful portrait of some rural regions in the
South.

The meetings at the Dolley Pond Church of God With Signs
Following are held every Saturday and Sunday night in the warm
months, which in this region means most of the year. On Saturday,

chores are finished earlier than usual, people get cleaned up, eat an early supper and walk to the church, sometimes for miles, carrying children too young to walk. Worshipers gather at the church sometimes two or three hours before services are scheduled to begin, as this gives a time for visiting and sharing local news. Sometimes spectators and even "furriners" may gather to observe and ridicule the cultists. But while such unbelief may be easily discerned by the believers, it is not tolerated without rebuttal when too impolitely overt.

The devout greet one another with a "holy kiss," mouth to mouth, accompanied by a vigorous formal hug. Men kiss men, and women women; the holy kiss is not exchanged with members of the opposite sex. Male members usually stand around in gradually enlarging groups and talk about blessings received in the last meeting or since then, as well as about crops and other concerns. Women do not mix with this male group but march directly into the church and seat themselves on wooden benches, surrounded by their younger offspring.[6] An adolescent boy would count it a privilege to be allowed to linger with the men's group outside the church, but he must not be a nuisance or he will be sent to join his younger brothers and sisters with his mother inside. Child care, at least in public, is an exclusively female occupation, and the boy must not make it necessary for the men to "mess with" him.

The arrival of the guitar (pronounced with a strong accent on the first syllable) player, the tambourine shakers, and the preacher is usually the signal to drift into the church, though informality is the rule throughout the meeting, with a minimum of initiative by the minister to spark the proceedings. Members newly met since the last meeting may gather around the "pulpit" and exchange the holy kiss and embrace, and after some chords on the guitar the meeting has begun. The first few songs, informally selected from suggestions by the congregation or by the preacher, are needed to warm up. But soon the spirit begins to move some members and they may jump up and down, caper about, and occasionally kick in passing the wooden box in which the snakes have been brought. The chanting of old familiar hymns becomes stronger and stronger,

[18

in the peculiarly highpitched and strident nasal tone which, in homogenized form, is better known to most Americans as hillbilly singing, commercialized in Nashville as "Grand Ole Opry" and in Durham by the tobacco-barn radio singers.

Communicants may clap as they choose to the rhythm of the guitar player and shout phrases like "Praise the Lord!," "Thank God for Jesus!," or "Hallelujah to Glory!" more or less ad libitum. With similar informality individuals may begin to pray for divine healing power in behalf of various members who are ailing, whether absent or (more usually) present. Everyone prays at the same time and aloud. Members may go to a sick person brought up to stand by the hurtle in order to stretch out a "healing hand," usually to the head of the ailing brother or sister. Praying may last ten minutes or more, at the end of which some people may speak, emergent from the Babel, in "unknown tongues." One Durham preacher was told by a newspaper reporter that he was speaking the word for God in an African dialect.[7]

The climax comes when the power is strong within the congregation, heightened by the clichéd preaching of the minister. A rope is then stretched out by a member to separate the audience from the snake-handling devout, and visitors are warned that the snakes are about to be produced. This precaution may be barely accomplished before an impatient believer snatches up a snake from the angry knot in the opened box. Removing a snake from the box is regarded as a supreme test of faith, for the constantly jolted reptiles are by then thoroughly aroused, and it is believed that they are most likely to strike when they are first touched. The box has been kicked, in a kind of half-jocular sin-baiting, because the snake represents the Devil, whom the spirit of God allows the true believer to overcome.

It seems possible that when held dangling by their middles, snakes accustomed to coil and strike may have their reflexes disturbed. Herpetologists well know also that some snakes will "play possum" when approached by human enemies. Also, it has been suggested that the body heat of the worshipers might have some drugging effect on the snakes. But none of these suppositions is to be relied upon, for the way that they are loosely held, the snakes still have enough free length to strike, should they choose; the snakes observed in meetings are still moving when handled; and human body warmth may just as well serve to make cold-blooded reptiles more active. Schwarz invokes as an explanation the cataplexia known to be true of some snakes, including rattlers. He tells us that "One brother held a rattlesnake (approximately four feet in length) in the mid-trunk region, and as he stamped around the congregation, shouting his praises to the Lord, the reptile hung limply, seemed to be cataplectic . . . and showed no response until the worshipper paused and became silent for a few seconds."[8] While by no means denying that rattlesnakes may become cataplectic, I can only assert that cataplexia is present, and then dubiously, in but one of the photographs of Durham meetings, and no local member is reputed to "cause" serpents to become limp. I regard the question of why more snake-handlers are not bitten as being unsolved and still open.

There may be some jostling to get snakes, but good manners of a sort are usually preserved even in this. However, shaking violently from head to foot, a believer with the spirit in him may grab a snake from a quieter or less aggressive member or from one whose interest in the snake is visibly flagging. The snake may be held in various ways. Sister Harden, the preacher's sister, was observed to hold a large snake before her in both hands at about waist level, eyes closed, body bent tensely forward in an arc, lips stretched into a tight oval open-jawed scream, while two other sisters stood behind her, one clapping, the other with the left hand clasped over the right fist, and both of them shouting also. Sister Minnie Parker, a buxom elderly gap-toothed woman — who walked barefoot among seventeen buzzing rattlesnakes in a homecoming service in the summer of 1946 — held a beautiful large timber rattler around her neck like a necklace, with the free neck and head of the snake along the outside of her left forearm, while cooing with closed eyes and a delighted expression on her face. A young woman in a store-bought dress held the thick middle of a very large rattler across her forehead with both hands like a coronet, the head of the snake over her right shoulder and behind her back, with the rattle reposing between her breasts.

There appear to be no special sex-differentiated ways of holding snakes. One man of about sixty at a Dolley Pond meeting had a small copperhead crawling from his open collar over his left cheek and across his forehead. Mark Braddam, said to be dying of cancer and barely able to see for the wide suppuration-soaked bandage tied vertically across the middle of his face, supported a large rattlesnake cradled over his outstretched bent left arm while holding its middle with his right hand. Preacher George Hensley allowed Brother Lewis Ford and another man to drape a crown of snakes on the top of his head; but such decorations do not stay long in position and the snakes may drop heavily to the floor, where they are possibly more dangerous since there they can gather themselves to strike. In yet another variation, Preacher Raymond Hays held a rattlesnake and a copperhead to his face at the same time in one Dolley Pond meeting.

A particularly admired gambit is to grasp the snake about midbody and then raise it slowly until the flickering tongue touches the nose of the worshiper, who meanwhile stares intently into the snake's eyes. This is to taunt and to overpower evil with the "spirit" in the worshiper. Another stunt is to "charm" the snake — to move the reptile close to the face, weaving one's head back and forth with the animal's until the snake's jaws brush one's lips. (During some fourteen months in India, I repeatedly saw "snake-charming" and battles of a snake with a mongoose. It seems probable that the weaving of the snake is a response to the charm of neither man nor mongoose, but results in both cases merely from the snake's following the warm-blooded animal with its infrared-sensitive head pits. That rattlesnakes and cottonmouth moccasins are pit vipers like the cobra suggests that the same mechanism is in operation here. The motion of the target may in fact inhibit the striking of the snake, which is accustomed or better able to strike a more stationary object.)

Besides snake-handling, there are other ways of testing the spirit. One elderly man held his hand over the flame of the kerosene lamp on the pulpit while a younger man lifted the etched-glass chimney for him; meanwhile an attractive young woman in a polkadot dress with white buttons and collar crooned ecstatically, eyes closed, as she held a Bible up in her outstretched right hand. Few of the Dolley Pond group claim to be able to swallow poison, though a glass of it is always kept on hand during services, in case "the Lord anoints one of us to take poison." It is said, but without verification, that some of the more fanatic members have drunk a solution of strychnine "strong enough that one drop on a grain of corn will kill a chicken."[9]

At one Dolley Pond meeting a hostile visiting Baptist minister suddenly emerged from the crowd of spectators and thrust a roaring blowtorch into the hands of a believer. "Try this!" he cried, grinning broadly as a ripple of laughter spread through the audience. The cultist stood a moment apparently dumbfounded. But suddenly a tiny sweetfaced granny in a dark dress and neat white pokebonnet darted forward, grasped the torch, and walked toward the skeptic until only the rope separated them. Looking the minister straight in the eye she held one hand in the middle of the flame. The skeptical physicist may still wish to point out that different parts of a blowtorch flame have different temperatures, but there can be no question of this little old lady's complete faith. Without a word, she handed the blowtorch back to the visiting Baptist, who turned it off and soon after left the meeting.

Another skeptic, Cecil Denkins, born in the Valley, claimed that the cultists used snakes that had been defanged or milked of their venom. He and a friend caught an eleven-pound rattlesnake in the mountains and carried it in a five-gallon milk can on the back of his truck to a meeting at Dolley Pond, believing that the cultists either would refuse to use it or one of them would die from its bite. But this rattler was taken directly from the milk can and fondled by the cultists. A few weeks later Cecil Denkins himself "got the spirit," joined the Dolley Pond congregation, and found he had the power to handle rattlesnakes.

Forty-year-old Tom Allison, not a member, is the official snake-catcher for the church.* He performs this service free. A deacon takes care of the snakes between services and feeds them rats, small chickens, and, allegedly, milk.[10] A few snakes have died during the services while being handled.[11] This is said to have happened with Mrs. Allie Harden, mother of the preacher at Dolley Pond. The cultists explain that some of their members are filled with a strong power "like electricity" and that snakes are shocked to death by this power. People at Dolley Pond say that when Mrs. Harden takes up a snake it immediately ceases to struggle and becomes "limp as a necktie." Officially, only one member of the Dolley Pond Church has died of snakebite: Lewis F. Ford, a husky two-hundred-pounder in his early thirties, son of Walter Ford, a deacon of the church. This happened in September 1945, and a funeral service was held later with the same fatal snake.

* In the literature a persistent assertion about the catching of snakes is that they are caught by "sinner-men" (Collins) or "unbelieving sinner boys" (Schwarz). That non-members, like Tom Allison, and Cecil Denkins before he was a member, should catch the snakes, appears to suggest some desire on the part of members for this public test of the intactness of the snakes. But should members wish to tamper with the snakes before meetings — though there is no shred of evidence to suggest that this ever happens — there would be opportunity to do so, so this explanation seems feeble. Furthermore, are snake cultists so hidebound as to suggest that all non-members are necessarily "sinner-men"? I think not; there is another reason for this, but I do not know what it is.

CHAPTER 3

Publicity and Persecution

THE death by snakebite of Lewis Ford at the Dolley Pond meeting in 1945 first brought the attention of a larger world to what had heretofore been a remote and inconspicuous minority cult in the Tennessee mountains. It was this event that was investigated by a Chattanooga newspaper reporter; the news found its way onto the Associated Press wire, resulting in much publicity.

Soon afterward, on a Sunday, the cultists went to Chattanooga and held a meeting inside the city limits. In a small tent with an oil-drum pulpit, on the eastern border of the city, nightly revival meetings of the now evangelical Dolley Pond Church of God With Signs Following were planned for the benefit of the city folk. At one of the first meetings a large crowd gathered, the street was blocked, and traffic jammed. Chattanooga policemen arrested Harden and Hensley, respectively the preacher and the prophet of the cult, and others and took them to the city jail. Members of the group were pleased with the attention they got and jubilant about being in jail "for the Lord" just like the saints and prophets of old. In the bullpen they shouted and sang, laughed and hugged each other. A dozen of them, released under bond, conducted a service outside the jail to pray for the policemen who had arrested them. Harden and Hensley, still in jail, sang all through the evening and into the night, praying the Lord to open the prison doors as he had done for Saint Paul.

At a preliminary hearing before Judge Martin A. Fleming —

attended by many relatives and friends of the accused — the two cultists were each fined fifty dollars for disorderly conduct. They refused to pay.* Nor would they permit a number of their friends to make up the sum. Paying a fine, they said, was against their religious principles and they would go to the workhouse first to pay it off at a dollar a day. But after several days on a road gang in the hot sun of the city streets, Hensley weakened. Friends hired an attorney and appealed the case. The two men were brought before Judge Frank Darwin who dismissed the charges. Immediately, in court, the congregation began shouting in praise of God for this deliverance — a modern miracle, a new way God had of opening prison doors.

About this time the Faith Tabernacle in LaFollette, Tennessee, was offered by its owner, Preacher C. D. Morris, as a possible sanctuary from the law for members of the snake-handling faith. With this offer, however, went the condition that snakes be handled in an orderly fashion, and by one person at a time. Preacher Shoupe of Kentucky later held services in the Tabernacle under these rules. But extreme local autonomy is the tradition in the religious groups out of which the cult had arisen, and many people resented such rules and regulations. It is said that from this period derive two branches of the faith in the southeastern states, one according to the Morris plan and another the original Hensley cult. The latter seems to have spread more widely in subsequent times.

But followers of the conservative faith continued to suffer accidents. Clint Jackson, a munitions worker in his early forties, was bitten in a meeting held near Daisy and died in July 1946. Public opinion was increasingly aroused against the snake-handlers by this event. An indirect blow was dealt the movement by a ruling of Judge Hamilton S. Burnett of the Tennessee Court of Appeals. The Court held that Lewis Ford, who died after being bitten in meeting

---

* This kind of intransigent, back up, joyful and prideful resistance to external authority is a prominent trait in Southern character, and not alone among rural folk. It sometimes takes a puerile form, as in the rash of Confederate flags and stickers and string ties among college boys in the early 1950's. But it is a distinct psychological reality. In more ominous form, in "citizens' " pro-segregation committees, it is an undying rebel yell proving who won the War Between the States.

251

in Daisy, Tennessee, had not died accidentally. His widow, Ressie L. Ford, was therefore not entitled to double indemnity by accident from the insurance company.

The insurance death was caused by being bitten by a rattlesnake in a religious service. One voluntarily handling a poisonous serpent is not accidentally injured when bitten by the snake. If you were picking blackberries in a field and received a bite, then that might be different.[12]

Harassed by both the executive and the judicial branches of government, the cultists now suffered another blow from the legislature. On February 4, 1947, a bill was introduced by Senator Willard Hagan and Representative I. D. Beasley in the state legislature of Tennessee, prohibiting the handling of snakes. The bill passed the house on February 28 by a vote of 70 to 0. The senate having already passed it, the bill became a state law when it was signed by Governor Jim McCord.

The next summer, nevertheless, the cultists started up again, and now began an amiable kind of cat-and-mouse game with the police that came to be characteristic of the cult here and elsewhere. Snakes were again being used in meetings, in defiance of "man-made laws" and in obedience to "God's commands." Word of this soon came to the ears of Sheriff Grady Head of Hamilton County. On Wednesday night, the twenty-third of July 1947, he called in all available policemen and deputies and took them in patrol cars to Dolley Pond Church. There they found a large crowd of spectators and a few cultists, but no services were under way. Harden was summoned by the sheriff.

A crowd including newsmen from Chattanooga and a representative of the Associated Press gathered around Harden and the sheriff, who continued to wear his hat and chew a cigar although he had entered the building. "You's in charge?" the sheriff barked around his cigar. "Well, now, I guess I am," Harden answered calmly, with a smile playing around his mouth. "Where's your snakes?" "We ain't got none here. As a matter of fact, I didn't know there was to be any services tonight. I just came down to see what the trouble was," Harden answered.

At that point a reporter interrupted. "You might as well go ahead and get your snakes and handle them tonight. You are going to be

arrested sooner or later, and you might as well get it over with."
The reporter, apparently disappointed at the prospect of traveling
all the way from Chattanooga without seeing snakes handled and
the first arrests to test the new state law, added, "Look, there are
a lot of us reporters here and we're all set for a big show. Get out
the snakes and let's get it over with."

Harden stood looking at the impatient man for several seconds
before answering him. "Well, now, I reckon I sure do appreciate all
that, mister," he said slowly, "but before I handle those 'snakes' I
believe I'll still wait on the Lord."[13]

It is strongly to be suspected, although not surely known, that
false information was in some manner deliberately planted in order
to reach the ears of the police. Having made a considerable production of this raid, the sheriff might be less eager to answer any future
cry of "Wolf!" and thus the cultists might enjoy some unmolested
privacy to continue breaking the law and mildly persecuting the
police. The reporter's suggestion was of course sound psychology.
But even this appeal to publicity was not enough. If they were going
to be arrested, they would still do it in their own good time, and
they would certainly make it as inconvenient as possible for their
harassers. The whole incident illustrates the amiable and folksy
quality of the transactions between the police and the cultists. Despite the cultists' shrewd teasing and police-baiting, good humor was
preserved, and mostly good manners, throughout. If there was no
zealous vindictive persecution, there was also no burning martyr-
dom. Each side recognized, even half-respected, the position of the
other. But each side still stood where it stood.

The sheriff's party searched the church but found no snakes. As
they were leaving, one of the brethren mounted the pulpit and
called out, "You folks be back Sunday. We'll have some serpents
if it's God's will." But the congregation did not wait until Sunday and
moved the meeting up to Saturday night instead, when a three-and-
a-half-foot rattlesnake and a smaller copperhead were handled in
the meeting. "Now where's the sheriff?," people cried. Sunday,
police came to services going full swing, with about a hundred
spectators outside unable to crowd into the church. But there were
no snakes being handled.

Frustrated once again, the sheriff was fast becoming an object of public amusement. So he changed his tactics from charging up in police cars in full force. Instead, he planted two plainclothes deputies, George Ely and Hughie Baker, posing as spectators from Chattanooga. At the end of a meeting in which they had observed snakes being handled, the two deputies put the whole congregation under arrest for violating the state law and confiscated the snakes. At this disclosure, there was a moment of startled silence, and then everyone broke into shouts of joy, jumping about and screaming, hugging and kissing one another, and buffeting the deputies laughingly as at a good joke. The moment of issue had arrived.

Since not enough transportation was available for the whole congregation, services were begun again while Ely drove to the nearest telephone and called headquarters for police cars. In town, attorney George Chamlee obtained bond of $250 each for the smiling little congregation, and the jail was full of the remainder of shouting prisoners, those who had actually handled snakes. The snakes were killed with a piece of sheet iron, out of sight of the prisoners, because it was thought that the sound of shots might arouse the congregation still further. When some of the members were released, the congregation promptly held a singing meeting on the courthouse lawn. At the trial, Judge Goodson held a brief hearing, with George Chamlee and Fred Hixson as defense attorneys, and ordered the twelve major defendants held for grand jury investigation.

Persecuted in Tennessee, the cult now began a history of slow spread over a number of states in the Southeast, a sporadic movement, but one destined in time to cover considerable territory. The national press reported a lantern-light meeting of snake cultists, with guitar music, in Euharlee, Georgia, in 1946, led by the Reverend Gordon Miller. In late August 1947, in Summerville, a county seat in northwest Georgia, Ernest Davis, a farmer aged thirty-four, took several gulps of a "salvation cocktail" made with strychnine, in one of the Reverend Miller's meetings.* He died five days later.

* *Time*, September 8, 1947. The Summerville meeting may have some bearing historically on a figure to be discussed in a later chapter. Summerville is south of Chickamauga, in the beautiful mountain country toward

As he was being buried, his wife lamented that "Ernest just had too much faith."

It may be well at this point to sketch out certain aspects of the cultural background of the snake-handling cult which doubtless facilitated its spread. The history of rural Southern religion which lay behind the experiences of George Hensley, the founder of the snake-handling cult, is not difficult to find. The rural South has long been a stronghold of low-church sects like the Baptists and the Methodists, the Holiness and the Pentecostal churches. In the Piedmont this trend has been reinforced by a secondary migration of Quakers from Pennsylvania down the Appalachian valleys. All these groups, which represent the extreme of Reformation anti-clericalism, have much emphasized the individual religious experience, without any priestly intervention, as a sign of the soul's closeness to God.

The roots of the movement lie deep in American religious history. John and Charles Wesley, under the auspices of the Society for the Propagation of the Christian Gospel, sailed on their famous mission to the Indians on October 21, 1735, and landed at Savannah, Georgia, on February 5, 1736. Alabama was the southernmost scene of their missionary labors, but Savannah was the center. John Wesley's *Journal* mentions at least one trip northward to Virginia. On December 2, 1737, he was in South Carolina on his way back to England; he left under local pressure of troubles with women, in particular, one Sophie, according to historians. But the seeds of Methodism had been well planted in America, and the sect grew and flourished. The Holiness and Pentecostal groups were offshoots of Methodism.

At this time, of course, the colonies were chiefly on the Atlantic seaboard, and the trans-Appalachian region was long a wild and bloody frontier.

Hungry Mother Mountain, where the cultist preacher whose autobiography is later to be discussed in detail was born. It should be stated specifically that Gordon Miller, whom I have never met, is not this preacher. On the best information available, Miller is apparently a Georgian, but in any case he was not born at Hungry Mother Mountain.

Times unfavorable to religion followed in connexion with the War of Independence; but, about the turn of the century, chiefly through the preaching of James McGready and two brothers by the name of McGee, a remarkable awakening passed through the Cumberland Valley in Kentucky and Tennessee — a region which had long been notorious for irreligion and violence. Taking place in such a population, assembled in huge camp-meetings, it was attended with physical manifestations of a remarkable order, which, under the name of "bodily exercises," are fully described in a curious but obviously well-informed article.[14]

This religious movement had appeared somewhat earlier in England. "Ranters" was the nickname of an antinomian sect appearing in the time of the Commonwealth, a chaotic left wing seeking primitive Christianity outside corrupt existing institutions. The two traits of this loose group were pantheism and antinomianism. The Quaker George Fox wrote of his experiences with them, on one occasion being much frightened by the antics at bedtime of a Ranter with whom he shared a room at an inn. Ranters were punished for "blasphemous and immoral" views, and the sect was rigorously suppressed by acts of Parliament. Many were absorbed into Quakerism, and the sect disappeared, although the tendency toward antinomianism reappeared occasionally in America among isolated rural peoples of colonial stock.[15] The same tendencies are apparent in the contemporary rural South, where there is a frequent "recrudescence of the ancient belief that ecstatic experiences are the work of the Holy Spirit — a kind of possession [which] . . . accompanied the Scottish-Irish revival in Kentucky in 1800–03."[16] Curiously, Quakerism is an established religious strain in the Piedmont South of the present study. But Quakers, in time, perhaps partly in reaction against the Ranters they had absorbed, were conspicuously quieter in demeanor and became notably restrained in seeking the Spirit; they grew from cult to respected sect in the prosperous days of Queen Anne, by codifying their beliefs considerably and stiffening into typical Protestant institutional forms. The Book of Discipline replaced a too rampantly autonomous Inner Light. Famous old Quaker names appear in the Piedmont region now as bankers and high university administrators — among the first to find the snake-handling cult opprobrious. But by this time, because of the upward mobility of its adherents, Quakerism was a denomination, and in class terms hostile to the new, lower-class cult. Thus, in the absence of such institutionalization as Quakerism underwent, the Ranters died out in England — only to reappear in essential ethos in the snake-handling cult.

Rural upper New York State was in early times also a source of aberrant American sects, but transportation and urbanization in the East have left the necessary conditions for development intact only in the mountainous areas of the rural South. In our time southern California and Florida also see the rise of such sects, doubtless owing to the migration to such places of numerous retired people of rural origin, with both money and a personal concern about the imminent hereafter. Indeed, one of the earliest snake-handling cults in the United States is said to have started at Los Angeles in 1906. Since the Hensley cult in Tennessee is reliably dated from 1906, this California sect is either independent in origin or a remarkable example of swift cultural diffusion.* It will occur to the anthropologist, however, that there are nearer sources to California than Tennessee for stimulus-diffusion of snake-handling, namely the snake-handling Hopi of Arizona. But no such non-white influence is evident in the modern snake-handling religion of the Southeast, and for various reasons it is ethnographically improbable.

Even more vexing ethnographically is the report of a snake-handling group started in the hamlet of Cherokee, North Carolina, by A. J. Tombleson or Tomlinson in 1903, and now led in other states by his sons. The same possibility of Indian influence arises here as in California, although I regard this as very doubtful in the Cherokee case, because of widely differing attitudes toward snakes. The Indians of Carolina would not molest snakes when they came upon them, but would pass by on the other side of the path, believing that if they were to kill a serpent, the reptile's kindred would destroy some of their brethren, friends, or relations in return . . .

The Cherokee regard the rattlesnake as the chief of the snake tribe and fear and respect him accordingly. Few Cherokee will venture to kill a rattlesnake, unless they cannot help it, and even

* See note 6, page 183.

then they must atone for the crime by craving pardon of the snake's ghost either in their own person or through the mediation of a priest, according to a set formula.[17]

Both the respect for the snake and the marked desire to avoid it seem the exact opposite of the attitudes of snake-handlers!

The groups in Kentucky are reputed to do more snake-handling than those in other states. But on the evidence presently at hand I regard the cult of Grasshopper Valley in Tennessee as being the center of origin of contemporary snake-handling proper. What seems probable is that the founding dates of such obscure sects as Tomlinson's are correct, but that — as is true of the Durham cult — snake-handling was grafted onto their ecstatic cults sometime after 1906. A great difficulty in this connection arises from another trait which modern Holiness and Pentecostal sects have inherited from primitive Methodism.

The characteristic feature of early American Methodism was the itinerant preacher, who without adequate education or remuneration traveled thousands of miles on horseback, preaching to small groups in pioneer communities, organizing classes and then making a regular circuit of his scattered "charges." [18]

This is distinctly the pattern still in the snake-handling cult. Visiting ministers are a commonplace, the only difference being that modern transportation allows the distances traveled to be much greater. George Hensley, the founder of the snake-handling cult, preached all the way from Tennessee to Florida; and in a subsequent chapter I shall mention the interstate travels of the Reverend Oscar Hutton and others as facilitating the diffusion of snake-handling cults in the South.

Because of this sporadic diffusion into widely separated rural areas, because it occurs in obscure and remote places, and because the mostly illiterate cultists are in any case more interested in dionysian experience than in apollonian historical scholarship, we must expect some incompleteness in our study which only further direct field information can remedy. Very probably new information will continue to emerge concerning local snake-handling groups. For example, as the present study nears completion, Dr. Jack Conrad of Southwestern University at Memphis, a former graduate assistant of mine, reports on a snake-handling meeting he attended in Kingsport, north of Knoxville, in 1943 while in his teens. The cultists had moccasins and rattlesnakes in the meeting, but no copperheads. They met in a tent and would crawl up the aisle on hands and knees to confess their sins and to testify in front at the mourners' bench. About fifty people, all white, were present, ranging from children to oldsters of sixty and seventy, with about even numbers of men and women. A guitar was played but there was no organized singing. Dr. Conrad had heard of poison-drinking, but he never witnessed it.

The attempt of the Dolley Pond congregation to evangelize the city of Chattanooga was the harbinger, perhaps, of the eventual extinction of the snake-handling cult; for its ethos is essentially rural, increasingly in conflict with the busy industrializing urbanism of the new South. Hensley's entanglements locally with the law in Tennessee doubtless served as a further stimulus to the spread of snake-handling into other states of the Southeast, notably Virginia, Georgia, North Carolina, and Florida. In the next chapter I shall describe in detail the vicissitudes of the snake cult in an urban center of North Carolina, and in a later chapter what may be the last stand of the cult in rural northern Florida.

CHAPTER 4

The Interstate Convention

BENJAMIN R. MASSEY brought the snake-handling cult to Durham, North Carolina. He associated himself in this purpose with a self-ordained minister, the Reverend Colonel Hartman Bunn, pastor of the Zion Tabernacle on Peabody Street in Durham. Massey, one of the leaders in Bunn's group, had been visiting a snake-handling ceremony elsewhere with his mother-in-law when they both felt the call to handle snakes. They said they knew that if God really wanted their wish to be realized, the snakes would be brought to them. They were nevertheless a little surprised when the leader chose them from among all those present and handed them the snakes. Later, Massey asked Bunn to initiate snake-handling in Durham, and soon afterward Bunn, at Massey's suggestion, had his first experience.

In the winter of 1947–48 police seized two copperheads during services at the Tabernacle. The snakes were examined by a state museum curator in Raleigh who pronounced the poison sacs intact and the specimens deadly, as tested on white rats. Bunn and Massey were convicted of violating a recently passed municipal ordinance prohibiting the public handling of serpents — the response of the Durham city council to reports of earlier snake-handling activities.[19]

Cases were pending against Bunn and Massey in the state supreme court when the following events took place. On October 6, 1948, Bunn announced to the local newspapers that there would be an interstate convention of snake-handlers in Durham October 15–17.

Present would be Oscar Hutton of St. Charles, Virginia (he had previously operated in Virginia and in Harlan, Kentucky), and three Kentuckians: Ottas Hurley of Wallins, Eli Sanders of Lejunior, and Roscoe Long. Also expected were cultists from Tennessee and West Virginia, in addition to Ledrew Tripp of Vanceboro and the Reverend Noah of Winston-Salem and High Point, North Carolina, together with many of their followers. Snakes would be available, a specialist who manifests faith by playing a blowtorch over his face would be present, and also others who demonstrate with poisons. *Life* magazine had asked permission to take pictures of the proceedings at the Zion Tabernacle.

Friday and Saturday, October 15 and 16, were to be devoted chiefly to those fasting and praying for the power of God. But night services would be open to the public, with Dewey S. Watkins of Durham leading the mass singing. On Sunday, October 17, the meeting would begin at 11 A.M. and last as long as anyone felt the spirit to continue it. No time would be allowed for lunch, inasmuch as many would be fasting anyway. The Reverend Mr. Bunn announced to the Durham press:

This meeting has been set to get the people who believe only in God and not the worldly traditions of religion — we are attempting to have it with as little form as possible. We will let the Holy Spirit be the leader as in the early church. We expect people to be healed and we expect revelations of the spirit.

We will have serpents for those who wish to handle them, but I would like to emphasize that this is not done with the idea of breaking a law. We have this experience from God, we enjoy it, it is the plain words of Jesus and we will not bow to man-made laws that contradict. We want no harsh feelings from anyone. I hope and pray that this announcement will bring a sacredness upon all who expect to attend. Let us stop from worldly fashions and return to the God of Power. This meeting is called only for such.[20]

In response to this public challenge, Police Chief H. E. King, promptly announced a policy of "wait and see." He reminded the public of the municipal ordinance against snake-handling. He pointed out, however, that there was no law against people's using blowtorches on themselves or taking strychnine or other poisons in religious demonstrations, so long as they did not injure the health or lives of other persons.[21]

Chief King did not have long to wait. On the first Friday evening of the convention, Captain M. M. Thompson led a squadron of ten serious-faced and businesslike policemen to the Zion Tabernacle. There were four Negroes in the crowd, three women and one little girl in pigtails who sat on the edge of her seat as the congregation responded to Bunn's appeal for the "spirit," with people jerking their necks, dancing, waving their arms, and collapsing onto the floor.* A white pulpit with red bunting was at the front of the church, the floor of which was filled with benches.

Just before the police officers entered, the Reverend Mr. Bunn relinquished the snakes he was handling to the visiting Reverend Oscar Hutton, a gray-haired man resembling a blander Will Rogers

* The unsegregated presence of Negroes in an otherwise white religious meeting may be startling to outsiders. The reasons for this are several. In the first place, snake-handling originated in mountain areas, many of which have very few Negroes and hence have fewer race problems; the situation in the Coastal Plain counties would of course be different indeed. It is possible that this racial tolerance moved about as a "cultural adhesion" with snake-handling in at least some of the places it invaded. In the second place, many of the laboring-class people in Durham are accustomed to working with Negroes in the Liggett & Myers tobacco factory, the cotton mills, and the local machinery company — and many of these have attitudes of racial tolerance which they feel are quite consistent with their fervent and sincere Christianity. It should be noted further that many of the people in this Piedmont region are descended from Quaker secondary migrants from Pennsylvania which, together with the fine Scotch-Irish intellectual traditions of nearby Chapel Hill, gives this region a somewhat different flavor from other parts of the South. Members of the best old families have for some time been meeting quietly with Negro leaders on social agency board concerns and the like in the Washington Duke Hotel. Many local people take pride in their belief that both their region and the state of North Carolina are commonly moral leaders in the southern states. Some substance may be lent to this claim by the fact that, during the troubles with segregation on buses in Georgia, the Duke Power Company without external compulsion quietly abolished segregation on the Durham buses with virtually no difficulty whatever. Unsegregated musical and other cultural events at Duke University and the North Carolina College for Negroes are increasingly commonplace in Durham, lunch counter integration was won in Durham in 1960, the Duke Graduate School was desegregated in the spring of 1961, and the University of North Carolina in Chapel Hill has for several years admitted qualified Negroes, both to the undergraduate school and to the Medical School. At least three North Carolina cities have even begun school integration and others will inevitably follow.

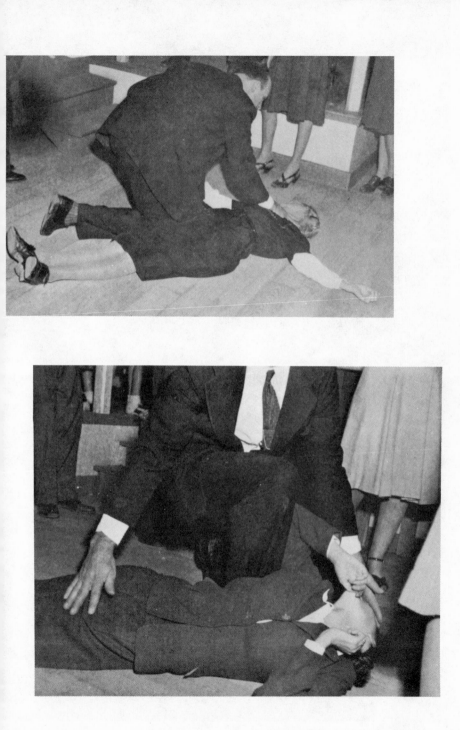

and widely noted for his snake-handling feats in Virginia. Hutton had two copperheads and a rattlesnake in his right hand and a Bible in his left. Responding to the applause of spectators in the crowded Tabernacle, Hutton was reaching for more snakes when the police arrived. About twenty minutes before, Bunn had asked several of his followers to check outside to see if police were around, and he was evidently disappointed that he had not been handling snakes at the moment of the raid. He asked the officers not to take all the snakes, but Captain Thompson pointed his finger at Bunn and said, "I am going to take them all."

Using a longhandled forceps made for the purpose the year before by Captain Glenn Rosemond, the police eventually confiscated the two copperheads and rattler from Hutton, a copperhead from the accordion player, and another small copperhead held in the hand of a young girl, placing them in a white metal can with a hinged lid. As the officers were having some slight difficulty in capturing the snakes, Bunn asked officer H. B. Strayhorn mockingly, "May I help?" Hutton placed his snakes in the can with the aid of a Durham member of the Tabernacle as a woman screamed, "Leave us alone! You are stopping the work of God!" Bunn patted the police officers on the shoulder and on the hand, smiled and said, "I love all the police, I feel so good I could kiss them all!" No such demonstration took place however.* Hutton cried, "They had Jesus arrested too for preaching!"

Bunn laughingly pleaded with the police to take him to jail, but the police made no arrests and left promptly with the five snakes. This behavior of the police was strictly proper, for under the city ordinance the snakes (1) had to be publicly handled, (2) must touch the naked flesh, and (3) must be demonstrated to be venomous. Since (3) had not yet been scientifically demonstrated and (2) must not be violated even by the police, sufficient legal reason for the forceps seems evident.

As the police left there was much shouting and groaning. The

---

* In one picture with caption in the *Durham Evening Sun*, October 16, 1948, Bunn has temporarily immobilized the raid as he stands, arms held wide, praying in the midst of police and congregation. See also the *Durham Morning Herald* of the same date.

accordion player who had been handling one of the copperheads broke into loud sobs, and he and the guitar player wept on one another's shoulders. An elderly woman in a flowered print dress gave out piercing cries, her shaking body rattling a long bench. Bunn cried from the platform, "Take me with you and the services will stop! But tomorrow we will really have a big one here. We have many more serpents left, we couldn't let you take them all tonight!"

As the raided gathering quieted somewhat, Hutton said:

In Cleveland, Tennessee, we handled snakes on the courthouse lawn. They told us to stop. We could not fight them but we returned later and handled the snakes and were not bothered. But in Winston-Salem when I handled a snake they put me under a $3000 bond. At about the same time a man there who had just shot someone else four times was put under a bond of only $600.

Hutton wore a brown striped suit and vest, blue striped trousers, and a shirt without a tie. By contrast, Bunn was clad in a neat navy blue double-breasted suit, with a white shirt and blue tie; he said:

We will do more preaching tomorrow on the courthouse steps as soon as it gets dark. You know when MacArthur left Leyte he said that he would return. So will I.

We will meet in the field across the street tomorrow if you will be more comfortable there. I tried to borrow or rent a tent, even from another preacher, but I could not get one. It makes no difference, we can do as they did in Kentucky, preach in the wide open spaces.

Bunn announced as a coming attraction the specialist with the blow-torch who was expected to arrive the next day.* The meeting then straggled apart, with much vociferous conversation.

---

* This personage, one "John the Baptist," is a handsome six-footer, bearded to the waist, who can also "speak in tongues." He habitually stands in meetings with his arms outstretched as if he were on a cross, his head back and eyes rolled upward. In this state he is touched by women communicants who are said immediately to be possessed of the spirit and to slide unconscious to the floor. This method is different from that of Bunn and other ministers who themselves touch their female parishioners, as our photographs indicate. In this the practice of ministers in North Carolina and Florida is evidently not typical of the Kentucky and Tennessee Fundamentalists: "Both because of their rigid moral code and their vulnerability to persecution, the brothers and sisters carefully refrain from the laying on of hands during the healing rites below the shoulders of any member of the opposite sex" (Schwarz, p. 409).

The Interstate Convention

The next day, Saturday, seven persons (including Bunn and Hutton) were served with warrants charging violation of the city ordinance against snake-handling. That evening the Tabernacle drew the largest crowd of the convention. After a brief snake-handling episode, Bunn turned the meeting to "healing of the sick, laying on of hands, and speaking in other tongues." The last was perhaps the most spectacular event of the evening. Bunn lined up about twenty-five female followers chattering simultaneously, and as he embraced them one by one they toppled over like tenpins.* Habitués of the meetings consider that Bunn handled serpents on this Saturday night meeting with more confidence than he had previously shown, taunting them by shaking their heads, passing his hands close in front of them, and draping them about his head like a halo.[22]

Sunday morning, shortly before noon, a few of Bunn's followers performed for newsreel cameramen at the Zion Tabernacle, an occasion which went officially unnoticed by the local police, as had also the Saturday night meeting. In the middle of Sunday morning, in fact, police chief King had left Durham, taking his evidence in the form of five snakes to Raleigh to be tested to discover whether their venom-injecting equipment was intact. Concerning the Sunday morning meeting for pictures Bunn said, "I mocked the law." He and the six other defendants were scheduled to appear in Recorder's Court on Monday morning, the same court in which he had been convicted the year before in the case then pending in the state supreme court. Bunn announced that he would keep on appealing, "because if I pay Judge Wilson I might not get to talk with the

---

* Photographs exist of this meeting, taken by the medical arts photographer from the Duke Medical School in the company of a visiting British psychiatrist who later wrote a brief note about the meeting for a medical journal. A number of Duke students and faculty were also present, and the *Duke Chronicle* published some news items on the meeting. The Duke Law School conducted a mock trial on the case later, which Bunn attended in person. Several people from Dr. J. B. Rhine's laboratory of parapsychology discussed snake-handling with the Reverend Bunn also: the handling of snakes with impunity is obviously a potential instance of the "PK phenomenon," psycho-kinesis, or the "power of mind over matter." Bunn did not understand the motive behind Dr. Rhine's investigations, but was impressed with the results. He said he would be glad to "submit himself to mental telepathy" if he thought he would be doing anyone good, just as he would submit his body for examination after his death if he had any unusual disease.

President." He also said, "I doubt that they'll come tonight. If they do, how are they going to get in? If you're friend, you'll stand right still [and passively resist the police by not moving aside]."

About three-thirty that same Sunday afternoon, Bunn moved the meeting outside the Durham city limits and hence outside the jurisdiction of the city police. Spirited serpent-handling rites were held from the back of a truck parked in a clearing in the pines on Route 70 or Raleigh Road approximately three miles from the city limits. Bunn stated that he had two reasons for having the meeting out of town: first, he did not wish to lose an unusually large rattlesnake to the police, and second, because an International News Service Telenews cameraman wanted to take photographs in a more rustic atmosphere. It is doubtless true that the Tabernacle setting — near a coal yard amid Durham back-street stores — would not have seemed sufficiently authentic and rural for the taste of metropolitan audiences and the meeting had necessarily to be stage-managed in this fashion.

About three hundred persons were present at the impromptu roadside meeting. Since it was given no advance publicity and was a last-minute arrangement, none of the police, not even a single state highway policeman, molested the affair. When one cameraman had difficulty with his camera, the handlers obligingly did a repeat performance with the snakes for another camera. Among those present were a middleaged Negro woman (a local Durham communicant of the sect); Paul Lee Dotson of St. Charles, Virginia, who said he had been bitten seventeen times by snakes without appreciable effect; and L. D. Tripp of Vanceboro, North Carolina. Unable to get strychnine Sunday in time for the meeting, Tripp performed with snakes instead, though poison-drinking was his real specialty. A photographer from *Life* magazine was present at this improvised al fresco meeting. Most Americans, unfortunately, have derived their notions of the snake-handling cult from this somewhat contrived and artificial situation.

Sunday night an estimated fifteen hundred cultists and onlookers attempted to crowd into the little building on Peabody Street. This time, as the squadron of police, again headed by Captain Thompson, entered, the Reverend Colonel Hartman Bunn headed for the rear exit, still carrying a copperhead snake. He was finally cornered against the wall of a building back of the Tabernacle, but apparently did not have the snake with him. Officers loosened his clothing and gingerly explored his person but did not find the snake. A number of people joined in the hunt, and Bunn was allowed to return to the crowded hall when most of the hunters had given up. Finally, however, armed with a flashlight and his special snake retriever, Captain Thompson found the snake in the grass, where Bunn had apparently dropped it in his flight.

But at a late hour Sunday night officers were still searching for the Reverend Mr. Bunn himself, waiting to serve another warrant for another violation, his third, of the municipal snake-handling ordinance. Police had made no attempt to serve the warrant as he resumed conducting the interrupted services, but it is unclear as to how and when he made his second exit. Some of his followers said that he had left because they thought he would be unable to post bond.

After the interstate convention broke up in this debacle, little was heard of Bunn and the snake-handlers for a time, the law evidently having decided to rest its case on the conviction of Massey and Bunn the year before. But on Tuesday, December 14, 1948, on a Superior Court appeal, Case Number 722, Bunn appeared in the state supreme court in Raleigh, still appealing the fifty-dollar fine levied after his original Recorder's Court conviction in Durham. He said that he would personally argue his case; not being represented by counsel is a rarity in this tribunal. Assistant Attorney General Wade Bruton, who appeared for the State, cited decisions of the United States Supreme Court in contending that "you cannot regulate what people believe, but if their practices endanger them the state can regulate these practices." [23]

Bunn told the court that some snake-handling cults in Virginia believe that people should be bitten by snakes to test the power, but "our doctrine is that no one should be harmed because we can't conceive God permitting anyone to be harmed." He said that his people made no argument that the State should not regulate their practices by requiring that snake-handling be done in cages or at a definite distance from other people. He did contend, however, that the Durham ordinance made no attempt to regulate but "It says we shall cease, making criminals out of our people and forcing some of them to break rocks on the roads.* It is not a question of law or for this court. It is part of the order of Jesus Christ and it is something that people following his word would do no matter what the law provides." Bunn said his only contention was that the ordinance was invalid because it barred "a religious practice followed in North Carolina for over 40 years without harm to anyone." He added, "Someone in this crowd" — he paused and indicated the courtroom thronged with his followers and others — "Someone in this crowd has been taking up serpents for over twenty years! We pick them up under the power of God. No one is induced or invited to take part in that ceremony, and in fact no child and no mentally deficient person is allowed to participate."

For the State, the assistant attorney general said that Kentucky and Virginia had state laws against snake-handling (the more highly publicized Tennessee law of 1947 had apparently escaped his notice). He said in other cases involving religion the court has upheld the right to any belief, but also upheld the right to restrict practices connected with religion. Bunn, dressed in a blue suit, stated coolly and forcefully, "We'd be willing to conform to a regulation, but not

* A single-sheet broadside, signed by C. H. Bunn and dated November 1948, shows two pictures of ex-serviceman Corporal Albert Maynard, in uniform in 1944 and wearing prison garb #509–53 as he served on the roads in 1948. Ralph Massey was also serving at the same time. The text quotes the Constitution of the United States and taunts the opposition with the allegation that only one city councilman served in the military service, "While . . . the Mayor of Durham sat at Home and enjoyed the comforts of American luxury." The mayor of Durham, a respected Jewish businessman, was over age for military service at the time; and the two councilwomen, one a much-admired granddaughter of Benjamin Duke, would not have been subject to military service in any case. The broadside further announced that there were two court cases on the way to the United States Supreme Court to test the issue. After the decision of the supreme court of the State of North Carolina, review was refused by the United States Supreme Court, which at that time had more serious invasions of personal liberty to rule upon.

a restriction which forbids us from even following our religious practices." The state attorney general was heard to remark later, "I've never heard a man plead his own case better."

Since Bunn still refused to pay his fine, the alternative, a thirty-day jail sentence, was ordered executed. On May 21, 1949, Bunn held a special farewell meeting and said that he would present himself to the Durham Superior Court on Monday morning "to be locked up if they wish." He would petition the Supreme Court from jail if necessary, still declaring that he would not pay his original fifty-dollar fine and requesting his followers not to pay it for him. When asked if there would be snake-handling at the farewell meeting, Bunn said, "Nobody has brought in any snakes this season. We let the sinners bring them in." He said, "I don't intend to pay anything, because all the money I have and all that's given to me is dedicated to the cause for which I'm persecuted — not for serpent-handling, but for the religion in which I so deeply believe."[24]

CHAPTER 5

Later History and Spread

IN DECEMBER OF 1955, having long since served out his sentence, the Reverend Bunn quietly reappeared in Durham and took up preaching again at the Zion Tabernacle. Since his return there has been no evidence of snake-handling in his services, currently broadcast over station WTIK in Durham for an hour on Saturday nights. Snake-handling in religious meetings was now a dead issue in the locale of the great interstate convention of 1948. The state supreme court of North Carolina had upheld the ordinance of the city council of Durham against snake-handling, and any municipality might on short notice pass similar ordinances. The states of Kentucky, Virginia, and Tennessee now had state laws against the handling of snakes in the public performance of religious ceremonies.

But meanwhile the snake-handling cult was spreading in other parts of the South. On July 15, 1951, Mrs. Ruth Craig, a fifty-year-old farm woman, held snake-handling services at her home near the rural village of New Hope, Alabama. She arranged the service herself and brought to it a glass jar a good-sized rattlesnake with ten rattles. "I'm going to handle the snake and anyone who doesn't believe had better leave," she told her fellow cultists. She then took off the jar lid and tried to get the snake out. It would not or could not come out, so she broke the jar. As the snake slid across the floor she tried to grab it, but it bit her rapidly four times on the upper arm and shoulder and then escaped through an open door.

Mrs. Craig quickly collapsed and soon passed into a coma from which she did not recover. It was the first such fatality in several years, the most recent previous death in the cult having been that of Ernest Davis from drinking a salvation cocktail in Summerville, Georgia, in 1947. The coroner ruled Mrs. Craig's an accidental death, since such services were not banned in Alabama.[25]

The Bristol (Tennessee-Virginia) *Herald Courier* for Sunday, November 8, 1953, carried an article and pictures captioned "Snake Handling Services." One picture taken out-of-doors shows a man in shirt sleeves and galluses, his eyes closed, his right hand raised. Beside him is a plump woman in a flowered housedress and apron holding a snake in both hands. In the background is a taller, younger, thinner woman wearing somewhat more modish clothes. The second picture is that of a woman looking perhaps younger than her stated eighty years, wearing glasses, a small-figured cotton dress, and a large black sunbonnet. The caption in full is as follows:

Mrs. Lloyd Freeman, a member of the Christian Church of God at Esserville, Va., in Wise County, is shown above handling a deadly four-foot rattlesnake as her husband, also a member of the church, and an unidentified woman look on. At right above is a picture of Mrs. Dosha "Granny" Fields, 80, member of the church who was bitten by a rattlesnake at recent services. She was a patient at the Norton General Hospital but since has recovered and been discharged. The Rev. Gordon Freeman, brother of the man shown above, is pastor of the church. Virginia law prohibits the handling of snakes in worship services. Sheriff Harold Fleming, of Wise County, said no charges had been preferred, as yet, against any member of the church.

Granny Fields' recovery from snakebite confirmed some people in their snake-handling practices. The accident of being bitten itself was of little theological moment, if only the "power" in them was demonstrated by their not subsequently dying from the bite. Indeed, several of the prominent leaders in the cult somewhat pridefully let it be known how often they have been bitten.[26] Tom Harden, leader of the Dolley Pond congregation, was bitten at least four times, and Paul Lee Dotson of St. Charles, Virginia, seventeen times. And according to one source,[27] the founder of the cult, George Hensley, said he had "been bitten four hundred times 'till I'm speckled all over like a guinea hen."

The snake-handling cult in California, mentioned earlier, appears to be authenticated by an event of this later time: in April of 1954, a seventy-two-year-old woman was bitten during a service at Long Beach, California. In much of this contemporary history of the spread of the cult we are forced to rely almost entirely upon press reports, since field work in all these remote places is manifestly impossible, and since a blasé public had become interested only in fatalities in the cults. Such reports, however, were coming in from both ends of the country. In June 1954, a snake-handler was bitten and died at Fort Payne, Alabama, and charges were filed against the lay preacher who had conducted the service.

On August 12, 1954, forty miles up the valley from Fort Payne, in a meeting held near Trenton, Georgia, Reece Ramsey, a man of sixty-seven, became the year's third victim. Ramsey had handled snakes for twenty years and was said to have survived ten earlier bites. But in a service conducted in the open by A. M. Walraven near Rising Fawn, Georgia, Ramsey was struck by a "satinback" rattlesnake three times on the right side of his head. He refused medical aid, but requested the preacher's daughter to sing "Only One Rose Will Do." After walking over to the preacher, Ramsey collapsed writhing on the ground. The preacher lifted him on his arm and the choir broke into a loud singing of "I'm Getting Ready to Leave this World," during which Ramsey died. The cause of death was listed as "not known," pending an investigation to determine whether the Georgia law against snake-handling with danger to others had been violated.

Sheriff F. C. Graham of Dade County, Georgia, went to Rising Fawn on Friday the thirteenth of August and later conferred with other county officials as to whether charges should be pressed against leaders in the cult.[28] Dade County is mountain country, made up of Lookout Mountain, Sand Mountain, and the valley between. Trenton, the county seat, is a small cluster of white houses lying in the midst of forest land and plowed fields. Reece Ramsey was a lay preacher from Tennessee and the cult is said to have been

Later History and Spread

driven from Tennessee and Alabama to Dade County. Sheriff Graham is a big white-haired man, six feet four inches tall. It is not known how he handled this large problem in his county.

In a remote mountain clearing about fifty yards from the Virginia border, near Harlan, Kentucky, some four thousand people gathered around for the snake-handling services that took place within a roped-off enclosure on August 21, 1955. This was a memorial service for the late Reverend Lee Valentine, who had been bitten by a large rattlesnake at Fort Payne, Alabama, and died during the second or third week of August. Sergeant Roy Cundriff led a squadron of Kentucky state police in the arrest of the preacher, Reverend William Vernon of Keokee, Virginia, almost immediately after Vernon began handling snakes in the service. These included four rattlesnakes and a "copperhead moccasin" which were confiscated and placed in two boxes as evidence of violation of the Kentucky statute forbidding public snake-handling.

As the Reverend Vernon was being led away under guard to one of the six state patrol cars he said, "I don't want any bond! I prefer to stay in jail, carrying on services and singing." Much of the crowd began to follow Vernon. At this point, the Reverend Oscar Hutton of St. Charles, Virginia, who had opened the services, cried, "I would rather die now with salvation I have than be in the place of the state police." He asked the crowd not to go away, for "There'll be more wonderful things!" Reverend Raymond Hayes of Cumberland, Kentucky, then picked up a lighted blowtorch and moved it up and down his arm. When suspicious police returned after Vernon had been jailed, they discovered hidden in the woods a third box of snakes, which no one claimed. Hutton said of his fellow minister, "Vernon got in too big a hurry. He tries to take over our meetings." Hutton claimed that with a little more patience they might have "conquered" Valentine's killer, the big rattler dubbed "Alabama" which they had brought with them, but which had been confiscated by the police. Valentine was the fourteenth member of the cult to die since 1940 as the result of snakebite received in meetings, according to the United Press accounting.[29]

About a week later, on the night of the 29th of August, 1955, a fifteenth (and very nearly a sixteenth) victim was claimed. Mrs. Anna Marie Covington Yost and her brother, Mansel Covington, were struck by rattlesnakes at services in Savannah, Tennessee. Both were at the same time under suspended ten-day jail sentences for illegally handling snakes. Mrs. Yost, a woman of forty-one, steadfastly refused medical aid to the end, firm in the local group's belief that prayer and the power of the soul can prevail over serpents. She died early next morning at her home.

Since Mansel Covington had broken his promise to desist, Judge John Caldwell of the Hardin County General Sessions Court canceled his probation, ordered him booked, legally attached his person, and sent Coroner P. M. Wade out to the country to the house of Covington's father, where communicants of the cult were praying in the yard, the victim himself being feverishly ill. Covington argued against leaving, telling the coroner that the group rejected doctors because it had faith in the Lord. "He argued about leaving and kept going on about Jesus and everybody else," Wade said. "Finally I asked him, 'Are you ready to go?' But he said, 'I won't go anywhere with anybody until they lay hands on me.'" Wade then pulled Covington by the sleeve and he came along "without too much protest." But again, at the doctor's office, Covington became stubborn and protested against antivenin injections. But he was finally persuaded to have them and was then taken to jail.[30]

The culmination of these events was reached when the founder and prophet of the snake-handling cult himself, George Went Hensley, was bitten on the wrist by a diamondback rattlesnake during a prayer meeting at Lester's Shed near Altha, Florida, on Sunday night, July 24, 1955. The aged prophet of the cult, now seventy, had been handling a snake for nearly fifteen minutes and was putting it back into a box when he was bitten. His whole arm turned dark and became enormously swollen. But he refused all medical attention and died "vomiting blood" early Monday morning. His wife, Sally, a native of Jackson, Mississippi, said her husband was conscious until the end and died saying, "I know I am going to go; it is God's will."

At two o'clock the next Wednesday afternoon, protracted funeral services began with a "family singing" at Lester's Shed, a reconverted barn used by the cult. After Bible readings and prayers led by the Reverend Obis Lassiter, members of the congregation testified to Hensley's "doing the right thing in giving his life to God." Several persons in the crowd of three hundred at the Shed swore their allegiance to the faith and vowed their determination to continue snake-handling rites. Following this, the funeral cortege made its way some two miles to Mount Olive Cemetery, where Hensley's body lies buried. The congregation then returned to Lester's Shed for more singing, prayers, and pledges to continue practicing their faith. One member said he had "no idea how long" the service would last; "it might go on all night and tomorrow too," at which the observer left. Hensley's widow said that she was going to move from Albany, Georgia, to the northwest Florida pinelands community of Altha, west of Tallahassee, "to continue her husband's work." It is to this same region in Florida that we shall return in a later chapter, after a study of the background of snake cultism in the Old World.[31]

The snake-handling cult is still vigorous at the present in some places. During the Fourth of July weekend of 1959, for example, a meeting was held at Forester Asher's home at Blue Hole, a hamlet in a remote hill section southeast of Manchester, Kentucky. In this Holiness Church meeting, James Estep, an unemployed miner of Arjay, demonstrated his faith by handling four very large timber rattlesnakes simultaneously. On July 19, 1959, one of these same rattlers bit Estep on the finger; he refused medical attention, saying "I'm letting the Lord do my doctoring." The Reverend Shilo Collins is the leader of this group of snake-handlers which, quiescent after a police raid in the summer of 1958, held numerous meeting in midsummer 1959; Estep was bitten after he and Collins had returned from making a radio broadcast. On August 9, 1961, sixty-year-old Mrs. Sally Hall of Stollings, West Virginia, became the nineteenth victim of cultist snake-handling. Bitten on the hand by a rattlesnake the preceding Sunday afternoon (August 6) during services at the Church of Jesus Only in Nolan, West Virginia, Mrs. Hall refused medical attention when taken to the home of Richard

Hensley of Nolan, and later to the home of the Reverend Kelly Williams of Switzer, pastor of the Church of Jesus Only, where the church members prayed for her recovery. On Wednesday morning her daughter, Mrs. Woodrow Sexton of White's Addition, coming to the Williams's house and realizing her mother's condition, rushed Mrs. Hall by ambulance to the Logan General Hospital where she died about noon, a few minutes after arrival.

Early in the first week of October 1961, the Associated Press reported that a twenty-three-year-old girl, daughter of Mrs. Robert Elkins, a leader in the snake-handling Church in Jesus of Jolo, in the coal-mining region of southern West Virginia, died from a snakebite received in a meeting attended by some two hundred people. Medical aid was twice refused. The minister, known only as Brother Carl, was "a handsome youth with hair combed back." It is reported that a solution of strychnine was also sipped by one communicant. Aroused members of the West Virginia legislature have promised a state anti-snake-handling law. In a meeting held less than a fortnight after her daughter's accident, Mrs. Elkins testified, "I'm letting God fight my battle. You think I'm going to let some of these little judges and lawyers make me back up on my salvation? No!"

} *THE SYMBOLISM*

CHAPTER 6

Snake Cults in Africa

PSYCHOLOGICAL interpretations of the snake cult will already inevitably have occurred to the careful reader of the foregoing. In any group ritual of such psychological intensity we must surely expect to find both inner meanings and the emotional communication of these meanings in cult practices. And, just as surely, there is much discernible phallic symbolism in the present snake-handling cult. That the meanings are unconscious, or at best preconscious, in no way militates against their reality or their demonstrability.

For example, in the meeting described in Chapter 1, the preacher in an interesting sequence talked about the meaning of snake-handling as an overpowering of the evil animal or Devil, requested that the Samson and Delilah ballad be sung, and after this explained that the young boy who told his mother Samson lost his power from laying his head in Delilah's lap (the head can be trusted only in God's lap) was not really telling her an "evil story" as she supposed. Then the preacher launched into a discussion of his own problems with the marriage laws and argued a preacher's right to perform his own impromptu marriages. His thought associations are completely clear, and the theme throughout is undeniably sexual.

Again, at the same meeting, after the preacher had variously dealt with women in a state of orgiastic ecstasy, why, then, had he to preach about the wonders of a religion in which such spiritual phenomena take place "without there being the least intention of carnal desires"? Can anyone doubt that symbolic communications take place in the cult and, further, that considerable acting-out occurs despite the preacher's bland over-protestation? But what is the status of a symbolism that is officially denied so explicitly and repeatedly? And in what manner is the symbolism still culturally present, to be so constantly exploited?

These psychological problems are illuminated by a great mass of ethnological facts which I shall proceed to demonstrate and summarize. Of course, not all the ethnographic facts cited are historically ancestral to our own tradition, which is here at issue. Nevertheless, they are descended from a common cultural ancestor, and they represent a system that is certainly germane symbolically. The culture-historical generalization I shall seek to demonstrate is that in the ancient eastern Mediterranean world, centering geographically, at least, in Egypt, phallus and serpent were symbolically equated in religion so explicitly as not to be denied; that attributes which belong properly only to the phallus were repeatedly projected onto serpents; that from or at least via Egypt this snake symbolism has spread widely in Africa, in some cases diffusing along the same known paths as the Egyptian harp, the concept of the "divine king," and the African immortality legends; and that the snake symbolism which spread anciently from Asia Minor into contiguous regions of northwest India is identifiable and identical with the snake symbolism that came from Semitic sources to Europe — and ultimately, here with complete cultural continuity, to modern America.

This snake symbolism coincided with the ancient culture area extending in a large arc from northwest India through the Middle East into Egypt, later spreading to pre-Hellenic Greece, and thence, reinforced from Semitic sources, into Christian Europe. This large-scale historic process followed known and well-established anthropological principles of diffusion. Furthermore, this diffusion can be documented ethnographically in such a way as to satisfy the most critical naturalistic and non-mystical mind — quite without precariously postulated *Kulturkreise*, culture-evolutionist *Elementargedanken*, or an unnecessary and undemonstrable Jungian "racial unconscious." It is a direct diffusion of "covert culture," nonetheless real for all that it is at times unwitting or unconscious in its culture bearers. But even the most succinct summary will require a long presentation of data; I ask the reader's indulgence in my adducing these until I can show their relevance to the main theme: the reality and the nature of the symbolism in the snake-handling cult.

First, a brief excursus into co-traditions in Africa and Asia that have the same historic origins — and one of which, in part, is ancestral to our own. Frazer has pointed out that in the Garden of Eden story there were two trees, the Tree of Knowledge and the Tree of Life. Only the first of these was forbidden to the primal parents (Genesis ii, 16f). The Tree of Life or immortality was to be theirs, but the wily serpent seduced Eve and Adam to eat of the forbidden Tree of Knowledge first. For this sin against the Lord they were cast forth from Eden and their re-entry forever barred by an angel with a flaming sword — since, if they had both knowledge and, later, immortality, they would be as gods. Man thus lost access to the other tree, the Tree of Life, and hence lost his first chance at immortality — regaining this only when the Son of God had expiated the sin of Adam. What seems meanwhile to have escaped our notice is that, at the Fall, the serpent himself ate of the Tree of Life and became immortal, by periodically casting his skin.[32]

The sometimes apocopated Semitic story is fuller in its African versions, diffused through Egypt from whatever were its original sources. One of the most curious and persistent elements in African folklore is the tale that has come to be known as "the Origin of Death" or "the Story of the Perverted Message." For example, among the Hottentot, who believed that the waxing and waning moon had immortality,[33] the hare was the messenger. Through malice or forgetfulness, the hare perverted the message given, "As I die and rise to life again, so shall you die and rise to life again," into its opposite, "As I die and do not rise to life again, so you shall also die and not rise to life again" — for which the Moon split the hare's lip with a stick, but not before the hare had put scratches on the Moon's face that may still be seen on clear nights. The Bushmen have a similar tale, but in this version a skeptical man was cursed at the death of his mother and struck by the Moon and turned into a hare; the hare still has some human flesh in his thigh, for which rea-

son the Bushmen cut this part out and do not eat it. The Tati Bushmen believed the tortoise was the first messenger, but the Moon was
so vexed at the tortoise's slowness that he sent the hare also, who
got to man first, but with a garbled message. The magic efficacy of
formulas and promises was such that man has henceforth been
doomed to death. Still another Hottentot story has another pair of
messengers, an insect and the hare, but the same dire results.

Among the Nandi the messenger is a dog but, insufficiently
honored by his hosts when being fed, the dog in a huff perverted
the Moon's message that people would rise on the third day after
death. The A-Louyi of the upper Zambesi tell a more complex story
of the Origin of Death. The dog of Nyambe the Sun died, and Nyambe, loving his dog, pleaded with his wife, Nasilele the Moon,
"Let the dog live!" But this she refused. Then Nyambe's mother-in-
law died and Nasilele in turn begged that her mother might live.
But, remembering the fate of his dog, Nyambe vindictively refused.
Thus, from a family argument over a dog and a mother-in-law, death
came to men, for a hare and a chameleon bearing opposite messages
from the gods ended the race with the faster animal victorious.
Among the Ekoi of Nigeria, the sky-god Obassi Osaw sent the frog
and the duck with opposite messages; but the duck fell to gobbling
palm oil on the way and got to mankind fatally second. On the
Gold Coast the messengers were a sheep and a goat, but the goat
unfortunately browsed along the way. The Ashanti have several
versions, also involving a sheep and a goat. The Akamba have a
bungling chameleon and a lying thrush. In Calabar there are a dog
and a sheep. All these African stories are evidently related.

In Togoland, God sent a dog with a message of immortality to
men, but the dog stopped off at a place where a man was boiling
magic herbs, thinking that they might be food to allay his hunger.
Meanwhile a frog, in an act of pure officiousness, went off to God
and told him falsely that men had said they had no interest in immortality. Angered, and believing the false messenger, God conferred immortality upon the frog, who seems to be dead in the dry
season when the harmattan blows but who comes to life again
when it thunders in the rainy season. Thus the frog, like the serpent,

has perfidiously obtained immortality for himself, but at the expense of men.

The Zulu "Old Old One" or Unkulunkulu sent a chameleon to men, but it dawdled on the way to eat flies and to sleep. Meantime the Old Old One had thought better of his idea and sent the lizard with an opposite message, and the lizard outran the chameleon. Other Bantu groups like the Bechuana, the Basuto, the Baronga, the Ngoni, and the Wasania have a similar tale. It is also found among the Hausa, who have undergone extensive Hamito-Semitic influences. Thus the belief is widespread in Africa that God intended at one time for man to be immortal; but this plan miscarried through the fault of the messenger entrusted with the word. Since Africanists are agreed on the diffusion of cattle culture from northeastern Africa down the east coast to the Zulu, and on the spread of "Semitisms" in culture through the Sudan westward to West Africa, we have two great corridors already established through which the Origin of Death stories might have spread from northeastern Africa to the tribes mentioned who have the story.

Even more important for our study are other numerous Africanisms regarding the serpent. These repeatedly contain the associated ideas of immortality and of creativity. Thus the Wafipa and the Wabende of East Africa say that the great god Leza one day came down to earth asking all living creatures, "Who wishes not to die?" Unfortunately, all men and other animals were asleep, and only the serpent was awake to answer "I do." Therefore he alone nowadays never dies, but renews his youth and strength every time that he changes his skin. The Galla of Abyssinia, most interestingly, have combined the motifs of perverted message and cast skin. The *holawaka* bird or "sheep of God" was once sent by God to tell men they would never die, but that when they grew old and feeble they should slip off their skins and renew their youth. As a badge of office the bird was given a crest which he wears to this day. But on the way he met a snake devouring carrion and begged the snake to give him some of it. The snake selfishly and repeatedly refused, whereupon the bird said he would tell the snake a secret, the message from God. But the bird perverted the message to: "When men grow old they will die, but when you grow old you will cast your skin and renew your youth." This is why men grow old and die, but snakes crawl out of their old skins and are immortal. Man's birthright was lost, over a mess of carrion; in punishment, the *holawaka* bird was given a painful intestinal ailment, for which reason he sits high in the trees and bleats constantly like a sheep.

Thus the Biblical tradition of the Origin of Death is but one of many obviously related ones in the Old World. In the African versions the creator sends a messenger, in various animal forms, with the promise of immortality to man. Through a mistake, however, whether by accident or by intention, the message is altered, and the messenger keeps his secret to himself or lies to man. The creator then curses and punishes the messenger, as the serpent in Genesis was cursed and punished—but the messenger has obtained the immortality, and man in any case is left mortal. Frazer believes that the story of the Fall of Man in the third chapter of Genesis is an abridged version of the myth which is more complete and understandable in its African forms. Indeed, it is otherwise unclear why God should be angry that man became *moral* (having knowledge of good and evil) through the good offices of the serpent; it is, rather, that a benevolent God would be angered because the snake and not, as intended, man, became *immortal*. And man, likewise, was punished because he disobediently ate the fruit of the wrong tree. Thus God, giving man immortality through the Second Adam, Christ, was only bestowing what he had always intended. The snake, or man's sinful nature, merely delayed this dispensation.*

Others have argued that man was punished because he sought the prerogatives of the gods, creativity and immortality. Thus sexuality was the sin of Eve and Adam; but the equally rebellious serpent got the gift of immortality which came to man only through later and complexer divine machinations. The serpent, an older god, the old Devil, is a constant rebel against God (as chthonic snake deities in Greece even threatened the sky-god, Olympian Zeus). The

* Again, much later, the serpent in the snake cult carries either death or salvation to immortality, depending upon sinful man's relationship to his creator. (A child's sexuality vis-à-vis his father is of course the perennial source of all such symbolisms.)

snake, with his immortality, is suspiciously even a little like unto
the gods. The snake, in short, on other African and pre-Greek
evidence, would seem at times to be no less than the high god himself! (This will be no surprise at all to psychiatrists, who have maintained all along that the "good father" and the "bad father" of man
are one and the same, but viewed with the son's ambivalence.)

This evidence suggesting that the serpent is an older creator-god
is rife with "Semitisms" of culture in Africa.* Thus the Ijaw of
Nigeria believe that pythons contain the spirits of the sons of Adamu
(himself a python and chief of the water spirits); women may not
mention his name or approach his temple, though priestesses take
the sacred snakes as husbands.[34] The Bavili think that the black
snake-deity can lift itself on its tail to strike people dead. Ndoma
is also the cause of man's thinking and reason.[35] The wisdom of
the serpent as the familiar of wise men, mages, and medicine-men
(e.g. Moses, Hermes, Asklepios) is a deep-rooted idea in Mesopo-
tamian, Greek, and Semitic cultures. Was, indeed, the serpent the
animal-familiar of the snake shamans Aaron and Moses, as it was
the totem of the Leah tribes? We have already noted the powers of
these mages at the court of Pharaoh; Moses' apotropaic brazen serpent that protected the people against snakebite in the wilderness
was worshiped for many generations in Jerusalem; and if Moses
could produce water in the wilderness with his snake-staff, this is
only what every rain-king in Africa was able to do, even that chief
African "divine king," the Pharaoh himself.†

* Note, incidentally, that "The tribe of Levi, and probably all the Leah
tribes, venerated a seraph, or winged serpent; the Rachel tribes, a bull"
(*Hastings Encyclopedia of Religion and Ethics*, 7:444). Note also that the
levite priest-shamans Moses and Aaron already had snake staves in Africa
at the court of Pharaoh. Note, further, that the image of Jahweh himself at
Jerusalem in Isaiah's time was a bronze serpent (Numbers xxi, 8; II Kings
xviii, 4; Deuteronomy viii, 15; Isaiah xiv, 29 and xxx, 6; see also Herodotus,
bk. ii, 75ff).

† As for the wisdom of the serpent, even Jesus tells his disciples to be "wise
as serpents" in their evangelism (Matthew x, 16). For the chthonic snake
attributes of even some of the Olympian sky-gods, see the abundant illustra-
tions and examples in Jane Ellen Harrison's great *Prolegomena to the Study
of Greek Religion*. From both classic Greek and Biblical evidence it is plain
that the snake was an ancient high god in the eastern Mediterranean, henothe-
istically demoted later to be the Enemy of a subsequent high god.

Outside of Egypt, Africa has two great centers of snake worship, West Africa and Uganda. So widespread and so ancient are African snake cults that Hambly postulates two origins for them: "My general conclusion [he says] is that python-worship is an indigenous factor of Negro culture; but on the contrary African ideas of rainbow snakes, snake monsters, and birth-snakes, are derived from Hamito-Semitic beliefs of southwestern Asia."[36] Respecting the latter conclusion, there are some interesting Semitic-African symbolisms that connect snakes and water: the python water-gods and rainbow-serpents in West Africa and the rainbow of God after the Flood; Moses' snake-staff from Egypt and the water from the rock and the African rain-kings, and so on.*

In any case, the African high snake god and creator is full of clear echoes of and parallels to Semitic myths. For example, in Dahomey the chief god is a snake, "their extreme bliss and general good," as Bosman put it in 1700. The snake is invoked in very dry, or very wet, or barren seasons, and on all occasions having to do with government. Even kings send presents to the snake. Sometimes the snake appeared to the most beautiful girls, inducing madness; such girls then had to enter the service of the snake temple; and before human sacrifices, these wives of the snakes danced with earthen pots on their heads, apparently to bring rain. The python god also opened the eyes of the first man and woman.[37]

The generally ancestral, not to say the specifically phallic, aspects of the African snake god are abundantly evident. In Nigeria, "any offense against the snake is an offense against the ancestor." In Nigeria, also, the python once stiffened his body to allow warriors to cross a river, and when the enemy came he relaxed and submerged them — a fantasy at once phallic and remotely recalling the

* It will be remembered also that the phallic snake-god Shiva of northwestern India, according to legend, gave rise to the Ganges through a fountain springing from his head. Likewise, in both Greek and Asia Minor rain-bull sky-gods and river-gods, the water rushes from a broken horn. Even more startling, since wholly independent, are the rain-snake parallels from the American Indians, to be presented in detail later. In all this symbolism the fructifying water proceeds from the phallic snake — which is entirely consistent with body symbolism and is a "condensation" of the dual functions of the phallus. The only diffusion we need invoke here is the diffusion of symbol-using Homo sapiens and his body.

Red Sea story. In Ashanti the *ntoro* is one of the two main elements in every man and woman, though it is transmitted only by the male — a recognizable parallel to the Pelasgian Greek snake god and later male logos, and to the Latin snake *genius lectualis*.[38] This African and European phallic snake symbolism I believe in each case to have been diffused from the same eastern Mediterranean source.

The phallic symbolism of African snakes is again suggested in their supposed hairiness, though in nature no snakes, African or otherwise, have any hair whatever anywhere on their bodies. The Akikuyu, for example, offer beer to the sacred snake, which intoxicates it, and then a specially appointed man can pull hairs from the snake, these being used as powerful charms. The rainbow-snake monster of the Zande in the Belgian Congo is thought to be covered with a powdery white substance and also to have a beard.[39] In Europe another high god, Zeus Meilichios, the "Zeus of Placation," is represented as "an enormous bearded snake, a well-known representation of underworld powers or dead ancestors."[40] I believe the African, the Semitic, the pre-Hellenic snake-ancestors and snake-deities — and indeed the abundant *nagas* or snake gods in India as well — are for both geographic and historical reasons probably all derived from the same ancient Old World and possibly Old Stone Age source, as we shall see. But what of the wholly independent Middle American concept of the Feathered Serpent or the bearded snake god Quetzalcoatl? Snakes no more have feathers than they have beards!

Need we invoke here a Jungian "archetype"? Or only that ubiquitous cross-cultural phenomenon, the human body and the propensity of man to body-image fantasying? In fact, it is the very impossibility, or at least the high improbability, of any culture-historical relationship between Old World and American Indian legends that must convince us of the body-image origins of some startlingly parallel symbolisms. No snake in the world, I repeat, has either hair or feathers; and yet, in the New World again, snakes are persistently associated with or endowed with these properly only phallic attributes. The Aztec association of feathers with a rattle-snake god is widely found archaeologically in the southern Mississippi River basin and eastward into the Southeastern Woodlands and may derive culturally from an ancient Mexican focus. Opler reports [41] a Lipan Apache myth of a rattler with hair on its head; and Madsen wrote that Nahuatl women south of Mexico City stimulate hair growth with rattlesnake oil, which makes the hair grow as long as the snake, though if care is not taken, the hair will twist like a snake in a rainstorm and strangle the woman or her husband — an American Medusa and with the same body-image origin! [42] In Peru, it is said that the god of riches was worshiped in the image of a horned and hairy rattlesnake, embellished with a tail of gold. [43] Stories of hairy rattlesnakes appear repeatedly — taken seriously by some narrators, treated as folklore by others. One of the earliest is that of Dudley in 1723; but as late as 1853 Aubry encountered hairy rattlesnakes in Arizona. [44] Hairy rattlesnakes are part of Ozark folklore; and Carvalho said that natives in Brazil believe that very old rattlesnakes grow feathers on their bodies. [45] None of these legends can have been influenced by the Greeks, the Akikuyu, or the Zande!

In addition to their phallic attribute of hair, the specifically sexual associations of the snake in Africa are also evident. For example, in the python cult at the Muzini River on Victoria Nyanza, "no man who spent the previous night with a woman is allowed to cross the river. A menstruating woman is forbidden to cross. There is a belief that any person with a deformation of the generative organs will be drowned in attempting to cross." [46] (Compare the belief — in South India! — that a Toda who had been bitten by a snake must not cross any stream whatsoever; [47] compare also the American rattlesnake legend that when a rattlesnake swims a river, it dies on reaching the other shore [48] — so similar is body-image thinking the world over!) As another example of the association of snakes and sexuality in Africa, "The Nuba and Abyssinians make a snake antidote from roots ground to powder by a virgin; such powder is proof against both snakes and scorpions." [49] (Despite the contrastive body-image, snakes and scorpions are also associated symbolically and repeatedly mentioned together in the Bible, a matter to be taken up later.)

The whole African complex of phallism, soul concepts, and the ancestor cult is perhaps best shown in West Africa.

The Ibo-speaking people of southern Nigeria believe that when a snake advances toward a woman, it does so as a sign that she has conceived. There is a belief in the reincarnation of a Ci at this time. The Ci may be either the spirit of a dead or a living person. The medicine-man is called in to say exactly what this Ci happens to be. Taboos will then be imposed on the woman with regard to eating or contact with certain objects. Talbot speaks of a tree which was supposed to give fertility to women. A python was coiled round the tree at certain seasons of the year. To Ibo and Ijaw people the snake typifies masculinity. There is a belief common to all Hausa women that if they dream of a snake, they have conceived. The Bavili of the Lango Coast classify certain snakes under the name Bobo, which means "bearing ones." In the same region the Fan make figures of the snake out of clay. This is done at the time when boys are ready for initiation. The sexual side of these rites is strongly developed, and throughout the ceremonies the snake is the symbol of the male organ.[50]

The Yao say that "if a dead man wants to frighten his wife, he may persist in coming as a serpent"; the Masai offer milk to such a snake-husband.[51] Hambly, who has gone more deeply into the African evidence in recent times than any other scholar, says that

It is not improbable that the reincarnation concept is logically fundamental to every form of African snake worship, snake cult, and snake belief . . .

A reincarnated ancestor concept . . . is of continuous occurrence from the Cape to Lake Rudolph, including the southern part of Madagascar . . . The snake, more than any other animal, is prominent in African belief and custom. There is a worship of the snake more definite than the veneration accorded to any other creature . . .

The most fundamental ideas of all kinds of African snake beliefs are those of resurrection and fecundity.[52]

These highly condensed paragraphs pretend to be no more than a sampling of the rich African materials on phallic snake cults. The points I consider to have been demonstrated are these: that in Africa there is a widespread symbolic equation of the snake and the phallus; that there is repeated projection onto serpents of attributes that belong properly only to the phallus (tumescence and detumescence, hairiness, the production of water, ancestorship, husband-hood, specific masculinity, and so forth); and that because of detailed Hamito-Semitisms in content the African area is an extension of the Egypt-India arc of snake symbolism which the African data at times expand and illuminate; and that, indeed, there is sufficient reason to regard these as merely further examples illustrating standard Africanist opinions about the diffusion of material and other culture from northeast Africa.

CHAPTER 7

Classic Near East Cults

ONE significant feature of the mass of African materials is that, although they are all variations on the same theme of maleness and paternity, we have no real reason to believe that the specifically phallic symbolism demonstrable behind them all was always *necessarily* conscious. Only in the case of the Tanganyika cults (note 50, p. 190) are we forced to suspect a quite conscious symbolism; the need to symbolize in the first place remains a motive for people to "forget" the meaning of their symbols, to which they will then react directly with compulsive "mysterious" magic ritual. Nevertheless, conscious or otherwise, the symbolic equation *snake = phallus* is ubiquitous in Africa and has been everywhere transmitted intact. Indeed, despite the obviousness of meanings in the snake phallisms of Africa, it is even possible to suppose that the manifest symbols and legends alone were diffused, but that each group had a ready unconscious understanding of the communications culturally mediated to them. So easily can people deny knowledge of what they already competently understand! But this should not surprise us much. We shall encounter the same "lack of understanding" again and again in American snake cultists, despite their undeviatingly sure exploitations of meanings; for the hysteroid denial of purposely masked and purpose-masking symbols can reach unbelievable extremes of naïveté in calling a spade a spade while yet blandly denying that it is one. However, for such cultural communications to operate we evidently need postulate no mysteriously and genetically transmitted "racial unconscious." All that is required is a constant and vigilant institutionalized repression of understandings and a common cultural need to repress. For manifestly there must be repressions before there can be a "return of the repressed," so spectacular and conspicuous in the American snake-handling cult.

A snake is not a phallus. Still less can we pretend that the human mind must everywhere and inevitably discover that they "are" the same. Far more economical of scientific theorizing, therefore, is the acknowledgment that symbolism can be diffused in much the same manner, and indeed in the same historical directions in the Old World, as we can establish that items of material culture have been diffused. No new mechanisms are required. Symbols are never *discovered* in nature, but as humanly arbitrary associations they are always culturally *invented*. Once cultural, they can be diffused; once inventable, they can be invented again independently. Thus it is probable that snake symbolism was prehistorically diffused in the same fashion as, if not indeed concurrently with, the concept of the "divine king" in the large contiguous region stretching from West Africa through the Sudan to Egypt and through the Near East to northwest India, the vast area of spread and the many secondary variations being indices of the time-depth. Similarly, but independently, an American Indian concept of the rain snake spread over much of the western United States and a concept of the feathered rattlesnake over much of southern and southeastern America, coming possibly from Mexico originally. The startling parallels we find between American and Old World snake symbolism may still be arguable in the familiar terms of diffusion versus independent invention that we employ for material culture. If independent invention is the presently preferable assumption, then the similarities may nevertheless be explained in terms of the same body image that is everywhere being projected onto nature.

In the diffusion of the African concept of the phallic snake, Egypt appears to be the critical region, either as the place of ultimate origin or as the intercontinental doorway to diffusion from elsewhere, whatever the direction. Perhaps it is only that our documentation is earlier and more complete for Egypt than elsewhere.

The snake has been associated with ideas of fecundity in Egypt since predynastic times, probably even preceding the neolithic Egypto-Mesopotamian-Indic rain bull. In dynastic Egypt the snake became the symbol of deity, and in time the snake hieroglyph itself became the written sign for deity.[53] The cyclic reflooding of the Nile and the rejuvenation of the soil by its silt, the endless death and rebirth of the sun, and the consequent idea of the cyclic immortality of the divine king, are together at the very core of Egyptian religion. The Pharaoh is the prototype of the widespread African rain-king or "divine king" who, in his prime, controls the weather and all fertility in nature until he must die and be replaced by another human embodiment of the immortal. The rain snake and the rain bull are his symbols throughout a large region and from ancient times.

In the welter of quasi-totemic deities that became the animal-headed gods of later Egypt, the snake of the lower Nile is unquestionably the most prominent of them all, and as such the snake was incorporated into the double crown of the Pharaohs of Upper and Lower Egypt. The belief in the reincarnation of the Ra-Pharaoh, which is the rationale of mastabas and pyramids, is also anciently intertwined with snake symbolism. Isis is often shown as a serpent, the guardian of the fertility orb Ra. Osiris likewise commonly takes the form of a snake; and Osiris is another ancient symbol of resurrection, who as the son Horus, is constantly reborn from his mother-consort Isis.[54] The Ophites, a Gnostic subsect, were still worshiping the snake in Hellenistic times, not long after Cleopatra and her asp. Snake symbolism is prominent even in modern Egypt: the popular belief is that as snakes grow old wings grow out of their bodies, but they never die.

The diffusion problem is involved with the crossroads of the Old World, the Eurafroasiatic Near East land bridge. Sooner or later in ancient times everything passed through this corridor—from Chinese silk to African ivory and Cornish tin. For reasons I shall bring out later, I believe snake symbolism to be of Old Stone Age time-depth in Egypt and to have spread since then with near-universality over the Old World. Certainly on the Neolithic horizon we have basic culture areas of truly intercontinental range in this same general area. For example, the so-called ritualization of cattle in East Africa forms a great continuous arc with the Apis-bull of Egypt, the Neolithic rain bull found everywhere in Asia Minor, the Iranian man-faced bull, the Mohenjodaran bull god of Neolithic northwest India (whence derives the phallic Shiva and his *vahana*, the bull Nandi), and even perhaps as far as the Toda dairy cult and the Dravidian bull gods of the south Indian peninsula (of which the young Krishna, avatar of Vishnu, is the prototype). In this "trait area" the ritualized cattle complex is as impressive in time-depth as it is in geographic area covered. Inasmuch as the Cretan bull worship can now be seen, together with the Thracian cult of Orpheus, to be a part of the Dionysian mysteries and their bull god — and these in turn the source of such diverse complexes as the Phoenician-Spanish bullfight and the Christian Eucharist — we have truly impressive evidence of vast diffusions of culture in the Old World.

But beyond the Neolithic bull god there lies the far more ancient snake god of the Old Stone Age. At the eastern end of our great culture arc, for example, snakes are the basic village gods of pre-Vedic India, and only later become attributes fused with the Mohenjodaran Shiva. The snake in India is so ubiquitously a symbol and cult object that the question might well be raised, can India have been an ancient source of snake worship and symbolism? The claims of India to such a role are not lightly to be dismissed.

India is the only country in the world inhabited by all the known families of living snakes. The chief characteristic of the reptile fauna of the Indian region is the great variety of the generic types and the number of their species, the latter amounting to no fewer than 450, which is nearly one-third of the total number of species known in the world, referable to about 100 genera, of which the majority do not range beyond the limits of India.[55]

Nevertheless, the complexity of cultural associations with the phallic snake (e.g., its association with immortality) would seem to suggest, rather, a Near Eastern or Egyptian origin. India, like Africa, is at the periphery of the total region in question. But before coming to deal with this central region of snake symbolism, Asia Minor, it may be well to discuss a third, also perhaps peripheral, region, the European — or at least its earliest well-documented forms in Greece. It should in no way be supposed that the Greek snake cults are directly ancestral to the snake cults of the southeastern United States: both are separate emergents from the same ancient common and continuous substrate. The immediate ancestor of snake symbolism in the American Southeast is Semitic, specifically Biblical. This ancestor, for various reasons, we leave until last.

The Pelasgian "chthonic" gods of pre-Indoeuropean Greece were without any question various forms of snake deities. The point is exhaustively documented in Jane Ellen Harrison's classic study, the *Prolegomena to the Study of Greek Religion*. When Pausanius saw the great chryselephantine image of Athena, patroness of Athens, in the Parthenon, he noted that at her feet lay a shield, and near the shield, a serpent. Who was this serpent? Pausanius surmised it might be Erichthonios, the "lord and luck of the state." [56] This snake deity was one of a very ancient type, not unlike the Latin *genius loci* or the Indic *Naga* or supernatural serpents: place deities and guardian spirits.

The snake among the Greeks was full of *mana*, was intensely sacred . . . because he is himself a life-*daimon*, a spirit of generation, even of immortality. But — and this is all important — it is an immortality of quite a peculiar kind . . .

Crecrops is a snake, Erichthonios is a snake, the old snake-king is succeeded by a new snake-king . . .

The individual members of the group of Crecropidae die, man after man, generation after generation; Crecrops, who never lived at all, lives for ever, as a snake. He is the *daimon gennēs*, the spirit, the genius of the race, he stands not for personal immortality in our modern sense, not for the negation of death, *athanasia*, but for the perennial renewal of life through death, for Reincarnation, for *palingenesia*.[57]

To the Greek, then, the snake was a form of the immortal "divine king" so plentifully illustrated in Frazer's *Golden Bough*, who dies and never dies. Again, "[the word] *pelōp* is one regular term for an earth-born monster and especially for a snake. Gaia herself in Hesiod [*Theog.* 159] is *Gaia Pelōpē*, the Python in the Homeric Hymn to Apollo [v. 374] is *pelōp*, etc." [58] The snake, as such, was immortality and deity itself; curiously, also, in classical days it was the general belief that all snakes, of whatever kind, were deadly.[59] That is to say, the numinous snake bore the power both of death and of life. The latter was especially true of the half-legendary snake-shaman or medicine-man, Asklepios. This physician-god saved so many souls alive that Hades complained to his brother Zeus that Asklepios was depopulating the underworld; therefore, to oblige his brother, the All Father blasted the purveyor of immortality. But Zeus repented him of his deed and restored Asklepios to life, "therefore his special symbol became the serpent which, when it sloughs its skin, seems to die and rise from its own dead self." [60]

The pre-Greek gods of the Greek world were repeatedly associated with the snake. I need only remind the reader that "from Minoan times in Crete we have the little ivory figure of a snake priestess, her dress encircled with bands of gold, standing upright with a golden snake in either hand." [61] The snake played an important role in the worship of the Great Mother, Magna Mater or Demeter, and snakes were an attribute of Athene, Erichthios, Hermes, Asklepios, Dionysos, and many other Greek gods.[62] Hermes was especially the phallus-snake. "Hermes, as Agathos Daimon, was once merely a *phallos*: that he was also once merely a snake, is, I think, a safe conjecture." [63] In any case, the caduceus or twin snake-wreathed staff is as much an attribute of Hermes as it is of Asklepios. The word "caduceus," meaning herald's wand, originates from his function as ambassador or nunciator, for Hermes was par excellence the mediator between the world of spirits and that of living men — that is, between gods and men — and hence the "messenger" of the gods. It is in fact difficult not to see in Hermes the lineaments of the ancient snake-shaman and his animal-familiar. Much as the immortal snake-physician Asklepios gave mortals immortality by curing them, so to speak, Hermes the death-stayer was also the intermediary between the spirits of the dead and man: Hermes is godhood and immortality in essence, he *is* the phallus and he *is* the snake. As a boundary god and spirit guardian of the land, his symbol was the phallic head on a square shaft, still surviving in the acorn-headed posts of the New England fence. In later Hellenistic times,

Hermes Trismegistus was still a magician-shaman who could even bring back spirits from the dead; and with that other life-restorer Orpheus, he was a forerunner of the great Christian conferrer of immortality. Hermes, it is said, once separated with his wand two serpents coiled in mortal combat; thenceforth he carried messages between enemies and his wand became a symbol of neutrality. Hermes also presided over coitus which may be why the two serpents on his staff are sometimes thought to be one male, one female.* Hermes is thus the bringer and the restorer of life — and, as the god of flocks and gardens, he is also the guardian of fertility as well. He is Psychopompos, leader of the souls, god of ghosts and the underworld. He, a snake to begin with, and carrying always the snake staff, is the very *daimon* of life and reincarnation. The snake is the spirit-soul, divinity, the male *logos* itself: the life principle.

Far down into classic times, snakes remained a part of sacred rituals. Arnobius, in fascinated preterition, pretended that the Bacchanalian rites were too horrible to recount — and then went on to revel in revolting detail over the rites "which the Greeks call Feasts of Raw Flesh (*omophagiai*) in which with feigned frenzy and loss of a sane mind you twine snakes about you, and, to show yourselves full of the divinity and majesty of the god, you demolish with gory mouths" still-living animals.[64] The scholiast on Lucian wrote that the Arretophoria ceremonies were the same as the Thesmophoria and

are performed with the same intent concerning the growth of crops and of human offspring. In the case of the Arretophoria, too, sacred things that may not be named and that are made of cereal paste are carried about, i.e. *images of snakes and of the forms of men.*[65]

The Christian circumlocution refers to the pastry *phalloi* of the ritual. These classic snake-handling rituals are abundantly confirmed by numismatic sources. There is "A whole class of coins of

* The curious symmetric "dance" sometimes observed between two snakes is always, however, invariably performed by two male snakes, conceivably with some reference to territorialism, rivalry, or combat. Coitus between male and female snakes is, for anatomical reasons, in an entirely different position and could never be mistaken for the "dance" which evidently gave rise to these Hermaic legends.

Ephesus known as cistophoroi [that] show us the sacred cista, its lid half-opened, a snake emerging.[66] As Jane Harrison was struck by the prominence of chthonic snake deities in ancient Greek times, so also another great Hellenist, E. R. Dodds,* has been impressed by the importance of snake rituals even in full classic times.

Another obviously primitive element is the snake-handling (*Bacch.* 101ff, 698, 768). Euripides has not understood it, although he knows that Dionysus can appear as a snake (1017f). It is shown on vases, and after Euripides it becomes part of the conventional literary portrait of the maenad; but it would seem that only in the more primitive cult of Sabazius, and perhaps in Macedonian Bacchism, was the living snake, as vehicle of the god, actually handled in ritual in classical times. Even Sabazius, if we may believe Arnobius, eventually spared his worshippers' nerves by allowing them to use a metal snake. The snakes in the Dionysiac procession of Ptolemy Philadelphus at Alexandria were doubtless sham ones.[67]

In the legends of Alexander and other great men, the phallic and godlike attributes of the snake are made quite explicit. A snake was seen lying by the side of Olympias, devotee of the Dionysian rites in Macedonia and mother of Alexander the Great, and from that time forth Philip of Macedon deserted his wife's bed. It may have been, Plutarch thought (*Vit. Alex.* 2), from fear of her enchantments or because "he dared not violate the sanctity of one wedded to a greater than he," namely, a god, the snake. Aristomenes was born of such a serpent, too, who visited his mother as Olympias, mother of Alexander, had been visited.[68] Plutarch wrote that the Macedonian men objected strenuously to the snake-handling of

---

* Dodds adds that in modern times, "Snake-handling is also practiced at Cocullo in the Abruzzi as the central feature of a religious festival" (citing M. C. Harrison and C. Ashby). Dodds was familiar with a journalistic report on an American snake-handling cult in Kentucky in which the snakes are "held high above the worshipper's head (cf. Demos. *de corr.* 259, 'holding over the heads') or close to the face. One man thrust it inside his shirt and caught it as it wriggled out before it could fall to the floor" — an oddly exact parallel to the ritual act of the Sabaziasts described by Clement and Arnobius (*Protrep.* 2.16: δράκων δέ ἐστιν οὗτος (Σαβάζιος) διελκόμενος τοῦ κόλπου τῶν τελουμένων, Arnob. 5.21: aureus coluber in sinum demittut consecratis et eximitur rursus ab inferioribus partibus atque imis). But Dr. Dodds hesitates to accept the opinion of Dieterich that the act in question "can signify absolutely nothing else than the sexual union of the god with the initiate" (p. 276).

their women, and said that when the serpents crept out of the ivy, the likna, and the thyrsoi of the women, the men were "frightened out of their senses." But however much the men disliked the maenadic orgies of their Bacchic women, they were too frightened to put a stop to them. The women were possessed, magical, and dangerous to handle; our modern diagnosis would be hysteria, i.e. the playing with symbols of sexuality, not the realistic engagement with real sexuality. The Macedonian men were intuitively right in being disturbed at their displacement by the "gods."

The use of snakes in the Greek mysteries was a basic feature of the Hellenistic rites. As MacCulloch writes:

The ritual use of a serpent in Asiatic and Greek mysteries is connected with the aspect of certain divinities as snakes. In the initiation to the rites of the Phrygian Sabazios, whose symbol and embodiment was a snake, a golden snake was let down into the bosom of the candidate and was taken away again from the lower parts. Clement of Alexandria calls this "the serpent gliding over the breast" — this serpent crawling over the breasts of the initiated being the deity.

This rite was also adopted in the Dionysiac mysteries . . . In these a snake was carried in a *cista*, the snake being the god himself. The cista, with the snake emerging from the vine leaves is represented on coins of the cities of Asia Minor of the Roman period, and Clement speaks of the *cista* in which was a snake, the symbol of Dionysos Bassareus, having previously spoken of the box in which the Kabeiroi exhibited the phallos of Dionysos to the Tyrrhenians to worship.

In the Arretophoria, performed for the fertility of women and fields, "sacred things which may not be named were carried about, made of cereal paste; i.e., *images of snakes and of the forms of men,*" viz., phalloi. Snake and phallos are here parallel as symbols of a deity, under both of which Dionysos was represented.

In the Eleusinia, according to Clement of Alexandria, some object was taken by the initiate from a *cista*, put into a basket, and from the basket again put into the chest. This object has been conjectured to be a phallos, for a representation of the mystic basket shows a phallos among fruit, and Dieterich thinks that what was done with the snake — drawing it through the bosom — was also done with the phallos. The rite was one expressive of sexual and mystic union with the god, as Zeus or Sabazios as a serpent had entered ["into the maid's pudenda"]. The god was hailed as ["Ye under the girdle"], according to an Orphic hymn. "In relation to the god both men and women were as female." In such a rite snake and phallos were one and the same, and women imitated the divine action. Such rites may have given rise to the stories of sons born of human mothers by divinities in the form of a serpent.[69]

With respect to god-snake fatherhood, the reference to Zeus is of especial interest; for the snake was evidently the symbol, or even the forerunner, of the All Father himself!

The Diasia was said to be the chief festival of Zeus, the central figure of the Olympians, though our authorities generally add an epithet to him, and call him Zeus Meilichios, Zeus of Placation. A god with an "epithet" is always suspicious, like a human being with an "alias." Miss Harrison's examination (*Prolegomena*, pp. 28ff.) shows that in the rites Zeus had no place at all. Meilichios from the beginning has a fairly secure one. On some of the reliefs Meilichios appears not as a god, but as an enormous bearded snake, a well-known representative of underworld powers or dead ancestors. Sometimes the great snake is alone; sometimes he rises gigantic above the small human worshippers approaching him. And then, in certain reliefs, his old barbaric presence vanishes, and we have instead a benevolent and human father of gods and men, trying, as Miss Harrison somewhere expresses it, to look as if he had been there all the time.[70]

So ubiquitous is the phallus-snake to symbolize the father-god! Indeed, the question might be phrased, Where is the snake *not* a phallic symbol? We have already found it so in all the great culture focuses of both the Old and New World — in Mexico, in the intercontinental Old World crescent from Egypt to India (and thence to the whole Indic culture sphere in Indonesia and southeast Asia), and in Greece and Rome (and thence to Europe and all its culture dependencies). What of the last great culture sphere, China and the Far East? Here, too, the snake is a well-established fertility symbol. "For example, in China the spirits of plants are thought to assume the form of snakes oftener than that of any other animal. Chinese literature abounds with stories illustrative of such transformations."[71] Is, in fact, the symbolism of the snake as phallus a universal human one? Or is it merely so ancient as to have now spread everywhere? In the New World is it an independent parallelism or a most ancient diffusion?

Conservative Americanists would immediately take refuge in "independent parallelism" — a polite enough way of admitting that neither their data nor their present methods are adequate to cope with such a problem. But if our ignorance enjoins upon us viewing American Indian snake phallism as probably an independent parallelism, nevertheless the immensely long passage of time since the Old World Stone Age similarly enjoins us not to close our minds to the remote possibility of diffusion even here. Is the snake-phallus symbol one with the Ur-culture of Homo sapiens, along with fire, furs, and flints? I think this possible. In any case, there are certainly independent *phrasings* of the symbol in the New World, for the Mexican plumed serpent is evidently also the arrow; Hopi and Andean snake symbolisms seem to embody other ideas as well, as we shall see — and, indeed, why might not the special concept of the snake-phallus as the rain bringer have been invented twice?

It is this very ubiquity of the snake-phallus symbolism which raises an obvious question: what other natural objects, through their shapes or other attributes, are *available* in the world for making such symbolic equations? There surely is no paucity of alternatives! The varied symbols for Zeus the All Father alone should suggest that these are indefinite in number. In some of his cults, Zeus is, of course, the bearded snake. But Zeus is also a bull to Europa, a swan to Leda, rain to Danaë, and an angry thunderbolt to gods and to guilty men — all of which (like the trident of Zeus, Neptune, and Dis) embody phallic symbolism. The Indoeuropean symbol for the fecund all-creating Sky Father is the tree with its multiple acorn-glans, the oak, whose mistletoe is the soul or gonadal "life" of the oak tree.[72] (Again, a *psychological*, though certainly not a historical, cognate of this is the New World belief that the rattlesnake leaves its venom glands on a rock when it goes to a stream or pond to drink; when it comes back, if some one has stolen these in its absence, it dies in convulsions by striking its head against the rock.) Similarly the fish, with its head demarcated by the gill openings, has frequently suggested the phallus with its glans to both Old and New World symbolism. The human body itself, with the head as glans, is a common phallic symbol not alone in Greek and Hindu religious art but also in many other parts of the world as well. The thumb with its thumbnail is another widespread phallic symbol, both in religious and in obscene gestures. The arrowhead is still another body-image parallel: in American Indian legends the hunter draws his arrow to shoot a deer who forthwith turns into a beautiful woman; in Europe and in India it is Love's arrow that pierces the heart of the lady. Indeed, some Old Stone Age magic cults shown in European cave paintings suggest unmistakably that phallus and spear are symbolically equated in hunting and coitus; the taboos on sexuality before war and hunting (and even the sympathetic magic influence of the wife who remains at home) are of course worldwide in scope. And knives which are explicitly and undeniably phallic have been found in such diverse places as Ceylon and Mexi-co (in one example the body of a man is the handle, the blade his phallus), which leaves no room for the rebuttal that these are sub-jective imputations of symbolism. In short, we must expect phallic symbolism to be as ubiquitous and as universal as the human body itself. All we need learn from this is *respect for the ethnographic fact of such symbolizing.*

But meanwhile I have too long delayed a discussion of the core of snake phallism in the ancient Near East, and its European cultural offshoots. The Hebraic origins of our religious culture are well known; and for an understanding of the snake-handling cult in the American South it is necessary to understand these historic back-grounds of snake-phallus symbolism. Fortunately, no problem can arise here concerning cultural diffusion versus *Elementargedanken* or archetypes or "racial unconscious." The transmission of this sym-bolism from the ancient Hebrews to the modern snake-handlers is here direct, demonstrable, and plainly culture-historical. No great mystery about cultural continuity can arise for anyone cognizant of the constant and intense preoccupation with the ancient cultural documents themselves, in the Bible-reading belt of the southeastern United States. As heirs of European culture and its past, these folk are sometimes poverty-stricken indeed; but they have the Book.

The snake, says the first book of the Bible, first brought evil into the world. Our mother Eve, tempted by the Serpent, offered the

Forbidden Fruit to old Adam, and they ate of it. This constituted the Original Sin of our kind, and for this they were evicted from Paradise. It is well to be reminded of the actual language of our source:

And the Lord God commanded the man, saying, Of every tree of the garden thou mayest freely eat: but of the tree of knowledge of good and evil, thou shalt not eat of it: for in the day that thou eatest thereof thou shalt surely die (Genesis II, 16–17).

Considering it is not good for man to live alone, God then created Eve out of Adam's rib.

And they were both naked, the man and his wife, and were not ashamed. Now the serpent was more subtle than any beast of the field which the Lord God had made. And he said unto the woman, Yea, hath God said, Ye shall not eat of every tree of the garden? And the woman said unto the serpent, we may eat of the fruit of the trees of the garden: But of the fruit of the tree which is in the midst of the garden, God hath said, Ye shall not eat of it, neither shall ye touch it, lest ye die. And the serpent said unto the woman, Ye shall not surely die: For God doth know that in the day ye eat thereof, then your eyes shall be opened; and ye shall be as gods, knowing good and evil (Genesis II, 25–III, 5).

As we have seen earlier, this story is of a familiar type, the story of the Origin of Death. It is one of the critical and pivotal events in Christian belief: for ever since Adam and Eve we have all been guilty of that original sin, and Christ is come to save us to everlasting life. The Primal Pair lost immortality to us; and the Son of God brought it back again through his death that was not a death.

As in the Hamito-Semitic versions that we have already noted in Africa, God then curses the serpent.

And the Lord God said unto the serpent, Because thou hast done this, thou art cursed above all cattle, and above every beast of the field: upon thy belly shalt thou go, and dust shall thou eat all the days of thy life: And I will put enmity between thee and the woman, and between thy seed and her seed; it shall bruise thy head, and thou shall bruise his heel (Genesis III, 14–15).

That the sin was sexuality is plain; for in the immediately following verse God curses women with pain in childbirth and saddles Adam with labor and endless economic responsibility for the results of his act. It is also made plain that he has lost immortality because of his deed: he has carnal "knowledge" to be sure — but he will die.

In the sweat of thy face shalt thou eat bread, till thou return unto the ground; for out of it wast thou taken; dust thou art, and to dust shalt thou return (Genesis III, 19).

They partook of what had been forbidden them (sexuality), and in punishment they lost what they might otherwise have had (immortality) — if we may read these statements literally. But — strange is the justice of Jehovah! — although man lost immortality, the original instigator of his sin, the serpent, did not. Man dies; but the snake-phallus is immortal in its resurrection. For in the Near East, the snake has long been credited in folk belief with immortality. This is evidently an etiological myth, arising from a peculiar habit of the reptile:* "Its long life and its habit of changing its skin suggest ideas of immortality and resurrection, or of purification, one festival being held at the time when its skin is sloughed." [73] Thus the snake's habit of casting off its skin and of reappearing bright and new after the process together symbolized immortality to the Semitic peoples, as it did also to the Greeks, as well as to others.[74]

Since the snake in the Semitic region is unmistakably the phallus, and since the snake's immortality is associated with its shed skin, we would venture still another explanation of an ancient Hebrew ritual, that of circumcision. Rationalist explanations can be multiplied, depending only on the ingenuity of theorists in achieving plausible conformity of the data with their own currently fashion-

* Perhaps the immortality of snakes as a notion also derives from the fact of their extraordinary tenacity of life. Decapitated heads of rattlesnakes have been known to bite, and fatally, hours after separation of head and body. Thus the snake-head is as immortal as that of the decapitated Orpheus in legend. Similarly, in an actual experiment, heartbeat in a "sidewinder" rattlesnake was detected fifty-nine hours after decapitation (L. M. Klauber, *Rattlesnakes*, 1:317). Nevertheless, *tenacity* of life is not the same as *longevity*: actually, rattlesnakes live only about ten to eighteen years, according to the species. Poisonous snakes in general are more fragile than most persons suppose; in truth, they must kill by quick depositing of poison and retreat, lest they be injured by the struggles of the small vertebrates which are their prey, then swallow at leisure their now harmless and immobile food. Large constrictors, obviously and necessarily, are built more durably; but their longevity in the wild state is probably limited to at most a few decades.

able etiological myths. The fault of such rationalist explanations is that they *are* rational. Let us not burden ourselves, however, with the thankless, and patently impossible, task of proving that people somehow must necessarily have reasonable reasons for their behavior; and still less must they have "good" reasons, that is, those that happen to make us intellectually comfortable. The present "irrationalist" theory at least has the merit of discovering (not inventing) its meanings solely in the data themselves, and solely in the fantasies of the people themselves. That the theory, exposed in all its stark symbolic nudity, may make us intellectually uncomfortable at first is of no matter — it was not elaborated in the beginning to make us comfortable — if only it correctly reproduces the beliefs (however erroneous) these people have held. That is, every single item of their beliefs may be wholly false (as we believe they are) and yet our explanation of why they held these beliefs may still be correct as phrased in their terms.

Man has sought immortality, evidently, since the first Neanderthals painted red ocher on human bones ritually buried in graves. Likewise, in the millennia since, the immortality of the soul has been a central preoccupation of European religion from its first dim origins in Egypt and the Near East. Now, sexuality, in this tradition (as Onians shows), depletes the life-stuff; each life we give to others depletes our own store of life; and for this reason sexuality must end in death (or loss of immortality), as in Genesis. How can man be saved from the fate of death after committing the "sin" of this sexuality? How give new life to others — and yet retain an immortality for himself?

This is a curious notion, from any modern point of view. Sexuality is "sin" destroying life (immortality for oneself), even in the act of giving life to another, *since life is conceived of as a finite substance or soul-stuff*. Only sexlessness, celibacy — "continence" — can preserve our life within us, which otherwise we "spend" recklessly in coitus, to our ultimate doom. But in this moral and metaphysical predicament, salvation comes through further symbolizing: phallus equals snake, and the snake obtains immortality by sloughing off its skin. Ergo, as the snake is immortal through sacrificing and leaving off a part of himself, so man also may be saved by ritually sacrificing a part of himself. If snake = phallus, then snakeskin = foreskin. The sinning organ and the whole man may be saved by a sacrifice of a part, an act of purification and a ritual means of regaining immortality through a magical symbolic act. The Semitic symbol paradigm is perfect. *Snake : immortal : sheds skin : : phallus : immortality : circumcision.*

Circumcision is the basic rite which seals the contract of the Chosen People and Jehovah, who thus again saves them from the consequences of Adam's act. Thus those who circumcise, Jews and Moslems, technically do not need Christ. However, the Hellenizing apostle Paul omitted this ritual requirement in his preaching to the Gentiles, and for this reason Gentiles most specifically need Christ, if they would attain to immortality. Pauline Christianity is virtually obsessed with "salvation to eternal life" which believers in Christ alone (the "circumcised in heart") will have in the imminent destruction of the world.

It is extremely important to note the "historical" context of circumcision as the Hebrews understood it. The Old Testament explains the matter clearly:

And this is the cause why Joshua did circumcise: all the people that came forth out of Egypt, that were males, even all men of war, died in the wilderness by the way, after they came forth out of Egypt. For all the people that came out were circumcised; but all the people that were born in the wilderness by the way as they came forth out of Egypt, they had not circumcised. (Joshua v, 4–5.)

Such *ad hoc* empiricism must arouse respect. But if circumcision were an established custom with the Hebrews, it would seem that they might already have performed the ritual automatically. The statement in Joshua makes it look, rather, as if circumcision were for the Hebrews of the Exodus a new custom, one arising perhaps from the new contract with the new monotheistic god — an unfamiliar and painful custom, concerning which they were neglectful and prone to backslide. Not even Moses was circumcised, until the emergency operation in the wilderness. Apparently circumcision was not an original rite among the Hebrews of the Exodus. They evidently learned about it in Egypt, as the text from Joshua implies and many an Egyptian mummy silently testifies — in that country already anciently obsessed with immortality and with the means of obtaining it.

Actually, of course, circumcision is an extremely ancient rite. According to Barton, "Circumcision among the Hebrews began far back in the Stone Age, but as late as the Exodus from Egypt and the conquest of Palestine — a time in the borderland of the Iron Age — flint knives were still used in circumcision." [75] That is, the events in Joshua occurred when there was already a full Bronze Age in Egypt, when bronze knives might have been used for centuries; indeed, in Asia Minor, the Iron Age had already begun, notably among the Kenites with whom Moses sojourned. For all the innovation of taking on a new God, the use of flint is a striking ritual conservatism — and one which points to Old Stone Age origins, when flint furnished the only available knives.

The Old Testament is specific about Zipporah's using a *flint* knife, somewhat hastily perhaps, to circumcise Moses when Jehovah threatened to kill him (Exodus IV, 24–25). Likewise Joshua made *flint* knives at Jehovah's command expressly to circumcise the Hebrews before they undertook the conquest of Canaan (Joshua V, 2). In each case, circumcision is done plainly to achieve magical immortality or immunity from death. It is at once talion punishment and sympathetic magic. The snake casts its skin and is immortal; man circumcises and is saved. But why the association of crisis-magic and circumcision with snakes?

The Egyptian origins of snake symbolism for the Hebrews are well attested to in the Mosaic books. Both Elohist and Jahwist versions in Exodus mention the famous magician's trick of the rod and the serpent. In the Yahwist version (Exodus IV, 3), the Lord showed Moses how to cast his rod upon the ground so that it became a serpent. In the Elohist version (Exodus VII, 9), the Lord commanded Moses that when Pharaoh asked miracles of them, Moses should tell Aaron to throw down Aaron's rod, which then became a serpent (Exodus VII, 10). The competition with the Pharaoh's sorcerers and magicians did not end this, however, in the Elohist version, "For they cast down every man his rod, and they became serpents; but Aaron's rod swallowed up their rods" (Exodus VII, 12).* It would seem that power over serpents was the especial métier of the Hebrews in Egypt!

But what had happened in the wilderness, before Joshua and his hosts took the Land of Canaan? And why the association of crisis-magic and circumcision with snakes? *Because Moses was a snake shaman already in Egypt, and because he served a snake god.*† After the Exodus from Egypt, the people murmured against God and against Moses in the wilderness. In the angry God's response, both God's messengers and the protection against them were serpents!

And the Lord sent fiery serpents among the people, and they bit the people; and much people of Israel died. Therefore the people came to Moses, and said, We have sinned, for we have spoken against the Lord, and against thee; pray unto the Lord, that he take away the serpents from us [did those same serpents kill the uncircumcised males among the Hebrews, as noted in the quotation from Joshua?]. And Moses prayed for the people. And the Lord said unto Moses, make thee a fiery serpent, and set it upon a pole: and it shall

* As we have seen, the snake staff as an attribute of the mage and medicineman or shaman was ancient in the eastern Mediterranean. The Hebraic symbolism might well have been borrowed additionally from Babylonian sources. For example, Ningishzida son of Ninazu, patron of physicians, has as a symbol "a staff round which a double-sexed, two-headed serpent called Sachan was coiled, and a form of this is the recognized mark of the craft of the physician to the present day. The serpent was chosen as the symbol of renewed youth and immortality [and health] because it casts its skin and renewed its youth, and because of its longevity." (E. A. Wallis Budge, *Babylonian Life and History*, London, 1925, p. 216.)

† The shadowy figure of Moses is evidently a syncretism of a number of persons and perhaps also a number of cults, including those of a volcano god, a bull god, a storm god, and a snake god. Freud long ago, in *Moses and Monotheism*, advanced reasons for supposing that Moses was an Egyptian. That anyone, and especially a Jew, should suggest this, has shocked most scholars out of seriously entertaining the possibility; nevertheless, it should be noted in this connection that the Moses-Aaron snake shaman of Pharaoh's court does seem to incorporate some elements of the familiar African snake shaman and rain-king (e.g. the rod and the water from the rock in the wilderness); the African "Semitism" of snakes and water-crossing and the Red Sea episode, as well as the plagues called down upon Egypt, similarly look very much like the magic of the typical African shaman or rain-king.

come to pass, that every one that is bitten, when he looketh upon it, shall live. And Moses made a serpent of brass, and put it upon a pole: and it came to pass, that if a serpent had bitten any man, when he beheld the serpent of brass, he lived. (Numbers XXI, 6–9.)

Would the jealous god have allowed to be set up for worship anything but his own image? This brazen serpent, in fact, was for a long time afterward a cult object in Jerusalem. But with the evolution of later conceptions of Jehovah, the old snake god of Moses suffered the familiar henotheistic displacement and denigration. It was Hezekiah who finally broke the Nehushtan or brazen serpent of Moses to which people still in his day burned incense (II Kings XVIII, 4). An echo of this seems to be preserved in Isaiah, for after Ahaz died the prophet admonished,

Rejoice thou not, whole Palestina, because the rod of him that smote thee is broken: for out of the serpent's root shall come forth a cockatrice, and his fruit shall be a fiery flying serpent (Isaiah XIV, 29).

And thus the shadowy old Levantine snake god of the Old Stone Age circumcising cult became overlaid with later gods, quite as the Olympians displaced the older chthonic snake gods in Greece. The Serpent in the Garden is already demoted to, at best, a culture hero who brought men knowledge; but already he is a malevolent deceiver also. The brazen deity of the old snake shaman Moses-Aaron is finally destroyed, and the serpent become an evil spirit and the adversary of the new god. In Isaiah, for example, the serpent appears to be the symbol of the adversary and evil itself:

In that day the Lord, with his sore, and great, and strong sword, shall punish leviathan the piercing serpent, even leviathan that crooked serpent; and he shall slay the dragon that is in the sea (Isaiah XXVII, 1; compare also Isaiah XXX, 6 and LXV, 25).

In Jeremiah the Lord uses serpents to punish the wicked:

For behold, I will send serpents, cockatrices, among you, which will not be charmed, and they shall bite you, saith the Lord (Jeremiah VIII, 17).

That they may not be charmed suggests that, conceivably, they once might have been. Elsewhere, serpents as the wicked, or as the punishment of wickedness, become a familiar theme in the Old Testament. The angry God will send bitter destruction and the poison of serpents to those who worship strange gods (Deuteronomy XXXII, 24). The wicked are compared to serpents and adders (Psalms LVIII, 4; CXL, 4). One must not look upon wine when it is red, for wine bites like a serpent and stings like an adder, and one sees strange women and says wicked things (Proverbs XXIII, 31–33). Of the "things which are too wonderful to me," one is the "way of a serpent upon a rock," and another "the way of a man with a maid" (Proverbs XXX, 19, 18), thus preserving, in Proverbs at least, the inveterate association of snakes and sexuality. Again, the voice of calamity is like a serpent (Jeremiah XLVI, 22). The prophet Amos says that one cannot escape the wrath, for it were as if a man fled a lion and encountered a bear, or went into a house to lean upon a wall, where a serpent bit him (Amos V, 19). And Micah (VII, 17) promises that nations shall lick dust like serpents in fear of the Lord.

The same symbolism continues in the New Testament. Jesus cries out in rage to the scribes and Pharisees, "Ye serpents, ye generation of vipers! How can ye escape the damnation of hell?" (Matthew XXIII, 33). In the Sermon on the Mount the figure is used contrastively: what man is there who if his son asked for bread would give him a stone, or if he ask a fish will give him a serpent? (Matthew VII, 9–10; compare Luke XI, 11). And John reaffirms the connection of snakes and immortality in a striking metaphor: "And as Moses lifted up the serpent in the wilderness, even so the Son of man must be lifted up: That whosoever believeth in him should not perish, but have eternal life" (John III, 14–15). The parallelism between Judaism and Christianity is here confirmed.

Paul refers to the serpent and Eve (II Corinthians XI, 3). James says that even the serpent hath of man been tamed, "But the tongue no man can tame; it is an unruly evil, full of deadly poison" (James III, 7–8). Revelation mentions "that old serpent, called the Devil" and "the dragon, that old serpent, which is the Devil (Revelation XII, 9 and XX, 2). Revelation also refers in confused apocalyptic language to the four angels bound in the Euphrates, who shall be loosed after the sixth angel trumpets:

For their power is in their mouths, and in their tails: for their tails were like unto serpents, and have heads, and with them they do hurt (Revelation IX, 19).

Thus in the Bible the snake has ranged in time from a high god to his very opposite, the archdemon. The serpent is procreator, teacher, punisher; immortal, phallic, and evil.

In this symbolism the serpent is inextricably intertwined with both life and death. As a phallic symbol he is associated with earthly life, and with life everlasting. As an attribute or agent of an angry God, he brings death and destruction. Thus the ancient snake, in Africa once (and perhaps in Asia too) the ancestor-god and the creator himself, although he still appears in the creation story, has been degraded to become the evil one — that snake god who with Moses was still the attribute of the rain shaman and the animal-familiar worshiped in the wilderness cult, in whose image men circumcised and were saved from death — and the once high god has become the mere punitive arm of deity. An extraordinary range of symbolisms! And yet (let us pause a moment) the snake in reality is quite none of these. From what source do all these mixed attributes come? From the human father: the snake symbolizes both the "good father" and the "bad father," and he portrays in all his basic ambiguity the child's ambivalent attitude toward his father.

For all his association with evil and with punishment and death, the Biblical serpent is nevertheless equally associated with godly knowledge and omniscience and immortality. Genesis, we recall, mentions two trees: the Tree of Knowledge and the Tree of Life. It was for eating the forbidden fruit of the Tree of Knowledge of good and evil that the primal pair were cast out of Eden (i.e., they became moral but not immortal). They were cast out, so the Bible says, lest, having disobeyed once, they now eat also of the Tree of Life:

And the Lord God* said, Behold, the man is become as one of us,

* The original has a Hebrew plural here, Elohim, which scholars intent on establishing a monotheistic God have argued is only "the plural of majesty." However, in this particular passage, that the partitive be attempted of the One and man become *like one of us* surely makes anything but an implied polytheism a forced construction, grammatically as well as theologically.

to know good and evil: and now, lest he put forth his hand, and take also of the tree of life, and eat, and live forever; Therefore the Lord God sent him forth from the Garden of Eden to till the ground from whence he was taken (Genesis III, 22–23).

This passage clearly suggests that fathers are ambivalent too, like the Zulu Old Old One who changed his mind, and jealous of their godly prerogatives. Still, if man were to be litigious, he could insist that he was allowed to eat of *all* the trees in the Garden, except the Tree of Knowledge, and this by God's express promise. Why then, by angry ex post facto decree, is he denied the Tree of Life, originally included among those allowed him?

As with the Greeks (until Orpheus-Dionysus), so with the Hebrews (until Christ): only the gods had immortality — and this they got through eating, nectar and ambrosia, and the Tree of Life, respectively.* Clearly, what the gods fear is, first, that man usurp the divine function of creativity (which he guiltily did in eating of the Tree of Knowledge); and, second, that man obtain immortality by eating of the Tree of Life (which was avoided, barely in time, by casting him out of Eden). Eden is the great symbol of that basic human institution, the family. The son, once having seized the father's prerogative of sexuality and procreativity, must leave the oral-dependent Eden of his childhood; henceforth he must produce sustenance for himself and for his own through his labor and knowledge and skill: he has "become like one of us," the fathers. The story in Genesis is also the great etiological myth of man's fate. Adam, man, can create new life, sexually; but he himself must die. It is the great merit of Christianity, say its adherents, that in the Messiah Jehovah redeemed his explicit promise made in Genesis and thus reversed the effects of Adam's sin, to give him now the intended immortality. But are not children allowed, in the familial symbiosis, a dependent sustenance if not sexuality? The "child's-eye" view

* That "cherubim" or wind-spirits were placed with flaming swords to keep the way of the Tree of Life has led some scholars to argue that this Tree was the date palm, the sexes of which exist in separate trees, the female of which must be fertilized either by winds or by the helpful knowledge of men; thus knowledge of the botany of the foodstuff is likened to zoological "knowledge" in men.

of the parents in the Eden myth is betrayed by the archaic body-image symbols that are used in the myth. The first sin, in symbolic form at least, was eating. And yet, curiously enough, in the Eucharistic sacrament or communion meal, all this is to be undone again — through eating!

CHAPTER 8

Religion and Psychiatry

CLEARLY, it is time now to examine these symbolisms for what they are: symbolisms. The fantasy of the Trees is an archaic one, psychologically that of simple oral incorporation. To obtain a quality, as to obtain a thing, both primitives and children follow the same method: you put it inside you, through the mouth. Thus, if life can be localized in the body, then "life" itself can be eaten: if an enemy's soul force is in his head, you eat his brains and collect his skull for your men's house; and to acquire the bravery of a lion, you eat his heart. Similarly, if words or morality are in the jaw, then you save your ancestor's jawbone. And if an enemy's strength and virility lie in his hair, then you collect scalps; the ancient Hebrews, some American Indians, modern Abyssinians, and others collect still more obvious trophies of virility.

In like fashion, if the procreative "life" of trees can be localized in their seeded fruits, then life or immortality can be plucked from trees and put inside man simply by his eating the fruits. Greek gods were immortal because they kept on eating the stuff of immortality, nectar and ambrosia. Tantalus became immortal, too, by eating these; but in his *hubris* or arrogance he killed his own son Pelops (a snake) and served up his flesh to the gods; for this he was punished in the underworld, where the fruit he sought to pluck always receded tantalizingly from his reach. This is true talion punishment; but what is still more interesting is the multiple replication of the same oral-incorporative symbolism in the legend, and the labile projection of the same envy motive into various persons in turn.

In the Garden of Eden Elohim, and later the serpent, were immortal because, quite simply, they ate the fruit of the Tree of Life. Adam and Eve, strangely, even "ate" the knowledge of good and evil (including *sexual* "knowledge") by eating the fruit of a tree! Surely this is symbolizing one physiological modality in the archaic terms of another earlier one!* In the Dionysian mysteries, the communicants drank the blood of the god (grape wine) and ate his body (the flesh of the slaughtered divine bull) and baptized themselves in the blood of the bull, in order to obtain the god's immortality. And in the Christian communion, the participants also consume the flesh and blood of the god as a means or token of their being saved for immortality.

The snake, in a similar manner, has frequently been the symbol of such naïve body-image thinking, though in other physiological modalities than eating. We have already noted earlier that, as the phallus, the snake has had imputed to him what snakes do not themselves really have: the hairiness of the Akikuyu mythical snake and others, the feathers of the plumed serpent Quetzalcoatl of the Aztec and the beard of the Greek snake god Meilichios. Since no snake in the world has hair or feathers or beard, it is obviously the phallus the snake symbolizes that has these attributes. As the phallus, the snake also has imputed to him other abilities which snakes do not possess in nature, namely making water and phallic reproductivity. Illustrating the first: the phallic Shiva produces the River Ganges from the top of his head, and various Indoeuropean and Levantine river gods from the bull's head, mouth, or horn; West African pythons produce rain, and may themselves be plainly seen in the rainbow; and Hopi snakes, who are connected in folk belief with the mysterious sources of water, will, if well treated in the Snake Dance, bring rain to the Indians after their release. Illustrating the

---

* It may be pointed out that even in our scientific language the acorn (glans) is placed between the lips (labia). Again, the motif of oral guilt (as in the Garden of Eden story) is obscure but persistent in African tales of the Origin of Death. A re-examination of these will show that almost invariably the accident of death is connected in some fashion with guilty eating.

89]

second: in Nigeria a legendary snake had the gift of tumescence and detumescence, and saved the warriors and drowned the enemy in water; the snake-entwined Shiva is in Hindu thought the *lingam* or male organ; African snakes seduce women, as the serpent did Eve; the Bavili *ndoma* is the source of man's knowledge and has the power of erection; Ijaw sacred pythons contain the souls and seed of the sons of *Adamu*; Dahomean serpents frighten beautiful girls and marry them; in many West African tribes snakes give women babies; and even after death, a Yao snake is often merely a dead husband trying to frighten his wife (among the Masai he is put into his place by being given milk).

Now at this point, if not before, we are sure to encounter the vast resistances of our own common sense in dealing with these data of symbolism. These things are simply not so, biologically. Not one of them. But who is the nature-faker here? Is it the anthropologist who faithfully collects and reports these outlandish data? *He* did not dream up these conjunctions of symbols in native folklore! Shall he then be blamed when he tries to listen to what his informants say? As biological scientists we agree on what snakes are and do. But as anthropological scientists, we must report what informants *think* snakes are and do. It is shocking to say, and open to misunderstanding, but the *truth* (nature) is irrelevant when we report the *fact* (fantasy) of what our informants say.

In the same way, when the psychiatrist reports faithfully what his patients say, we forget — in our discomfort at the report — who said it. Why, the fellow is crazy! Yes; of course. But the fellow who is crazy is the patient, not the psychiatrist. Thus both anthropologists and psychiatrists seem professional liars when they most scrupulously report what their respective informants have said. As for the data of psychiatry, are we to assume that the same ideas that drove the patient crazy will leave us emotionally unmoved when we contemplate them? Must (or can) psychoses be caused by genteelnesses that still leave us comfortable when we know them? Furthermore, does an especially marked psychological imprisonment in one's own culture *especially* qualify one to improvise and pass judgment on alien ethnography?

Meanwhile, all the skeptic has to do is to follow the anthropologist into the field or the psychiatrist into the clinic, to repeat the same observations. Perhaps it is too much to expect that he who wishes to deny the data will put himself to any great trouble in seeking them out. However, he will get nowhere (at least with those who have exposed themselves to the data) by loudly and simply reiterating the evidence of his own "common sense" — that is, his own cultural fantasies and his own personality defenses.

There is a certain kind of aggressively commonsensical mind that is quite incapable of self-examination, and hence incapable either of psychiatric or anthropological thinking. It is characterized by a stolid naïveté which is unable, in psychological matters, to take the "as if" position — which is certainly as important in social as in physical science — and hence has a built-in obtuseness and semantic rigidity that debars him from being a linguist or even learner of foreign tongues, an ethnologist or student of foreign ways, and a psychiatrist or student of alien symbol systems. These disciplines all equally make him impatient and anxious, and he must hasten to rebut them with his right thinking. He cannot tolerate the hypothesis that an animal may be Pferd or a cheval — because he *knows* that it is a horse.

But speaking his own language, even "like a native," does not make a man a linguist! This is the major difficulty in all the social sciences: by virtue of having a mind and a culture, each man in the street is sure he is therefore qualified as an expert both in psychology and in anthropology. He even thinks he "knows his own mind" when in fact he knows neither his own nor those of men in other cultures — since one function of the mind is to disguise our psychic problems from our awareness.

A snake is not a penis, granted — and the moon is not made of green cheese. One does not have to believe what a schizophrenic or a primitive says, in order to believe that *he* believes what he says. What the anthropologist and the psychiatrist both need, mainly, is willingness and ability to listen to what people say. But to listen clearly one must first filter out his own cultural and psychic "noise," i.e., common sense.

Now for various reasons, chiefly our own repressions, most of us have a further difficulty, beyond common sense, in dealing with the symbolic language of neurotics and of men of other cultures. And this is because the *content* of what they say is so often specifically anxiety-arousing. Of course; that is why the masking symbols were invented in the first place. For the purpose of symbols is just as often to hide as to convey meanings. Also, in dealing with the vast outside unknown, it has frequently been humanly comforting to project onto the world a control in body-image terms that we do in fact have over our bodies, but do not in fact have over the world. We can make water; but can the Hopi make the world-phallus water his fields? (Is this not anxiety-arousing — both to the Hopi to rediscover his real impotence, and to us to understand his gross symbolic language? If this is uncomfortable as an insight, does that make it untrue? If the fact is untrue, is the insight?) And in dealing with the vast unknown within us it is often necessary to invent symbols to mask or to deny threatening realities that arouse anxiety. We can seduce women: but do *snakes* make babies? For these reasons the man of common sense will be shocked anew to discover that the ethnologist and the psychiatrist are much more practiced skeptics than he is himself. They believe automatically very little of all that they hear. The snake-cult minister has *told* us he is a professional holy man, interested only in spiritual miracles — and how shocking to learn from his symbolic acts and words that he *means* he is seducing women and thumbing his nose at God!

No animal, it is safe to say, save man himself, has been so subject to human nature-faking, tall stories, and outright lies as the snake. Man has more myths by far about snakes than about any other single animal. Small wonder, when the snake is man's own sexuality!* The important question to ask is, what do these lies about the snake mean? Indeed, the entire traditional symbolism of the snake is laden with the kind of biological nonsense that is fraught with psychiatric significance. For if the alleged behaviors do not occur in

* Even in the simple matter of reporting objective and verifiable dimensions we all know how elastic a snake is. Perhaps tall tales about the size of fish run a close second to snake stories, and for much the same reason.

nature among real snakes, what other source is there for these stories than man's own projecting, fantasying mind?

Consider, for example, the childlike candor of Fabricius' story about the legendary Lettish "house dragon," and the equally childlike candor of the Christian commentator named Einhorn. Einhorn is much puzzled by this Lettish mystery; but simple quotation should clear the matter up for moderns.

"Some of them rear dragons, in their houses, which steal crops, which they bring back to their own people; others nourish huge serpents, etc. . . . This nation has also had just such an evil and horrible god of wealth [like Pluto], whom they call Puke . . . but the Germans . . . call him the dragon." This dragon was still kept by many people even in Einhorn's day. He would steal riches and crops and bring them to the people who entertained him. "He is fiery-red in appearance and flies quietly through the air like a burning fire. He is red when he is hungry; when he is well-fed with the corn he has stolen, he is quite blue and horrible to see. If any householder wishes to keep him and gain wealth through his services, he must prepare a special chamber for him . . . which must be kept perfectly clean . . . nobody must enter there, except the master of the house, and those whom he would have within . . . not everyone must know what sort of chamber it is." He must always have the first share of all beer and bread and other food, otherwise he will consider himself insulted and burn down the house. He is often to be seen in the evening, but those who keep him do so in great secrecy, and either cannot or will not say much about him.[76]

Can the "primal scene" fantasy of any neurotic be any plainer than that?

Snake fantasies at times tell us their meanings even more specifically. Consider, for instance, the persistent folk belief that a snake stings. This is a demonstrable distortion of the facts, and it clearly reaffirms the underlying phallic symbolism of the snake. The psychiatrist in his jargon would correctly insist that the snake has an "oral biting" mode of aggression! But in folk fantasy there is a displacement to a phallic-sadistic "sting" and noxious insertion (that easily recalls the coitus-death fantasies of hysterics and other neurotics). Naturalistically, far better symbols here would be the scorpion, and, though an imperfect *female*, the worker bee — which do sting in more obviously "genital" fashion. Though the snake, as we shall in a moment see, is a far more complete multiple body-image symbol* than any other creature, it is interesting, incidentally, that we find this "genital" aspect [77] continually reinforced through the serpent's repeated association with the scorpion in the Bible, together with the repeated metaphor of stinging.

A comprehensive survey of world folklore about the snake will discover this *multiplicity* of body-image symbolizing. Though admittedly (and by far) preeminent, the phallic symbolism of the snake is by no means the only one. *Once selected as an unconscious body-image symbol, the snake expresses every psychosexual modality of the body.* Though it is true that the snake is a phallic symbol, and very commonly, it is oversimplifying to suggest that the snake is only this. There are many other body-image symbols besides, and we must proceed to demonstrate these, in order to present a fair and well-rounded picture.

First, the oral symbolisms. As we have earlier remarked, one of the most persistent, and wholly false,[78] folk beliefs is that snakes can suckle, and that reptilean snakes like mammalian milk. This fantasy is found very widely: in the Bronze Age Cycladic mother-

* The oedipal completeness of the snake symbol is remarkable: the actually oral-aggressive snake is in "stinging" here accused, and unjustly, of (incestuous) "genitality" in body modality — incestuous necessarily in this context, in which biting is denied, since it is the same mother who is the oral object of frustration as well. The oral-biting wish, denied and projected, becomes the phobia of being bitten (a reality-testing repetition compulsion in the snake-handling cult), and the guilt-tabooed milk becomes the poisonous semen "sting" (again a component of the snake cult, as also is the persistent fantasy in folklore of feeding snakes milk). Small wonder, then, that the snake is the embodiment of the id, of oedipal evil in man, and his Enemy, as projected into the Devil! Fragmentation or dissociation of the individual psyche and hysteroid-paranoid projection of these components to the "outside" gives us both the Devil (id) and God (superego). For symbolically, of course, both in folklore and in the snake cult shortly to be examined, the snake is projectively the father also. As we have seen already, the snake is both ancestral creator and angry killer (or agent of the angry God), aggressor and punisher, biter and bitten, swallower and swallowed, container and contained — and as such is the perfect symbol in body-image terms. Since, in all that folklore alleges, the snake is not biologically these things in objective fact, then it can only be so in subjective fantasy. If, in each tale, we read "snake" simply in the appropriate body-modality, then the symbolism in each case immediately becomes clear — with the proviso that, for the snake, the body-image modality is likely to be multiple.

goddess of Crete, with two snakes held in her arms who seek her exposed breasts; in the European and American folk myth that snakes milk cows, and another that a bowl of milk is the best offering to be left on the doorstep for a snake. But this association of snakes and milk is not only in our own cultural tradition. The Maya of Middle America believe in an imaginary snake, Ekoneil, which glides into the houses of nursing mothers, covers their nostrils [sic] with its tail, and sucks their breasts. The Tarahumara of Mexico subscribe to "the belief that this snake Elaphadeppei milks cattle or sleeping women." [79] The Hottentot of South Africa believe that serpents come by night for women to suckle them, and bite them if they refuse. [80] "In Eastern Sonora [Mexico] the people believe that a harmless kind of serpent comes at night and suckles at a woman's breast, putting its tail into the mouth of her child." [81]

Again, in Welsh tradition the wings of mythical flying snakes arose because they had drunk women's milk spilt on the ground and had eaten sacramental bread, [82] — an interesting symbolic doublet and statement of our psychosexual growth.* Contrastive is the European belief that venom is transmitted through the mother's milk, even if she had been bitten long ago, in pregnancy [83] — a highly over-determined fantasy, involving both talion, displacement, and projection in its symbolizing mechanisms. A symbolically related myth is reported by Mauyduyt from Louisiana: a person, if bitten by a rattler soon after having drunk milk, would quickly die; again, there is the frequent belief that snake rattles will soothe and pacify teething children if worn as a necklace or in a bag so that the child may chew them. [84] There is an ancient European legend, now having crossed the Atlantic, of the child who periodically mysteriously disappears; when followed, he is found to be feeding milk to a snake; when the snake is killed, the child pines and dies [85] — a tale that embodies both the castration fantasy and the imaginary playmate, and

---

* Compare the flying (i.e. phallic) snakes of old Semitic and modern Egyptian folklore. Flying snakes are of course just as unreal as suckling snakes; but once we employ the snake to symbolize man, then it is inevitable (because of human anatomy and man's universal familial nature) that everywhere we will first find snakes suckling women and then returning later as flying serpents, having incorporated the father's masculinity, "power," creativity, immortality (*sacramental bread = god, father*).

in addition, perhaps, projection and symbolically disguised onanism.

The "oral biting" motif is evident in medieval stories.

Notable in the monkish accounts of terror and pain is the vision of Alberico, a boy of ten, who was conducted through hell by the apostle Peter and two angels. Alberico encountered first a dismal valley where many souls were standing immersed in ice, some only to their ankles or knees, others up to their breasts or necks; just beyond was a fearful wood of gigantic trees, bristling with thorns, from whose sharp and spiny branches were hanging by their breasts those heartless women who had refused to nourish motherless babes with their own milk; to each breast clung a snake, sucking that which had been so cruelly denied.[86]

In medieval French architecture,

serpents are represented suckling the breasts of women. Women are seen by visitors to hell suckling serpents as a punishment for refusing nourishment to their children. Some frescoes in Byzantine churches show a parallel to this. Lucian says that in Byzantium women pressed serpents in their hands and gave them the breast . . . The story of Caradoc, which forms part of the French Perceval cycle, relates how a serpent fastened on his arm and sucked away his life. He was saved by a young maiden presenting her breast to the serpent, which took the nipple in its mouth. Cador then cut off its head, but with that also the nipple, which was magically replaced by one of gold. A close parallel exists in a Gaelic folk-tale, and less close in a Scots ballad.[87]

(Caradoc is psychosexually suspect in the displacement and projection, but the maiden well performs the double role of women.)

"Oral incorporation" fantasies are evident in other myths. One of these is that the mother snake swallows her young when danger threatens.* Among the Atsugewi, one contest for power by two

---

* A thoroughly implausible tale! Snakes, like all reptiles, are solitary animals and receive no mammalian maternal care; the story probably arose because recently born snakes were found still near their mother (if rational in origin) or else it is a familiar projection of oral incorporation fantasies (if irrational). Experiments show that an adult rattler's powerful gastric juices would in fact kill a young snake, if swallowed, in about twenty minutes (Klauber, *op. cit.*, 2:1244, 1249). How birth from the cloaca, which is a fact in some snakes, could be connected with the oral-incorporative fantasy can only be explained by the existence of a false inference that such "excretion" followed a prior "eating," which is not the case.

shamans involved the eating of a rattlesnake;* the winner was the one who could eat without vomiting.[88] The oral incorporation motif reappears in the Indian myth of Saint Guga or Gugga,

also known as Zahir Pir, which is usually taken to mean "the saint apparent"; but Harikishan Kaul says that the proper form of the word is Zahria, "poisonous," because in his cradle he sucked the head of a snake. He is regarded as an incarnation of the Naga Raja, the snake king, and there seems to be good reason to believe that he is a snake-godling turned into a saint.[89]

The familiar fantasy of "oral pregnancy" is all that is needed now to complete the paradigm — and this is evident in an American Negro method of hexing: if powdered rattlesnake is put on an enemy's food or in his coffee, he will be filled with little snakes in four months.[90]

There are also a number of interesting oral-biting "talion" stories in various folklores. In Texas, a present-day folklore remedy for snakebite is for the victim to bite off the head of the offending reptile; in New Mexico, a person bitten by a rattlesnake should grab the snake by the head and tail and bite it in the middle, whereupon the poison in the person's mouth will kill the snake and cure the bite. It is difficult to say whether this method was taken from the Indians or from a traditional European one. For, on the one hand,

In the Rudo Ensayo written in 1763 there is described a method employed by the Opata of Sinaloa. Catching the snake's head between two sticks, they stretched its body out by pulling the tail; the snake-bite victim then bit along the snake's body, whereupon the snake swelled up [*sic*] and died, and the man recovered.[91]

* This competitive snake-swallowing is to be placed, psychologically, beside the goldfish-swallowing contests among Harvard undergraduates in the late nineteen thirties. Again, both the Excalibur and the Aaron-Moses stories find symbolic parallel in an American Indian tale reported by Meigs: "A Kiliwa shaman once made two little mounds of earth and stuck a sliver of wood between them. No Indian in the tribe could lift the sliver. The shaman flicked the stick aside and it became a rattler; he seized it and it was once more a stick." In this context, Klauber was impressed by the "inventiveness of individual shamans. For example, among the Ute and Southern Paiute some shamans sucked out poison; some, a symbolic snake; some, blood; and some applied the suction to the top of the patient's head." To all this, however, the psychiatrist will only shrug and say Plus ça change, plus c'est la même chose!

On the other hand, the European belief goes back at least to Pliny the Elder:

All men possess in their bodies a poison which acts upon serpents; and the human saliva, it is said, makes them take to flight, as though they had been touched with boiling water. The same substance, it is said, destroys them the moment it enters their throat.[92]

(Again a complex symbolism, involving identification, displacement, and projection; although these stories are psychologically germane to one another, they are probably independent in both hemispheres historically.) And, finally, regarding oral biting,

Another popular fallacy is that a rattlesnake will commit suicide when hopelessly cornered, by sinking its own fangs into its sides. No poisonous snake is susceptible to the poison of its own kind. Two cobras in a fight know this. Neither reptile tries to strike the other. The combat is a live swallowing match.[93]

(Compare poison swallowing as a symbolism in the snake cult, wherein an earlier introjected "spirit" or "power" overcomes the poison — but probably we have cited enough examples to indicate that the snake is involved in oral fantasies in folklore.)

Since the snake is so commonly a phallic symbol, we might anticipate that it would embody phallic "urethral" symbolism as well. In classic psychoanalytic theory, this would of course mean the association of snakes specifically with fire and water. Probably the American Indians best express this doublet in their widespread symbolizing of the serpent as lightning and as rain. Brinton remarks on the association of snakes with thunder and lightning in the myths of several tribes. "Because the rattlesnake, the lightning-serpent, is thus [through fertilizing rain] connected with the food of man, and itself seems never to die but annually to renew its youth [by changing its skin], the Algonkin called it 'grandfather.'" Spence writes that "The snake, besides being symbolized by lightning in many Indian mythologies, is also symbolical of water, which is well typified in its sinuous movements." Brinton notes that in a Chippewa pictograph a manitou brandishes a rattlesnake as a lightning symbol. Dorman states that the Algonkin in general consider lightning to be a great serpent. According to Hagar, the Micmac had a legend that thunder is made by seven flying rattlesnakes, crying to one another and waving their tails as they crash across the sky; a flash of lightning is produced when they dive for their prey. Webber records the Sauk-Fox superstition that rattlers come out of hibernation at the first clap of spring thunder. Dorman and Hudson state that the Algonkin Shawnee think thunder is the hissing of a great snake.[94]

But this Indian symbolism is not confined to Algonkin groups. Mooney says the Cherokee have a mingled reverence and fear for snakes, because of their connection with the rain and thunder gods. A rattlesnake's killer will be driven crazy since he has offended these gods. If a rattler has been killed, the head must be buried an arm's length deep in the ground, and the body hidden in a hollow log; otherwise rain will come in torrents and the streams overflow their banks. Gilbert notes the usual connection of snake and lightning also in Cherokee thought. According to McGee, the Sioux connect the stroke of lightning with the snake's strike. The Flathead believe that whipping a snake will bring rain.

The Isleta Pueblo custom is to put fetishes under any tree that has been struck by lightning, one of these fetishes representing a rattlesnake, probably Ikaina who is the rattlesnake god associated with war, lightning, and the sun. According to the Hopi, Sun Chief (D. C. Talayesva), "Serpent deities live in the springs and control the water supply" and the Snake and Antelope ceremonies are performed to propitiate the snake deities who will then assure the supply of spring water and of rain; for "When snakes are pleased with their treatment they were quiet and would bring rain as a reward." The Keres and Tewa Pueblos also have snake dances which are primarily prayers for rain, brought by the rattlesnakes well entertained and placated in the snake dances.

The Navaho have no rain dance, but they also link the rattlesnake with lightning and rain and under no circumstances will kill one. Bourke found that rattlesnake doctors among the Mohave were also rain doctors; Kroeber tells a Mohave myth about a great rattler who brings rain and thunder. Among the Klamath, the rattlesnake makes rain, and his rattling is the thunder. The Kato of California sing rattlesnake songs to stop excessive rain; among the Chukchansi, a man who had been bitten by a rattler and survived could stop excessive thunder and lightning by shouting to it to stop. The Opata of Mexico believe that if one had been bitten by a rattlesnake it meant he had been struck by lightning; the Huichol believe that lightning is a powerful snake, and fire is another one, namely the rattlesnake. Dorman says that Tlaloc, the Toltec thunder god held a golden snake in his hand to represent lightning; this association of snakes and rain is also Mayan.

Nor is the rain serpent symbolism exclusively American Indian, for it is also frequent in Africa and the Near East, as we have seen. The idea appears to be Hindu as well, for in a Rajput painting of an episode in the Ramayana epic, the siege of Lanka, the rain-arrows from the sky — some of them shown as living serpents — fall on Rama's army of men and monkeys, the snakes doubtless being sent by the Naga (snake) Raja, Ravanna.[95]

The urethral water-fire symbol association, it might be argued, is already "given" in nature because of the meteorological association of lightning and of rain. But man does not have to associate parts of his own body and his physiology with the weather! Nevertheless, for one example, the Hopi make a quite arbitrary connection, in a complex symbolism, of snake-phallus-arrow-lightning, in their own explicit statements. Weapons symbolize the warriors' specific maleness, they say; the warrior gods, of whom the warriors are the representatives, are explicitly ithyphallic; the images of the gods are made of lightning-struck wood; the lightning-snake is the arrow of the gods; and the lightning striking the cornfields is the act of fertilizing them. Finally, "The act of shooting [an arrow] is said 'to typify lightning striking the corn-field, an event which is regarded as the acme of fertilization.'" (The rain is, then, symbolically the urine-semen.)

Nowhere does the assimilation of the war-gods and of their representatives, the warriors, by the idea of fertilization appear more clearly than in the case of their weapons. In the myths the war-gods receive from their father the bow and arrows or lightning bolts as real weapons of war, to be used in their fight against enemies and monsters. In the ceremonies, however, we find just the reverse associations with lightning; there the lightning is not the destructive arrow of war, but the rain-bringing, fertilizing phenomenon. It is ceremonially represented by the lightning frame.[96]

In one of the ceremonies, the rain-snake is made to emerge, like a pantograph, from the altar, as phallus-arrow-lightning. The "fiery serpent" of the Near Eastern classical countries is, of course, another phallic-urethral association with fire, as is the Lettish house serpent. Fire-handling in snake-cult meetings is also a natural cognate libidinally and symbolically.

The specifically genital, as opposed to phallic, symbolisms of the snake are of course as much present in the Americas as elsewhere.

The Tarahumaras think this [harmless *Diadophia regalis arizonas*] is the most poisonous snake of all and believe it strikes poison with its tail . . . The Indians call [*Thamnophis eques*] bakalátchi and think it changes color when angry. There is also a racer or whip snake, sometimes 5–6 feet long but very thin. The Indians say that when it is enraged it beats a person with its tail.[97]

Compare Pliny on several of these points.* The Tarahumara, therefore, have the fullest (or most fully reported) snake symbolism of any American Indian tribe: the ejaculating and tumescent phallus, and the sadistic fantasy of coitus, together with the other symbolisms (hair, Medusa, and so on) mentioned earlier. The tumescence-detumescence fantasies about snakes appear to be associated with myths of changing color. When enraged, some Indian snakes are supposed to darken and swell up, or to shrink to half their normal length when sneaking away. Beverly wrote in 1722 that the snake's colors become more brilliant in the act of charming its prey (in one

* With respect to "stinging" with the tail, compare the legends that each time a snake "stings" it loses a joint in its tail; that when a rattler dies, it leaves its fangs in the victim; that if one sucks a rattlesnake bite his teeth will fall out; that Negroes with red gums can suck out snake poison, but a blue-gummed Negro would invite disaster; that snake fangs are barbed and lost when it bites, and the snakes die after biting anyone (both in Pliny); and also the legend of the Fatal Boot in which a man is bitten and dies, and much later son or sons, or a father, son, and grandson all die of the fatal boot in which the fang is embedded — or three successive husbands of a widow, which recalls the black widow spider and vagina dentata fantasies (Klauber, *op. cit.*, 2:867, 1217, 1249–1251). The coitus-death motif above appears again in the story that when a snake swims a river it dies on reaching the farther shore (Klauber, *op. cit.*, 1:464).

case a rabbit, which, unfortunately for the legend, lacks color vision). The colors of the rattlesnake are more beautiful when it is animated by resentment; in one story reported as early as 1642, the person bitten takes on the colors and pattern of the snake biting him.[98] After a snakebite at Isleta Pueblo,

Application for treatment must be made direct to the snake father, or doctor, who must find the offending snake. The victim then spit [*sic*] into the snake's mouth, which caused the snake to cure the man, for, after the patient spit, the snake swelled until it burst and died, and the man recovered. No woman should approach the snake-bitten man, lest she should instantly swell up.[99]

(On the other hand, among the Muskito and Sumo of Central America, the patient himself would die if he saw a pregnant woman — but in any case both tumescence and pregnancy appear in these fantasies, especially in the talion-spitting instance.) Some of these tumescence fantasies reach the dimensions of out-and-out tall stories: the hoe-handle bitten by a rattlesnake which swelled so much within an hour that it popped out of the socket; in another case a bitten hoe-handle swelled enough to give a farmer lumber for twenty five-room houses; and Peg-Leg Ike who, bitten in his wooden leg, despite his efforts and those of friends to chop it away, was choked by the growing timber, though his sorrowing survivors had enough kindling to last them all winter. The inevitable talion-punishment in this sequence, of course, is that of the snake who bit an automobile tire and was himself blown up for his pains.[100]

The connection of snakes with pregnancy is also notable. It is believed that if a patient undergoing treatment for a rattlesnake bite sees a pregnant woman, he will surely die (Honduras and elsewhere); that pregnant women are immune to snakebite (Southeast), or that a rattlesnake bite is always fatal to a pregnant woman; that snake rattles (residue of their "rebirth") facilitate childbirth — a belief found among Negroes, Kentucky lowlanders, Blue Ridge mountaineers, and pioneers in the Northwest.[101] There is also, as with pregnancy, a connection of the snake and menses. As we have seen earlier, the Yuki term for rattlesnake indicates that the source of its danger lies in menstrual blood, which they consider the deadliest of all poisons. This is perhaps related to the Hopi and other Pueblos' belief that the smell of a woman is highly offensive to a rattlesnake, angering it so much that it bites her. Californian Indians carried medicines with various smells to keep snakes away and prevent snakebite. By contrast, there are many stories that dwell on the offensiveness of the odor of rattlesnakes, which are largely fictitious. Indeed, why are animals with a keen sense of smell (e.g., dogs) so often bitten, if snakes smell so strongly? Nevertheless, in the South, the snake's presence is widely thought to be betrayed by the smell of its venom; one nineteenth-century writer thought the smell was due to excess venom coming out through the pores of the skin; and one unknown variety of snake was thought to kill if one merely touched it or the venom it exuded from its sides.[102] If the snake is the phallus, then the widespread use to cure snakebite of split animal poultices — mouse, chicken, pigeon, swallow, kid, lamb, and even cow have been reported in Asia, Africa, and the Americas [103] — would also find its transparent symbolic rationale. Perhaps the use of an egg is related to this also.

It is in this same context that we should examine carefully the alleged behaviors of snakes in symbolic terms.

Rattlesnakes have some peculiar, but often praiseworthy, preferences in biting. They won't bite children, at least until they have reached the age of seven. They won't strike a person from the rear, nor will they bite in water. Also, I was advised by one of my correspondents that rattlesnakes will bite only men, not women. This chivalrous attitude they must have inherited from their distant relatives the European vipers, who have long made this distinction. But our uncivilized rattlers seem not to have adopted the code of refusing to bite naked people.[104]

The indubitably genital symbolism of the snake, in any case, is repeatedly evident in a variety of snake stories. One of the favorite ones in the days of buckboard travel is of the snake that got coiled around the felloe of the wheel and was thrown into the lap of one of the riders, usually of course the girl; which serves a girl right if she will go out riding alone with a young man. At the same time, if one disturbs two snakes in the act of mating, the snakes will die.

In any case, snakes have since ancient times been thought (erroneously, as if they were mammals) to travel in pairs, and the remaining one to wreak vengeance on anyone who injures its mate. Old World folklore has it that snakes "fascinate" their victims, which is interesting in view of the fact that *fascinum* is a Latin vulgarism for the phallus; on the other hand, a Cherokee who sees a rattlesnake will suffer later from photophobia, and even seeing a snake in a dream causes sickness. Incestuous first-cousin marriage among the Maidu invites punishment from the ancestors in the form of snakebite. The Cora of northwestern Mexico wrap a rattler's fang in an oak leaf and wear it as a love charm, and the venom is a powerful aphrodisiac. If a Maya man sees snakes in a dream, he will quarrel with his wife; if he dreams of a naked women, he will see a rattlesnake the next day. New England Indians ate rattlesnakes to promote longevity; Cherokee did the same to make ball players more terrifying to their opponents, but with the unfortunate side effect of making them cross with their wives.[105]

All the above are, for various reasons, highly dubious legends. And yet some snakes have, in biological fact, verified behaviors almost fatally available for suggesting further genital symbolisms in folklore.

Certain cobras have the power of ejecting venom by spasmodic movement of a poison gland, in such a way as to spurt the poison through the air for a considerable distance. Loveridge says, after considerable experience in East Africa, that "beyond doubt the cobra does aim at the face."[106]

No one avers that venom is semen; but is this ejaculatory behavior a source for the many Near Eastern beliefs in fire-spitting serpents? Is this the "fiery serpent" of the Bible? But before we accept too easily this rationalist explanation, we should note that the same symbolism is alleged by American Indians of snakes that do *not* have this ejaculatory behavior biologically. The Omaha believed that some rattlesnakes could shoot or project venom for at least a hundred feet. And the Tarahumara believe that the same species of snake who sucks women's breasts can ejaculate its poison onto people and raise blisters on the skin. If a rationalist explanation is adequate for Old World snakes, we still need an "irrationalist" explanation for New World snakes! The fact remains that snakes are believed to indulge in all kinds of behavior that we cannot actually observe them performing in nature; but in each of these cases from "unnatural history" we can observe the origin and symbolic significance of the alleged behaviors, in the human mind. Probably the most unarguably and explicitly phallic symbolism is given us by the Japanese peasants, who warn their daughters not to indulge in the unladylike behavior of taking a nap in the fields, for there are snakes that enter women's genitals and can not be pulled out because of their scales.[107]

Perhaps further examples are hardly needed for persons familiar with world folklore regarding the snake. One need only keep his symbolic ears open for the next snake story he hears — say, the fabulous hoop-snake that puts its tail into its mouth (like the Hindu Sesha in an autistic-narcissistic eternity of bliss, the completely regressed and self-satisfied god-baby) in order to roll after the guilty person and whip him to death. Such stories tell as much as TAT's! Doubtless the most compendious symbolizing of all is found in the legend of the major avatar of Vishnu in India: the infant Krishna, after killing the cannibalistic ogre-mother sent by his enemies, after slaying the monstrous bull who interrupted his dalliance with the cow maidens, and after killing a great serpent sent to destroy him, went to the castle of his "uncle," usurper of his throne and kidnaper of his mother — only to find his entrance to the castle barred by the head and trunk of a great elephant swaying back and forth at the gate. One can only admire the persistence of this Indian Oedipus at symbolizing.

The fantasies of neurotic patients are in no wise unlike the body-image symbolisms that we find in folklore. Thousands of patients, in snake pits and out of them, have contributed to our knowledge of their snake symbolism. But before we apply these ethnographic insights to our study of the snake-handling cult, let us summarize the psychiatric insights available to us from clinical and psychoanalytic studies. The snake is an "uncanny" creature. A response to the uncanny, as we know, comes from the triggering of affect-laden associations in the unconscious — somewhat as the *déjà-vu* phenomenon comes from a similar triggering of earlier dream-associations. The uncanny is the "un-kenned" and the unknown — that is, except to the unconscious!

The snake is an uncanny creature primarily because, like the phallus, it has an independent and autonomous will of its own. Its uncanniness is also associated with its nature as a castrated, or projectively disclaimed, member, pleasurable and dangerous, good and bad at the same time. It has a life of its own, like the phallus and like the repressed wishes of the autonomous id: it becomes erect and detumescent independently of the conscious will. A snake's posture and erection, especially of the cobra's tumescent hood, is a herpetological fact fatally available for human symbolizing. Not able to telescope into his own length (unlike the turtle, a favorite phallic power animal for the medicineman's sacred rattle in America) the roused serpent can move only with the universal-joint motion of the airplane joystick. This swaying, in naturalistic terms, is merely the habit of some pit vipers of following a moving warm-blooded animal with their infrared-sensitive organs — which has led men to believe that they can charm and control serpents. Just as uncannily, the snake "fascinates" birds, so that they fall helpless from their perch to become his prey — a fine disclaimer and denial both for Adam and for the "hypnotized" hysteric woman.

All these beliefs come either from misunderstandings of snake behavior or from anthropomorphic projections onto them of men's fantasies. The African, the American, and the Asiatic rain snakes all have the same origin, physiologically if not historically. Historically, the richest elaboration of snake symbolism in the New World is undoubtedly in Mexico and the Southwest, and in the regions of the United States secondarily influenced from this focus.* In the Old World, perhaps, the greatest focus for the dif-

* As we have seen, the Huichol-Tarahumara have the most complete symbolism available in modern ethnographic studies of American Indians; archaeologically, the southern Mississippi and Southeastern snake effi- the Aztecan region of Mexico and its plumed serpent. In addi- laborate Hopi snake dance, and the snake ceremonies of other her in effigy, paint, symbolism, or in actuality, rattlesnakes are

fusion of snake symbolism has been the Hamito-Semitic Northeast Africa–Southwest Asia–Southeast European region. The best anciently documented of these (and most immediately significant for modern American snake cultism) has been the area occupied by the Biblical Hebrews. Indeed, one could make a strong case for the theory that the Hebrews, or at least their Egyptian component in the Exodus, were snake cultists: the centrally Hebraic folk practice of circumcision is at once a painful castration threat from the tribal fathers, the sanction of an almost compulsive loyalty to a "fossil culture," a magic sign of membership in the tribal group submitting to the Mosaic snake god, and a magic way of getting immortality by imitating the serpent's shedding of his skin.

Snakes *are* the gods, and *are* the deathless element in each man; snakes are essential immortality. And, like Orpheus's deathless little finger and Osiris's immortal member, snakes do not "die" (i.e., become detumescent) until nightfall and coitus-death. In all these things the snake is the "uncanny" creature, like the phallus possessed of an independent and autonomous will and life of its own. But as an independent and "castrated" phallus, the snake is also (in neurotic fantasy) the *victim* of unconscious oral aggression against the father, onto whom is here displaced the original oral-biting aggression against the frustrating mother at weaning, and now with the oral-incorporative wish (if by incorporating the father one may possess the mother). In talion, the snake, "castrated," now bites and kills. Therefore one may be, and is, enjoined to kill him (the return of the repressed, now suitably rationalized). Again, the snake placed tauntingly to the lips and mouth in the snake cult is another neurotic "return of the repressed" — but under talion danger again, for the castrated snake-phallus is not bitten but *bites*. This also fits the familiar infantile stance of paranoid projection: "It is

carried in the dances of the Mandan, Pomo (here defanged rattlers are waved in the faces of attendant women to frighten them), Nisenan, Yokuts, Western Mono, Chunut, Tachi, Paleuyami, Wukchummi, Yaudanchi, Choinimni, some Wintun (Nomlaki), Luiseño, Diegueño, and California Shoshoni — in view of which, similar Cheyenne, Arapaho, Cherokee, and New England dances must be regarded as peripheral outlyers, although snake symbolism as such, outside of specific dances, is very frequent in the New World.

not I but *he* who is evil and malevolent." But the feared father protects as well as punishes: if, then, in talion punishment the snake does not bite me, then I am, by very God, demonstrated to be guiltless (or have in any case escaped the wrath). Drinking poison is the identical gambit in parallel form: an oral incorporation of Power will not kill — if only one has faith in the somewhat witless benignity of the Power, or, alternatively, if one has already incorporated the spiritual power of the father which will render the new incorporation powerless. But only the triumphant paranoiac drinks poison; most paranoids are afraid of "poison," i.e., talion punishment for guilty oral wishes.

The snake has a cleft tongue, says folklore, because he tells lies, a literal kind of double-talk. But whose is the *double-entendre* of the innocent conscious — and guilty unconscious — sly symbolism? Projectively we say the *snake* lies (denies oedipal guilt); all the while it is we who so deny. Thus it is the projected discrete serpent that is the Devil, or the instrument of the Devil (sexual or incestuous desires); hence he (snake, phallus) must be spurned and killed (as must these desires), lest we be killed. Therefore, to handle the snake, without the punishment of death, means either (1) that God the father is being royally hoodwinked in this dangerous game, or (2) that God grants genitality to the (incestuously) guiltless. Snake-handling is then an anxious testing and abreaction of guilty terror. To "dominate" the snake is to dominate guilty and dangerous sexual desire. But neurotic symbols "eat their cake and have it too," for snake-handling is itself obviously erotized. The snake is both the ancestral or oedipal father, giver of life, God — and the phallic Devil, instrument of God. The snake is both death and life, and immortality as well; the godhood of the father and the sinfulness of the son; the instrument both of pleasure and of its punishment. As the prime symbol used by human beings, the snake must always and everywhere be preoccupied with man's basic concern: the human body image and its life and death or immortality. The snake represents every modality of our body's guilts and needs.

It is in such jungles of unconscious symbolism that the neurotic wanders, lost. And if he mistake these phantasms of the frightened child-mind for the real shapes of life, then he lives in the permanent nightmare of the psychotic. Is sacred culture the neurosis of a society of persons, and heir to their forgotten past? In any case, snake-handling is now one trait in a bona fide subculture, and must be accorded all the ethnological respect we give to a trait in any culture. If it is in some ways a sick subculture, let us now nevertheless examine it. Perhaps the snake-handler is in some sense as "crazy" as the psychiatrist's patient. But if so, let us seek the psychiatrist's understanding and use his method, the careful and detailed study of a life history.

THE PEOPLE

CHAPTER 9

Biography of a Cult Leader

WE HAVE now traced the history and presented an external description of the snake-handling cult and its vicissitudes. We have also discussed the ethnography and symbolism of the snake, particularly in its Biblical setting. But a merely ethnographic account remains somewhat alien to us psychologically until we can discern the inner meanings of snake-handling to the actual people who practice it. If, once again, the present analysis may tend to emphasize the social distance of these people from ourselves, a sympathetic and deeper psychological understanding must nevertheless aim at making them at least intelligible to us.

We must ask ourselves such questions as these: What are these people like, psychologically? What is the meaning of the strange and dangerous behavior of handling deadly serpents and drinking deadly poisons? At this stage, of course, we know the rationalizations and the culture-historically patterned rationale of the cultists. But these leave us scientifically unsatisfied, for they form only the superficial manifest content of the behavior. What does the behavior mean in terms of specific personalities and their cultural predicaments? What does snake-handling do for them affectively? What phatic communications are actually taking place? What kind of people join the cult? And what are the personalities of their leaders?

Since snake-handling is now illegal in the states of its origin and early diffusion, it has been necessary to go to Florida, where the

113]

cult still survives, for the material that follows. Our purpose requires a study of the life history of one person, preferably one closely identified with the snake-handling cult. The following, therefore, is the condensation of an extended biographical account, obtained from a prominent Florida leader himself, the Reverend Beauregard Barefoot.*

Beauregard Barefoot was born about 1910 on a farm near Hungry Mother Mountain in northwestern Georgia. He was named for the well-known Southern general in the War Between the States, but if the general's family had any remote blood tie with this sharecropping family, it had long been disclaimed or forgotten. As a result of an almost compulsive industry, the father and, through different personality traits, the son were both "upward mobile" economically, though the culture and general social outlook of both father and son remained that of the "cracker" or rural poor white. It is possible that his being named for a prominent Southern hero had something to do with the youngster's fantasies about himself; certainly it had to do with the ambitions and the attitudes of the parents.

Shortly after Beauregard's birth, the family moved from Georgia to a northwest Florida hamlet where the father became a small poultry farmer. Beauregard was one of eleven children; three sisters had preceded him, making him the first son. He describes his father as a sternly just and honest man, quite undemonstrative. His mother was a member of the Southern Missionary Baptist Church, a rigidly fundamentalist group which prohibits smoking and drinking. All her life she wanted her first-born son to become a Baptist

* The Barefoots are a numerous and well-known family in the region, and the name Barefoot appears on monuments of the War Between the States and of both World Wars standing in front of the county courthouse. Barefoot is a bona fide family name, but it is not the real name of the Florida cultist minister. The material was collected by a onetime student of mine, Mrs. Henry Lehrberger, formerly of Miami. To protect her fellow Floridian, the names and other data specifically identifying him have been disguised, as is usual in psychiatric case histories, but all psychologically relevant data have been taken, largely verbatim, from Mrs. Lehrberger's report. I have sought to be scrupulously faithful in summarizing her descriptive account, though she is in no sense responsible for the interpretations in the chapters following, which are mine.

[114

minister. The father, however, was apathetic toward this ambition, being wholly absorbed in his own struggles to get ahead. Neither parent had had any formal education in the backwoods Georgia of their day.

Only twenty-one months after Beauregard's arrival, his mother gave birth to twins; and these, together with the additional three brothers and two younger sisters (one boy died at two of an intestinal disease), soon withdrew attention, in this hard-working family, *alienation* from the first-born son. As Beauregard himself remarked, "There wasn't much time to give me love and affection." He felt that he was different from his brothers and sisters and never "went around" with them much. When he was young, he said, he had a violent temper and would often fight with his younger brothers.

At fifteen he had tuberculosis, as did one of his sisters, and he *healing* believes that without faith in God he would never have been cured. He did not finish high school. The book he most often read as a child, he says, was the Bible. As far back as he can remember, he always wanted to be a Baptist minister, doubtless at the instigation of his mother, with whom he always retained a tie, though this seldom was given any overt emotional expression by either. At one time, however, he fantasied becoming a lawyer, but his lack of formal education soon frustrated this ambition.

Beauregard tells several anecdotes about his childhood. On one occasion, the teacher sent him with his cousin to get a bucket of water for their one-room country school. The boys decided to play a joke and put some filth in the water; but, before returning from the spring, Beauregard said to his cousin, "You know, I can't do this; I haven't told anyone except you, but I want to be a preacher and I can't be playing this sort of trick." Another story is about his mother. "This story comes to my mind which shows what an honest woman my mother was. When we were kids, we would buy candy for eggs. One day I tried to buy some candy with a rotten egg. But when my mother found out, she made me exchange the bad egg for a good one."

Another anecdote, of considerable psychological importance, concerns his father:

I once heard my parents talking about what a good worker I was and that was true. I will say that I have always been a hard worker and was always sure to get my work done well. I remember once when I had influenza, I felt terrible about not being able to do my work. A few days after I had gotten out of bed, I was helping my father with the crops. I was so very tired and weak that I could hardly stand up, but I didn't want my father to think I was lazy. Every time that he turned around, I would sit down. I was able to sit down 25 or 26 times and had a pretty good rest. But he never saw me.

At the dinner table, my father told everyone what a good and smart worker I was. And that sure made me feel good because my father thought that I was good and smart and I was able to fool him at the same time. And that's the way that I have been right along. I would always do my job very quickly so that I could go over to my cousin's, and my parents would see that I had done my job and would let me go. I was always able to know what my parents desired and was able always to please them for my own gain. And I am still that way today. I don't know what you call it, but I always had a certain understanding of people. Why, I think that I am the only minister in Tallahassee that can claim that every person in his church wants him to stay.

When asked if he got along with his brothers and sisters Barefoot replied:

No, I won't say so exactly. You know how brothers and sisters get into fights. I was always more rash than any of them. I had a temper and would act right upon my feelings, and I am still that way to this very day. I believe that in the long run, people are going to act on their inner feelings — if a farmer wants a piece of land bad enough he is going to work for it and get it. But my folks would sometimes have to watch out after me so that I would not fight with my [younger] brothers. Even to this day I would like or enjoy a good fight. I would very much like to join the army or any other fighting organization. But my religion takes the place of these things for me, and these things are against my religion.

Although our family was large, I would say that I was not greatly influenced by my parents or my brothers and sisters. You see, twenty-one months after I was born, my mother had twins, and there wasn't much time to give me love or affection. I can't ever remember hugging or kissing my father or mother.

Asked if he were close to any particular brother or sister, he said:

[116

No, I was always a little different than they were. Right now I have two brothers in Tallahassee who don't belong to this group. One started out as foreman in an orange-picking outfit and he did so well that he and his partner got them their own grove for theirselves. The other is a bus driver in Tallahassee. The first is probably ashamed that I am his brother. The other, a big husky fellow, seems to accept me just because I am his brother.

When my father died, in 1933 about the time of Roosevelt's inauguration (which I attended), he left the plantation to his children. It was worth $15,000, or $1,500 apiece. Every one of them has that property to this day, but I sold mine to them right away because I didn't belong there.

In speaking of his father in another connection, he said that everyone in the family agreed that on his father's tombstone ought to be put, "Here lies an honest man."

Barefoot was then encouraged to talk about his family. He mentioned that although his younger, bus-driving brother did not approve of the snake-handling religion, he had come once to a cult meeting after he returned from the army. At that time his brother said that he would never have been able to survive if he had not known that his family and friends at home were praying for him. He would not make a testimony of this because he disliked talking before a large number of people. Barefoot said that his brother, who had resented having to go into the army, had been extremely cruel to the Japanese soldiers and had boasted of never returning a Japanese soldier alive. Although he said that his other brother in Tallahassee avoids seeing him, he was surprised to learn that this orange-ranching brother had once contested a statement that Beauregard was trying to take money from the people of his church.

Asking the interviewer if she had any difficulties in understanding people, Barefoot admitted that it was easy for him to know and understand other people's motives; but he added that he found it much easier to understand uneducated people than educated. He said that he had never lost on a business deal and that he always knew whether people were being dishonest with him. On another occasion, when riding in the car of some friends of the interviewer from his church to another part of town, Barefoot did almost all the talking during the entire ride. He asked her what a certain psychologist at the University of Miami thought of him and said that he thinks everyone he speaks to can't help but know that he has been sincere and honest.

The interviewer reported:

In the first part of our talk, the Reverend Barefoot told me that he has a need to obtain the things he pursues. If he doesn't achieve his goals, he feels hurt. For instance, if he wanted the pencil that I was holding in my hand at that time, and if I refused it to him, he would feel extremely hurt.

I asked Mr. Barefoot how his mother felt when he broke away from the Baptist Church. He said that she was very disappointed at first, but when she saw how very sincere he was about his religion and the many changes it brought about in his life, she accepted his actions. His religious change also pleased Barefoot's younger brothers, who were relieved because Beauregard no longer tried to fight with them. He remarked that his religion had taken away his fighting desires. He said that before his mother died, she made a testimony in one of his meetings in order to please him.

The interviewer inquired about the moral training Barefoot had received.

My mother gave us a good moral training. She believed in having one wife — she didn't believe in divorce. I wouldn't go as far as she says. Some of these things depend on the situations. To have one wife is best, but if two people don't get along it's sometimes best that they divorce. I have two people in this church that are divorced. My mother stressed the importance of high morals, and she was very careful about bringing up her girls to be very virtuous. If any one of them would have had an illegitimate child, she would have nearly died.

She didn't believe in drinking or smoking. But all my brothers smoke. And I don't believe that it is wrong to take a drink if you don't do it to excess. I smoked when I was a boy, and although my Dad didn't want me to, he told me just not to burn up the barn.

The interviewer remarked that "Perhaps it is sometimes good not to be too strict about these things." Barefoot replied:

I don't know. I have a little boy, and I would certainly not want him to smoke until he is grown up. It's not healthy for the body;

I've been told that too much smoking makes one less mentally alert. Our bodies are weak enough without making them worse. My mother also didn't want us to go around with persons who did not have a good reputation. However, she taught us to be nice to everyone. I allow every type of person to come to this church. I know very well that some of the women who are raising their hands here on Sunday walk the streets as prostitutes on other nights. But I think that they should have a place to pray here as well as anyone else.*

The interviewer then inquired about his own wife and marriage.

Mr. Barefoot seemed surprised when I asked about his wife and remarked that no one had done so before. His wife is not an active member in his church group; in fact, she rarely attends. In the early part of their marriage, she had no respect for his religious pursuits and felt that he wasn't honest about them. However, now she is convinced of his sincerity and looks up to him and respects him and his religious beliefs. He said that the spirit of God would have been a great blessing if it had been only for the changes that it had caused in his marital relationship. Before this change, he and his wife had much discord, and there was much jealousy between them. Now the jealousies and antagonisms that formerly existed between them have been dissolved.

They still disagree on some things. For instance, she believes in getting their son Christmas presents, whereas he does not believe in celebrating Christmas because no one really knows the date of Christ's birthday. He understands his wife's point of view that his son may be jealous of other children who receive presents; however, he feels that it is more important for him to save money for his son's education.

His wife is not a well woman, and in a way she has not been a normal wife for him. Not that he doesn't love her, but it's something that can't be helped. She has had a very painful female disorder, and although she has been to every good doctor in Tallahassee, no

---

* In another interview, "When asked what his position was in matters concerning sex, Barefoot said that he has performed marriages, but he does not usually like to do so. He stressed the importance of love in marriage. He told a story of two persons in his congregation who were in love but could not get married at present because of the divorce laws in Florida. When he found that they had been living together, he advised them to wait until they were married. He told them that they should have respect for what other people think. He did not refuse to let them come to church as he said most other ministers would have done."

one has been able to help her. The Reverend Barefoot has encouraged her to have a greater faith in God, but to no avail.

With respect to his own sickness in childhood,

He wouldn't say that his experience with tuberculosis was the most important factor influencing his religion, but he does think that if he hadn't had faith in God, he would not have been cured. Being healed can be an experience which shows that you have the spirit of God.

When asked what "the spirit" is like,

Barefoot said that it was like a quickening analogous to electricity. To the question, How do you know when you have the spirit?, Barefoot replied that it is manifest in various ways: healing, happiness, the dance, quaking, handling the snake, and trance-like experiences. The only prerequisite to join the snake cult is to "get the spirit." Barefoot compared the spiritual awakening to a physical awakening. The latter, the water birth, comes when you are born. The former must come later in your development. He referred to the section of the Bible that stated this.

A number of incidents illustrate or prove to Barefoot the power of mind over matter. He said that he

sometimes gets feelings that he is needed, and when he calls his friends to "check up," he finds that his friends usually do want or need him. In reporting an incident which occurred in his congregation, Barefoot implied that his knowledge of a certain love affair, which he had without being told, was due to some special power.

Another time, after he had received the "gift of tongues," a high school teacher told him that what he said sounded a lot like Cherokee. But Barefoot had never lived up in the western North Carolina mountain country where the Cherokee live and, besides, his parents had left northwest Georgia soon after he was born, even before he could speak English. On another occasion, that of the second raid on his meetings by the Tallahassee police, "He had a feeling that the police were coming one night, and sure enough they did."

In a third interview, the Reverend Barefoot was asked about the beginning of his ministry. After he had decided to break away from the Baptist group, he traveled about the country from one church group to another — Moultrie, Thomasville, Valdosta, and Waycross in southern Georgia, and up into Eufaula, Hatchechubbee, and Phenix City in eastern Alabama.*

He remained with one group, which was similar to the religion of the Church of God in Tallahassee, for two years; however, he could not accept many of their dogmas, as the bathing of the feet ceremony, and men and women sitting at opposite sides of the room.

Barefoot's first church group in Tallahassee was held in a large tent outside the city limits. When he first started to build this present church, the Mt. Pisgah Temple, he was working with two other ministers, whose dishonest intentions he soon realized. After breaking his relationship with them, he bought the property for his church and began building.

At first his church service was very similar to the formal procedures of other churches: beginning with prayer, then sermon, requests for testimonies or for members to perform by playing the piano or singing, and closing with a prayer and benediction. Gradually, however, through a series of accidental occurrences in the services, the formal procedures were discontinued. Barefoot soon found that the people were much more responsive to a more spontaneous service. He also did not like to be "tied down" to form. His present group is one of the few churches that has no definite order in the ceremony; one can dress, act, feel anyway that he pleases. He said he hopes that the remaining formalized procedures in his service will soon disappear.

Snake-handling began in his church in 1947 when a cultist from Georgia who had known the founder, George Hensley, visited his church, and told him about the practice, and showed him the supporting Bible texts. Later he heard that this man had been bitten by a snake. "In order to satisfy his curiosity as to why the man was bitten, Barefoot rode over two hundred miles to see him. As he had expected, he found that the man was a fraud, and this fact explained to him why the man had not been successful with the snakes."

* This does not agree with his statement in the first interview that "he first began preaching outside the city limits of Tallahassee because he had gotten the call there." Possibly the line between "testimony" and "preaching" is so ambiguous that he might easily be mistaken. But the traveling around to various places does seem more like the action of an itinerant preacher than that of a mere layman.

The Reverend Barefoot says that his group is now the largest of its kind in the country, and people from all parts of Tallahassee are members.

Barefoot told me about several of the most faithful members in his group. One, a guitar player, had become a member after a sequence of experiences: the man, after hearing Barefoot speak at a tent meeting, got the feeling that one day soon he would join the group; Barefoot saw this man several weeks later and predicted that the man had or was going to have family discord; not long after this prediction, the man's wife left him and he turned to Barefoot for guidance. Now this man has married again and appears to be very happy.

Barefoot said that every one of his most loyal members have had an experience, such as a healing experience, a prediction miracle, or other comforting or revelation experiences from the religion. Such experiences give the people faith in God and enable them to be the most fervent members in his group. He emphasized the value of a religion of experience, as his religion was. Such a religion can not be formal, because everyone must feel free to act as they feel.

People are not encouraged to handle snakes in his group unless they are certain they have the feeling of power over snakes. No one in his congregation has ever been bitten while handling snakes "with the spirit of God." Asked what he would do if he were ever bitten, he said that he would certainly go to a doctor.

He said that he had never handled poison or fire, but some people do. He recognized that there is no evil in these objects, as there is no evil in the snake — the evil is in man, and handling these dangerous objects shows power of good over evil.

In the course of a discussion, Barefoot stated his belief that "in the long run, right will prevail."

He gave the following example to illustrate what is right and the relativity of righteousness. Some people do not think that it is right to disturb the normal functions of reproduction. However, in some cases it is wrong if one doesn't intervene. For instance, he knows of a couple, the man a low-grade moron, the woman a loose and careless person who, he thinks, should not have been permitted to have children. Now the man has run away from his wife and the poor children are running around the street without enough to eat. When I remarked that the people who don't seem capable of raising children have more than those who do, Barefoot added, "Well, perhaps God has wanted it this way. There must be a reason for it.* It's the people, the poor people who seem to have the greatest faith in God, and who knows?, they may outnumber the others, and God's name will then be more greatly proclaimed."

Like many other snake-handling ministers elsewhere, Barefoot has had some difficulties with the local police. They have confiscated snakes that were being used in meetings in each of the three raids they have made on the Mt. Pisgah Temple. Barefoot (like Tom Harden at Dolley Pond and the Reverend Bunn in Durham) takes obvious delight in baiting the police by letting word get about that snakes will be handled at a certain meeting and then, when the police are in evidence, innocently concentrating on testimony, speaking in tongues, or the laying on of hands to cure the sick.† As yet, this has resulted in no permanent interruption of his cult, for there is no state law in Florida prohibiting snake-handling, nor is there any present municipal ordinance against it in Tallahassee. Barefoot frankly enjoys his triumphs over the police and delights in throwing up to them the constitutional protections of freedom of religion. He also likes to bait Fate with rash and daring risks. "In this interview,

---

* This is one of several instances when the interviewer agreed with or made an amiable comment to Barefoot — only to have him delicately retreat or reverse his position. Maybe one shouldn't be too rigid with a son about some things? — No, (sententiously) it is bad for him, the body is weak enough already. Yes, maybe some people ought not have children? — No, (unctuously) it is God's will [and where would I get my clientele otherwise?]. In conversation, Barefoot almost makes a fetish of being "stickery," with direct but mildly expressed disagreements, which constantly reiterate his "integrity." He is not a comfortable colloquitor, does not really know how to converse, must constantly dominate and set his companion right, and requires that at all times his own truth prevail. He is capable of long monologue in a twosome also.

† In Durham, after serving his jail sentence and giving up the handling of snakes in services, the Reverend C. H. Bunn has instituted Saturday evening radio broadcasts of his meetings, a large proportion of which in 1960–1961 were devoted to attacks on a well regarded and competent local police chief, who thus far has been too dignified to deign reply; Bunn's comments on the judge of the Recorder's Court that sentenced him have seemed to some respectful townspeople remarkably unrestrained in language. But the noisy defiance of public authority has been typical of snake-handling ministers from Hensley and Hutton in the early days to Beauregard Barefoot in the late days of the snake-handling cult: it is an intrinsic part of its ethos.

as in others and in his sermons, Barefoot mentioned the big thrill that he gets from taking fast rides on his motorcycle."

The theology of Beauregard Barefoot is interesting.

He believes in an all powerful God, who enables man to perform such arts as healing, raising the dead, handling serpents, etc. Everyone who has the spirit of God in him is capable of performing some of the above acts, but only the Apostles are capable of all. Barefoot believes that one of these days all of these powers will come to him, that is, if he is not killed first. Already he has been endowed with the powers to heal, to speak in unknown tongues, and to handle snakes.

He spoke of his religious ideas constantly throughout this interview. "Good is God. God is Good. Eventually Good will prevail. God is all powerful. Eventually Good will prevail. God is all powerful. If God isn't capable of everything then he isn't God. Snake-handling isn't a test of God — the snake is a stupid animal guided by instincts. Every person that I have spoken to who handles snakes has told me that snakes can't be trained. The snake represents the Devil and handling them shows how good has power over evil [a statement perhaps not entirely consistent with an earlier one that there is no evil in the snake but that the evil is in man, an apparent inconsistency that is itself significant].

Barefoot stated that when God came to man, he was capable of performing the acts that are written in the Bible. There are about nineteen of them, such as healing, raising the dead, handling snakes, fire, etc. Everyone that has the spirit of God in him is capable of all. He thinks that one of these days he will be able to lift the dead, but he will probably be killed before he does that. These powers do not come to people all at once. The power of healing came to him in 1938[?], the power of the unknown tongues in 1933[?], and the power to handle snakes only came to him four years ago. He mentioned the sudden appearance of these powers to many of the apostles. He himself thinks that he is destined to be an apostle. Otherwise why do people in his congregation look up to him? Why does he seem to be more powerful than they?

He seemed to attribute the evil in man to the Devil, as an outside power causing man to do evil. He told me about an incident of a man who was trying to prevent him from being arrested by saying that he was crazy. When the man tried to make a statement about this before the courthouse, Barefoot had all of his members sing so loud that none could hear him. He went to this man and said,

"Let's you and I go to the state hospital and have our minds examined. (People always say you have what they themselves have. If a person has something wrong with him, he will always push it on you. I know very well that that man is crazy.)"

Barefoot also spoke of the power of the mind over the body. He feels that this faith in God was partly responsible for his being cured of tuberculosis, which he had when he was fifteen. At this point I mentioned something that my brother [then in medical school] had told me concerning the importance of hope in the cure of patients. "See," said Barefoot, "he admits the powers of mind over body. Why, if someone were to go to the state hospital and speak to those patients and help them mentally before they go through all that rigamarole, half of the patients would be cured to begin with."

I inquired whether he had read many books other than the Bible in his youth. He answered that the Bible was one of the only books he had read as a child. During the interview, he pointed out several passages that he seemed to rely on heavily, as the story of Adam and Eve. He affirmed the previous statement that he had made about not believing every word in the Bible.

At the time of the interviews, the Reverend Barefoot was about thirty-eight, though he looked younger. He was a handsome, dark-haired man with seemingly endless physical energy and eyes that are commonly called magnetic. His manner was pleasant, accessible, and helpful; he was a friendly and likable person, with much charm. Besides his career as a preacher, Barefoot often works as a carpenter, a trade he learned at home.

CHAPTER 10

Psychology of a Snake Cultist

The case of the Reverend Beauregard Barefoot, seen in its cultural context, is an absorbing one. In it we can clearly see the relation between the minister's personality and the institutionalized cultural history of his region and his cult. We can discern in his life the complex interplay between a rigidly compulsive and pleasure-prohibiting cultural background and an individual adaptation to it of a peculiar kind. We can likewise now begin to see the special needs of the communicants and the cathartic services provided them by the personality of the minister of the cult. Not less interesting is our emergent understanding of certain pathogenic elements in the culture.

When Beauregard Barefoot was born, his then relatively poor parents already had three children, all girls. Thus, while he was not the first child, he was the first male and was welcomed as such — by his mother as her first-born son and, even in this undemonstrative family, her evident favorite; and by his father as a boy who would become a good worker and helper about the farm. As Freud has pointed out, behind a person's assurance and his sense of mission we can often discover a mother's love for her favorite child. That Beauregard was his mother's favorite is perhaps best shown in the fact that it was he whom her ambition selected to become a Baptist minister. Beauregard felt he was "different." In later life he thought he was destined to be an "apostle" (God's chosen one); in early life he was destined to be a preacher (mother's chosen one). And, though he does not exploit it, he is perfectly aware of a parallel: both he and Christ were carpenters.

But this advantaged situation was disrupted when he was barely able to walk and talk — by his mother's having twins when he was only twenty-one months old, a time when the infant is still struggling with problems of oral and physical mastery of the world. The birth of a younger sibling is ordinarily traumatic enough to a favored child, but the coming of twins to a family now totaling six and ultimately to include ten children caused an especially severe displacement. As Beauregard himself puts it, "twenty-one months after I was born, my mother had twins, and there wasn't much time to give me love or affection." From his account of his later relation with his mother it is evident enough that she did love him and was even in her way proud of her favorite's success. But in this hard-working family (indeed, an upward-mobile one after they came to Florida) the arrival of five more children after the twins must have constantly and considerably preoccupied the mother throughout the rest of his childhood. Beauregard felt both favored and deprived.

As a result, he became unusually sensitive to the signs of others' love and approval. Several items in his story indicate this. First is the minor incident of the pencil, when he said he would have felt very hurt if he had wanted it and the woman interviewer had not given it to him. Again, there is the talk about his son (an only child), with whom Beauregard closely identifies himself; in a discussion of jealousy, he remarks that he "does not believe in celebrating Christmas" and had argued with his wife about omitting the gifts only to accede when he realized the boy would be jealous of other children (even though he is the only child in his family). This somewhat atypical stand is a suggestion in Beauregard of the well-known "Christmas neurosis," in which sibling rivalries and a sense of being loved or unloved emerge with a peculiar emotional intensity at this season.

His rather taciturn father's interest in Beauregard was apparently satisfied when the father was able to believe that his eldest son was a good worker. But it is interesting to note that the boy liked to get away from home to his cousin's when, instead, he might well have identified more with his father and have joined with him, beyond the minimum, in the endless chores about the farm of an upward-striving family. Notable too is the fact that he quickly sold his share of the farm when his father died, sure that he "didn't belong there." We are entitled to take with a grain of salt his statement that he was a hard worker. Certainly he got into a vocation entirely different from his father's. It was the younger sons who kept their shares in the father's land, and perhaps in particular the orange-ranching son, who more closely identified with their father vocationally than did Beauregard.

Indeed, his vocational identification was ultimately the ambition of his mother. She emphasized strict and rigid morals in her household; she was a member of the Southern Missionary Baptist sect, a dourly pleasure-prohibiting fundamentalist rural group which frowned on smoking, drinking, divorce, and unsanctioned sexuality. It is significant that Beauregard broke away from his mother's church but became a minister in his own — and developed in it much more relaxed rules about bodily indulgences and sexuality in his parishioners. The mother was disappointed for a time, but it was she who came over to his position, not the reverse. The father, though not so religious, was as honest and hard-working as she. The atmosphere at home was a compulsive work-demanding one — and a household in which Beauregard could never remember hugging or kissing his father or mother. If such "affect-starvation" was at all as characteristic of his parishioners' background as it was of the Reverend Barefoot's, then the contrastively exaggerated physical expressiveness and bodily contact in the snake-handling religion is entirely understandable. One gets in church what he didn't get in childhood.

Beauregard's childhood was a life of hard work and of little expressed affection. Curiously, Beauregard's only mention of his sisters in the later interviews was of the one with whom he had shared tuberculosis. With his younger brothers he seems mostly to have fought. He was rash, impulsive, quick to turn anger into action, hot-tempered, and violent; his parents often had to protect the younger boys from the wrath of the eldest. That the boy felt this way is a measure of his rivalry with those who had displaced him; that he was allowed this much expression shows his parents' ambivalent guilt over an unfulfilled emotional bargain: they could neither give him enough love or the conviction of it, nor entirely punish it out of him, nor force him to repress his hostility. Beauregard's main tie was to his mother, not to be replaced with lesser ties to father or brothers. He was "different." Instead of going around with his own brothers, Beauregard preferred to get out from under the home situation as often as possible and play elsewhere, at his cousin's.

Beauregard's personality stands out clearly against this background. His identification as preacher is feminine, in superego terms, and represents the incorporation of his mother's ambitions and ideals. But it also incorporates his father's attitudes as well, for with the passive support of his father he was able to sabotage his mother's more rigorous prohibitions.* For example, the father winked at the mother's edict against smoking and took only the realistic view that he should not burn down the barn. Nevertheless, Barefoot's feelings about this are somewhat mixed, and he is similarly strict about too-early smoking by his own son. The moral identification is here again with his mother. The body is already weak enough, he says, without our weakening it further. On the other hand, in the matter of masculine identification in hard work, Beauregard was able completely to outwit and hoodwink his father, getting highly valued public praise before the family, which he knew he did not deserve.

This work incident is a peculiarly important and significant episode in Barefoot's life. The context of the story is especially interesting in its moral blandness and insensitivity. After hearing his parents talking about what a good worker he was, he says it is true and that he had always been a good worker; then he immediately tells the story of his fraud and his pleasure at his parents' praise —

---

* As for his siblings, the chief value of his religion was that, despite some masculine protest of aggressiveness (his aggressiveness toward men was not overtly expressed in masculine terms but deeply masked and dissimulated), his religion reduced his combativeness with his brothers and, later at least, his discords with his wife. But he is somewhat fascinated with (or envious of) the army career of his brother, who was particularly savage in killing his Japanese prisoners.

and goes on to generalize about his ability to "understand" people
and to "please them for my own gain." The episode is worth re-
peating in full:

I once heard my parents talking about what a good worker I was
and that was true. I will say that I have always been a hard worker
and was always sure to get my work done well. I remember once
when I had influenza, I felt terrible about not being able to do my
work. A few days after I had gotten out of bed, I was helping my
father with the crops. I was so very tired and weak that I could
hardly stand up, but I didn't want my father to think I was lazy.
Every time that he turned around, I would sit down. I was able to
sit down 25 or 26 times and had a pretty good rest. But he never
saw me.

At the dinner table, my father told everyone what a good and
smart worker I was. And that sure made me feel good because my
father thought that I was good and smart and I was able to fool
him at the same time. And that's the way that I have been right
along. I would always do my job very quickly so that I could go
over to my cousin's, and my parents would see that I had done my
job and would let me go. I was always able to know what my parents desired and was able always to please them for my own gain.
And I am still that way today. I don't know what you call it, but
I always had a certain understanding of people. Why, I think that
I am the only minister in Tallahassee that can claim that every person in his church wants him to stay.

This event is critical to an understanding of the character of Beauregard Barefoot. Even the sequence of his remarks is an unerringly
accurate statement about his personality.

That he was allowed, in view of his recent illness, to work at all
is of course a commentary on the family culture (or class or regional
subculture) with respect to work and illness: it is a statement of
the demanding expectancies environing him. But how he met these
expectancies is significant also. It is in his own context that we
must view his remark that he can always understand people to his
advantage and can always manage to please them, particularly uneducated people (like his parents) in his church; educated people
he finds harder, because they have more of what he uses — superior
insight and intelligence. Thus he externally "pleased" his mother
by becoming a minister — though departing far from her compulsive

counsels, and giving only a much-iterated lip service to them, as we shall see. His father he "pleased" in terms of his father's values — by pretended heroism in which he flatly cozened his father. Father permitted what mother prohibited — but then it was easy to fool father too. This is, in fact, the pattern of Beauregard Barefoot's whole personality and ministry.

It is the pattern especially of his pretense and practice about sexuality. Barefoot is particularly revisionist about his mother's sexual prohibitiveness. Ferenczi describes acutely the effects on the child of the official pretenses he is expected to believe, when he already knows better about sexuality through his own experience.[108] When the child first dimly discerns the facts about reproduction he must wonder about his parents. Sexuality, he is given to understand, is for the purpose of producing children. But the official phatic pretense maintained by the parents — exaggerated in Beauregard's family by the total absence of public physical affection — is that this is the whole story. There is no suggestion that sexuality is pleasurable. The child is then left with a problem in judgment, to the solution of which only his own personal experience can contribute. He is clever enough to have discovered that his own genitals are a source of pleasure, but this only adds to his difficulty. There are several answers to the problem. He may say, "What a wicked and sinful person I am to have pleasurable sensations in my genitals — how different I am from other people, and how depraved!" Or he may say, "What a lot of hypocritical nonsense this is!" * and generalize from his own experience to that of other people: "Of course

* This feeling is vividly reported by a college student of twenty-two: "When I was much younger I often had the idea that perhaps life was just one big pretense, that everyone including my family were all trying to fool me and that some day they would disclose to me that nothing was true. An example of this is that I felt that perhaps my parents did not really like me, but were only making believe they did." Unusually inhibited, he said that he had practiced neither onanism nor coitus until the previous year. He felt contemptuous of his mother that she should have had coitus and had a mildly compulsive voyeurism of males (to see if they were really like himself?), but never had any homosexual experience and has since happily married. This conviction that "It's all a big pretense and they're all a bunch of hypocrites" is so common as to be normal among youngsters of college age in our society. It is also a prominent feature of the problem of belief-unbelief in the adolescent religious crisis.

the genitals give pleasure, but for some reason people insist on pretending that this is not the case, and so the only way to please them is to go along with them in this conspiracy of dishonesty; let us therefore pretend with them all that sexuality is sin, but at the same time let us continue enjoying it."

Painful though it must be to students of ethics and moral theologians, we cannot avoid the conclusion that lying and morality are somewhat interconnected. To the child everything seems good that tastes good; he has to learn to think and feel that a good many things that taste good are bad, and to discover that the highest happiness and satisfaction lie in fulfilling precepts which involve difficult renunciations. In such circumstances it is not surprising — and our analyses demonstrate it beyond the possibility of doubt — that the two stages, that of original amorality and of subsequently acquired morality, are separated by a more or less long period of transition, in which all instinctual renunciation and all acceptance of unpleasure is distinctly associated with a feeling of untruth, i.e. hypocrisy.[109]

But hypocrisy remains, if our intelligence prevents our introjecting the "morality." It is the peculiar predicament of Beauregard Barefoot, an intelligent man, to have remained caught in this limbo between the child's knowledge of himself and the unreal demands of his culture. In a sense, he thus even has the right to proclaim his (introspective) honesty, though he is not honest in his overt cultural practices. It is also notable that "morals" in his ministry remain defined on a very primitive level, as if morality had only to do with simple prohibition of all the fleshly indulgences in his culture. His concern with what people think makes his morality far more shame-sanctioned than guilt-sanctioned. And, preoccupied with personal sin on this psychosexually primitive narcissistic level, how can people in his region have any real perception of larger, allo-individual, more complex *social* ethical issues? In such a situation the culture must come in for indictment far more than the individual. And if, in a narrow fundamentalist rural world, a man has no knowledge of alternative cultural dispensations, if he has no intellectual platform from which to assess and criticize his culture, what can he do? Faced with the culture's impossible demands and in need of love, he adapts himself and becomes as spurious as the absurd cultural pretenses require him to be. The Emperor has no clothes — but a person must live!

Thus the less genuine and complete the introjection of the parental culture, the more sought for is the appearance of probity and the louder the protest. In this light we may examine Barefoot's constant preoccupation with "honesty." We must recall the anecdotes in which he reiterates his parents' honesty and, even in childhood, his own. Again, his mother was disappointed in the direction his ministry took, but in time was convinced of his "sincerity." His wife long questioned his "religious" probity, but in time she acquiesced in the resigned tacit agreement that it was at least as honest as her own hysterical defenses. And now "everyone," including the Miami psychologist who ought to know, is convinced that he is "sincere and honest." (But are the police? the larger society? the Constitution of the United States? God?) Truly, an experience of revelation is required to sustain such a faith. There is indeed a relativity of righteousness. And prostitutes must have a place to pray like everyone else. But what kind of an honesty is it that has to protest so much?

True, the incident of the candy exchanged for a rotten egg shows that honesty was highly valued in the family; and on the father's tombstone would be put "Here lies an honest man." But his father constantly sabotaged his mother's greater strictness. In one's innermost mind can one trust such a father? An honest man indeed lies. Besides, can he not go one step further and hoodwink the same father who helps him hoodwink the mother? The sins of the son are merely the sins again of the father — and of all the cultural fathers.

In this same context, Barefoot speaks proudly of his ability to "understand" people and to please them for his own gain, as he did his parents. "I don't know what you call it, but I always had a certain understanding of people." But what is this understanding, finally, but the ability to play their game and to exploit them? And what is this honesty but knowledge of oneself? Barefoot is quick enough on some occasions to recognize dishonesty in other people:

in the bitten, fraudulent preacher from whom he had learned snake-handling, and in the two minister-colleagues who were plotting to get the gospel house which he somehow himself eventually obtained. Indeed, he was surprised and pleased to learn that his brother the businessman had defended him against a charge of dishonestly mulcting his followers; his reiterated protest of honesty is an indication that he did not expect to deserve this of life, least of all from a brother who presumably knew him well. But the brother is plainly projecting his own integrity in his unsuspicious judgment of Beauregard; such people are exploitable, since "foolish."

In Barefoot's constant preoccupation with what people may think of him lies the clue to his insecurity with other people — and with himself. Still, he never lost a business deal with anyone (apparently a business deal can redound only to the advantage of one person, not of both). One gets the impression that he has no real taste for close cooperation with sibling figures any more than he had with his brothers, and that "honesty" in dealing with other people is mere surefootedness in getting what he wants — mere window-dressing for motives which "everyone" employs in the battle of life. There is even the suggestion that physical closeness is distasteful to him (he did not like the foot-washing in one church, or the men sitting all together), which may reflect the attitudes formed in his childhood. On the other hand, he is much interested in the surreptitious-seductive and titillating-dangerous contacts with his female parishioners (without, he avers, even the least suspicion of there being anything sexual in it) — an undoubted reaction to the lack of physical affection in his childhood. He is a snake-teaser.

Like most of the snake-handling ministers, Barefoot also takes a decided pleasure in baiting authority figures such as the police. In this whole game, the prohibited act is the handling of snakes. But he will handle them anyway, for a greater Father has told him he can do so with impunity. One recalls here his own father's tacit connivance at breaking the mother's rule against smoking. A more powerful authority permits what a merely powerful one forbids (above the police is the Constitution, and above the Constitution, God). This principle is extended from smoking to symbolic sexual permissiveness as well. Sexuality is sin; the snake is evil, the Devil — but we will hold to it and play with the dangerous thing with impunity, supported by the "spirit" of the Father. Certainly, with or without a father's emotional assent, Barefoot's attitude toward the women in his cult is blandly, if surreptitiously, exploitative sexually. He is able piously to marvel that the young women swoon into his arms "without there ever being any sexual element in it." He is especially adept at embracing a line of jerking, spirit-quickened hysterics, one by one, and causing them to slide to the floor in ecstasy. His wife's jealousy and distrust of his religious practices in the early days was no doubt intuitively well founded; but since she has attained to her own protective "female troubles" the couple has reached a modus vivendi. In this he recalls the Reverend Bunn: what are we to think of a man who insists to the attorney general of North Carolina that a minister has the right to perform his own personal marriages himself should the occasion arise?

And what of aggression? Barefoot would "like nothing better" than to get into a fight, to join the armed forces. But his ministry prevented this (there are chaplains in the armed forces!). His religion has taken away his desire for fighting, and "these things are against my religion." One detects, however, the same ambivalence about the expression of aggression as about the expression of sexuality. At times he says he would enjoy a fight, and he does enter into fights (under the protection of his religion and the Constitution of the United States). But he had been sickly, and the body is "weak enough." He views himself not as a strong man but as a shrewd and clever one. In this connection we should recall that he once fantasied himself in the career of the more overtly oral-aggressive "masculine" lawyer, but because of educational lacks and weaknesses in himself chose instead the "feminine" identification (mother) with the ministry. And each of these remains an attempt at oral mastery, dating from the epoch of his major trauma.

Religion, then, is for him a feminine, mother-provided façade, which in superego terms his father tells him he need not take entirely seriously, and within which he may exploit women sexually — confident always that he can comfortably outwit such father figures as the police or the law, as he had outwitted his own father. Over-protesting a sincerity of belief in his mother's nonpermissive religious values, he recruits a great many female converts by the impressive candor of his look into their eyes, at the same time himself taking his father's more relaxed views about sin and sexuality. But, symbolically, in this he oedipally seduces his faith-laden mother.

Barefoot nevertheless is ultimately afraid of his father: for though God continues to endow him with such supernatural gifts as speaking in tongues and healing the sick and handling snakes, God will probably "kill him" some time before the final gift of raising the dead is given. A just Father may discover a boy's fraud and kill him! Snakes cannot be trained, no more than sexuality can be subjugated or the unreconstructed id denied. God is all-powerful. But anyone who has the "spirit of God" in him is capable of the nineteen supernatural acts that seem to contravene the laws of God's secular and naturalistic world (again a discrepancy between knowledge and pretense). In this there is also some unstable element of reconciliation with the father, just as there is some reconciliation with the male in the "holy kiss."

But on the whole, Barefoot allows the grizzled and tearful old cracker farmers to take care of themselves while he concentrates on the women, especially the younger ones. With men, his relationship is fearful-suspicious and paranoid; he is ever ready to project his own hostility and distrust into them. There is a paranoid streak in him, but it is not the major one. In handling snakes, one only borrows God's omnipotent power. Though "stronger" than his parishioners who "look up to him," Beauregard is not God, nor even Jesus. Nevertheless, he comes close to megalomaniac claims to omniscience and omnipotence: he implied that he knew of the illicit lovers in his church through some special power; when the spirit comes into the snake-handler there is a psychokinetic "power of mind over matter"; he had a "precognition" that the police were coming; and he has the mysterious "gift of tongues." He is a good enough natural psychologist to understand the predominantly paranoid mechanism of projection: he is well aware of the projection of the would-be helpful man who tried to protect Barefoot from the police by calling him crazy. On any joint trip to the state hospital to "have his mind examined," he knows that he would be acquitted. He knows that he is not crazy.

And he is right. He is in fact well adapted to his social reality. Though Beauregard Barefoot has some traits (and some guilts) that might be termed neurotic, there is no real evidence that he is psychotic, as many of his enemies have rather loosely alleged. For while his beliefs about handling snakes, drinking poison, and raising the dead may seem to us wholly out of touch with biological reality, nevertheless it must be emphasized that these are in him cultural traits, not individual psychotic or schizophrenic beliefs. Indeed, he holds some of these beliefs less trustfully and more realistically than do some of his communicants. He is well and even shrewdly adapted to his situation. Nor is he genuinely a psychopath in the sense that his behavior is simply antisocial "acting out" of impulses, inconsistent with his local culture. His personality fits more closely the technical classification of the "psychopathic character." [110]

In the restricted and precise modern analytic understanding of the term psychopath it is clear that we must go beyond the old legalistic definition of simple moral insanity in persons who "don't know right from wrong." Possibly this old notion is responsible for the journalistic cliché that psychopathic crimes are committed by morons. But this does not correspond with the clinical reality. The psychopath is not stupid, but often, in fact, clever; and at whatever IQ level he stands it is the hallmark of the psychopath to *regard* himself as a clever fellow. Those who are actually not so clever get caught. But so far as "moral insanity" is concerned, the psychopath typically has a perfectly adequate "ethnographic" knowledge of his society and its shibboleths and of what it considers right and wrong. He simply isn't having any. Or else he regards himself as an exception, and believes that the rules that may apply to others do not apply to him. His tested ability to escape around and through the naïve moral assumptions of his stolid contemporaries inevitably constitutes for him evidence of his cleverness and superiority. Snakes cannot be "trained"; nor can the psychopathic character.

In reality, the problem is not an intellectual (cognitive) *deficit*

137]

but an emotional (affective) *misgrowth*. In the second volume of his biography of Freud, Ernest Jones writes of this kind of personality with great appositeness:

The first of [the "unanalyzable" types Freud] labeled the "Exceptions." After a disquisition of clinical value on the particular type of renunciations a patient has to make during a psychoanalysis Freud called attention to a class of persons who blankly refuse to do so since they regard themselves as exceptions to the iron laws of nature. With such people the explanation of much unreasonable, and also injurious, behavior turns on their secretly cherishing the belief that they are exceptions to the rule that society justly demands a certain standard of conduct; they are free of such rules. The analyses of such cases disclose that, usually in early life, the patient has in fact suffered unjustly from some ill-treatment or accident, so that he feels that society owes him some recompense, while he owes it nothing. Freud described as such a type King Richard III, at least as delineated by Shakespeare, and he expressed his admiration for the skill with which the dramatist wins some degree of sympathy for the "hero" by adumbrating the meaning of his behavior rather than by bluntly insisting on it. In conclusion Freud suggested that women as a whole tend to regard themselves in the same light because of the part of the body they felt themselves in infancy to be deprived of.[111]

In the present instance, Barefoot clearly regards himself as a special case — the preferred but traumatically dethroned favorite of his mother. He is "superior" to his parishioners. He is "different" from his brothers and sisters in his sternly patriarchal, demanding, at least verbally religious family. He prefers, for whatever reasons, to play with his rascal of a cousin, though he is also capable of piously rejecting some of the pranks suggested by the cousin — in a slightly holier-than-thou tone, and he offers this childish virtue to the woman interviewer as evidence of his early election to grace. Meanwhile, playing away from home spares him some of the close surveillance of his parents and the tattling of his beleaguered younger brothers and sisters.

If his mother withdraws, or does not adequately show, her earlier love, then he may please her with lip service to religiosity; but clearly he is no longer obliged to take it too seriously emotionally, since she has not kept her part of the tacit bargain. Indeed, this religious seeming, in which he has become professionally quite skillful, is merely the handle with which to manipulate and to exploit those who do take, or must pretend to take, such religious injunctions seriously. His conscience is not a compulsive's; he is no seeker of responsibility. Nor is he a depressive Atlas bearing the world's woes. Any moral influence of his father's justice rolls like water off a duck's back. Nor is he compulsive in feminine superego terms (mother) either. He likes informality in his church and would slough off procedural rules one by one with even less compunction than he would slough off his mother's moral injunctions. And he is able to be entirely clear that he does not take the whole Bible literally, as do most Fundamentalists. That is, he is quite able to make his own independent judgment of the worth of parental truths.

Likewise, so far as sexuality is concerned, the snake-handling drama itself (and certainly as he practices it) contains a great deal of the sly return of the repressed in its sexual manifestations. He is particularly preoccupied with the Adam and Eve story — but he will lurk about Eden nevertheless and have commerce with the Serpent, despite the angry and jealous God who would keep creativity as his own. And despite the angel of death with the flaming sword, who more than a little parallels the snake.

His "superiority" to his communicants consists precisely in his Nietzschean position "beyond good and evil," in his slyly and joyfully inducing others to break the rules without their even knowing it. He can be as contemptuous of the female's pretenses as he is of the male's rules. The ineffable experience of some of his repressed female communicants is clearly an induced, if sometimes unwitting, public orgasm. Clearly, the snake and the fruit which Jehovah forbade may be seized and enjoyed, if only we can outwit God with our "faith." Such faith is merely pretending to believe things we know better about. And we shall be as gods, knowing good and evil to be mere arbitrary parental fiats — and the parents' motives and sincerity not to be trusted at that.

CHAPTER 11

Psychopathy and Culture

Now we must deal with the psychopath and the psychopathic character in some of their large social contexts. Many questions need to be asked. What are the relationships between these psychiatric types and their society? How are psychopaths and societies involved with one another in culture change? And what, perhaps, are the identifiable pathogenic elements in the societies themselves? To attempt some answers to these questions, we embark in these final chapters on a psychiatric ethnography of these segments and subcultures in our society and their relevance to the whole. But first of all we must examine more closely the dynamic meaning of the psychopathic life history.

How do the psychopathic types adapt to the peculiar socializing pressures that play upon them during individual growth? We must ask this, for the psychological conflicts arising from a child's problems of socialization take in these types a quite different direction from those of the neurotic or the psychotic. In the psychopath, the ego remains relatively intact, nourished by the mother's sufficient emotional sustenance in the early years, though deep resentment toward her is still present because of unsatisfied and unmastered longings. In this the psychopath differs from the schizophrenic in ego structure. The more severely rejected schizophrenic "lacks" the integrative ego and self-image built upon accepting and approving attitudes in the parent, though severely deprived psychopaths do grade imperceptibly into the schizophrenics. But, relatively speaking, the psychopath has had at least enough acceptance for him to have in turn accepted the world in ego-adaptive terms. Primary pathology, however, also resides in the psychopath's attitude of recalcitrance toward and non-identification with the father, the characteristic main source and sanctioner of superego introjection.* For the man who does not in the last analysis love and respect his father must have some pathology of the conscience.

In psychopathic types, basic hostility to the father still remains, but a hostility now dissimulated and directed outwards onto society at large. In Ferenczi's sense, both psychotics and neurotics undergo autoplastic distortions of the self; but the ego of the psychopath continues the struggle, with attempted alloplastic manipulations and modifications of his environment, while he himself remains morally unchanged. The psychopath hates. He remains not intellectually but *emotionally* unsocialized. The psychopath is a basically unsocialized animal who nevertheless lives in society, in Jenkins's conception. He acts out without repression his anti-social wishes, using his astute knowledge of people and of his culture only to exploit them and to protect himself against detection and punishment. Conscience, the morality of his tribe, is not built emotionally into his character, but like a lurking Javert remains only the hated policeman outside, who exists only to be evaded. William and Joan McCord well characterize the syndrome of psychopathy:

The psychopath is asocial. His conduct often brings him into conflict with society. The psychopath is driven by primitive desires and an exaggerated craving for excitement. In his self-centered search

* Some qualifications are necessary here. The classic picture of psychopathy in which the father is the brutalizing foil of revolt and non-identification, presupposes a patrist ethos which may already have ceased to exist in contemporary society. The psychopath shaped in contemporary matrist society seems to show a shift in hate objects corresponding to the change in the primary socializer and identification figure. Captain Ahab sought to kill the Moby-Dick that had maimed him; but sadistic attacks on female objects seem to preoccupy the fantasies in contemporary horror movies. (The dominating-denying female has been made explicit in Leslie Fiedler's provocative study of *Love and Death in the American Novel*, New York, 1960.) As between patrist and matrist foils for revolt, Beauregard Barefoot may represent an interesting transitional case (the matrist-patrist dichotomy of historic societies comes from another stimulating study, Rattray Taylor's *Sex in History*, London, 1953).

141]

for pleasure, he ignores restrictions of his culture. The psychopath is highly impulsive. He is a man for whom the moment is a segment of time detached from all others. His actions are unplanned and guided by whims. The psychopath is aggressive. He has learned few socialized ways of coping with frustration. The psychopath feels little, if any, guilt. He can commit the most appalling acts, yet view them without remorse. The psychopath has a warped capacity for love. His emotional relationships, when they exist, are meager, fleeting, and designed to satisfy his own desires. These last two traits, guiltlessness and lovelessness, conspicuously mark the psychopath as different from other men.[112]

The psychopath, in short, tends to "act out" rather than to form neurotic symptoms of conflict between the superego and the id, or psychotic conflicts between the self and reality. The psychopath typically produces much suffering and unhappiness — a repayment life owes him from childhood — but often (in the adult psychopath at least) with very little conflict, guilt feeling, or suffering in himself.

Whereas the neurotic suffers from excessive inner conflict, the psychopath makes others suffer from his lack of inner conflict, as Jenkins puts it; for Jenkins, the psychopath is merely the extreme on a continuum, so that the question is not so much one of categorizing — not *is* a given man a "psychopath"? — but rather *how* psychopathic is he? (which may explain why some psychiatrists have, or profess to have, such difficulties in diagnosing a psychopath). The dynamic gamut may therefore run between the extremes of *compulsiveness* and *impulsiveness*, between inhibition and exhibition of the forbidden wish. Whereas the neurotic compulsive person is hog-tied from all useful action by his conflicts, psychopaths "dramatize primitive impulses into real action" (as Bartemeier phrases it). But in their origins, psychopaths are of several different kinds. Levy discriminates the indulged and the deprived psychopath in this fashion: "The deprived psychopath is defective in his capacity to develop 'standards.' In the indulged psychopath, standards are well understood, but are taken lightly." [113] The deprived psychopath is the product of parental cruelty and rejection; the indulged, of parental conflict. The deprived psychopath would correspond to our concept of the moral schizothyme; the indulged, of the moral cyclothyme. Beauregard Barefoot would probably better fit into the indulged rather than the deprived classification, though still with some ambiguity perhaps. Barefoot is also a case of what Jenkins calls adaptive delinquency; for he integrates adaptively and co-operatively with a distinct subcultural group in a pseudo-social solution; he is not the maladaptive criminal lone wolf, certainly not in the typologically pure form — a still further reason for rejecting the new term "sociopath."

Jenkins is doubtless right in believing that the psychopath is merely one extreme on a continuum with normal people and that clinical psychopathy is a difference in degree, not of kind, from that elusive fiction, normality. And yet this difference in degree is true with respect to all neuroses and many psychoses as well as psychopathy. But why do some psychiatrists insist there is no such clinical entity as psychopathy, and why do others as stoutly maintain that this type of disorder is clearly definable? In this the shrewd remarks of Bromberg greatly aid our understanding. He discusses the question of social transference in order to bring out some possible reasons for our difficulty in diagnosing the psychopath.

Each member of society is unconsciously identified with aggressive, rebellious or asocial impulses released overtly by the psychopath. Each "normal" member of the society defends himself against the encroachment of his own unconscious aggressive impulses by projection to the person already in trouble with society. Hence the psychopath bears the full weight of social reaction formations.[114]

Bromberg considers that the notoriously varying difficulty of psychiatrists in clinically discerning psychopathy is related to the individual psychiatrist's personality; differential diagnosis is a function of the varying subjects, not of the unvarying object involved in judgment. It is the psychiatrist's own understanding of himself, the variable threat to the psychiatrist's defenses that his psychopathic patient poses, and, most important of all, the psychiatrist's degree of penetration of the psychopath's distinctive defense mechanisms.

In general, one may say the more the psychiatrist loosens the restrictions upon his personality, ingrained and nurtured by his traditional place in traditional psychiatry, the less the psychopath appears to be a distinct diagnostic entity. The various mechanisms which we, by agreement, call "neurotic," the displacements, condensations, reaction-formations, ritualistic bindings, tensions, guilt reactions, seen in neurotic individuals, are also seen in the psychopath once the defensive structure thaws out.[115]

Dalmau further aids us to see behind the characteristic façade of the psychopath. Behind a pleasing and seductive charm the psychopath maintains a destructive, aggressive energy steadily directed outward. His total lack of superego is, however, only apparent. In psychopaths, Dalmau believes, the superego is not so much absent as projected. This formulation explains especially well the mixture of paranoid and psychopathic defenses in Beauregard Barefoot. In psychopathy, Dalmau says, there is

a relative dissociation of the superego with projection of its role onto society in terms of getting caught and punished. Projection is an ego defense closely related to paranoid defenses and those defenses predominate in the psychopath. I've heard a psychopath rage against the police officer who caught him, but never at himself. There may be several ways of explaining the apparent lack of superego in the psychopath. Whether the mechanisms of projection, denial, undoing, dissociation and reaction formation are all responsible or one more than the other is not as relevant as the fact that the superego is functionally detached from the personality and projected onto society. In order to understand more clearly the behavior of the psychopath, let us keep in mind that the core of the superego is formed by the parents and what the child believes the parents expect. Later on society extends the role of the parents. The functional elimination of the superego then becomes equated with a symbolic murder of father and mother; the persistent attack against society also carries the same symbolism beyond the intrapsychic structure . . . The instinctual behavior of the psychopath is quite possibly a reaction formation against a massive, repressive superego. It is the threat of this overwhelming superego that forces the psychopath to deny its existence and project it symbolically onto society and even then he is not free from it [hence] . . . *the need for expiation through external agencies such as hospitalization, jailings, accidents and victimization through acts of fate* . . . The psychopath, perhaps more than any other patient, uses reality as a vehicle for symbolic behavior, and transference conflicts are acted out in stage-like representation . . . The psychopath uses the death drives as a boomerang without awareness that what he throws out will hit him in the back of the head . . . His violations are frequently so flagrant that he seems to be begging to get caught. Once caught there is a denial of any personal responsibility for being caught, even blatant proclamations of himself as a victim of persecution by the police in a beautiful paranoidal shift. Then of course he is "forced by circumstance" into a dependent repressed position to justify further his rage and the next opportunity to ventilate it against society.[116]

A purely dynamic interpretation of the genesis of Barefoot's personality in these terms would be that a severely compulsive father produced a reactively impulsive son. That is, the demands of the parent were too overwhelming to be made a part of the intrapsychic structure of the child as an internalized conscience. Instead, his ego adaptations remain always in a stage of defensive warfare against a permanently external and threatening superego or paranoid persecutor. In God, the police, the courts, the state, and society at large he refinds in repetition compulsion the massive and repressive superego model of the father. The snake must be dominated, but is still potentially dangerous; as unteachable as the psychopathic id, the snake is also made into one's still external superego-judge, a dramatized and symbolized Fate. Reality itself is systematically distorted to fill this role in Beauregard's private drama, and his acting out is skillfully contrived to seduce the needed punishments from society. Nowhere more than in the psychopath is a man's personality equivalent to his fate.

Psychopathy is notoriously so refractory to the best efforts of the therapist as to give currency to the cliché that the psychopath "never learns" or "never learns any better" morally, despite repeated punishments. Although this refractoriness is clearly a transference phenomenon — in which the therapist is persistently placed in the role of a harsh and punitive parent, thus arousing again the typical paranoid and psychopathic defenses of the patient — many psychiatrists consider psychopathy a primary constitutional or even a hereditary trait in some persons. Indeed, an older term was "constitutional psychopathic inferiority." On the whole, Dalmau takes the psychoanalytic position on the psychogenicity of psychopathy. He believes that

The emotional damage in the psychopath may basically occur anywhere from birth to Oedipus; it may occur in the latent or puberal stage. It appears that the anethopath, or true psychopath, forms at a very early stage whether through difficult birth, allergic reactions, eczema, or at later stages with the birth of siblings and other situations which may establish the basic destructive rage pattern through the de-fusion of the life and death instincts. The child feels distress and experiences this as an external attack that gives basis to the paranoidal ideation and a punitive destructive superego.[117]

But despite his emphasis on environmental and psychogenic factors, Dalmau states:

However, my conviction is that a rejecting mother or punitive father only reinforces a pre-existing psychopathology. The basic lesion is always intrapsychic and divorced from external factors except as these serve to reinforce the paranoidal position. The psychopath brought up in an ideal home would still be a psychopath because of his intrapsychic distortions. The rejecting attitude of most parents of psychopaths is a countertransference reaction provoked by the aggressive, defiant child . . . *A hereditary basis for psychopathy may be formulated on the non-specific basis of intensity of instinctual drives.*[118]

The primary constitutional or hereditary factors in psychopathy have been argued in still another way by J. J. Michaels, who, like Dalmau, is alert to both constitutional and developmental factors. We have perhaps insufficient confirmation in Barefoot's life history of Michaels' thesis that the psychopath represents a quasi-constitutional failure in sphincter discipline which becomes a generalized indiscipline characterologically.[119] Nevertheless, Barefoot does display many of the standard traits of the urethral personality — its flamboyance, exhibitionism, dramatic flair, sensitivity to and preoccupation with the opinion of others, rashness, impulsiveness, slyness, ambition, quick temper, daredevil tendencies, and responsiveness to shame rather than to guilt.[120] Again, the classic "playing with fire" is another aspect of the psychopathic character which we find in Barefoot. As Fenichel writes, impulsive actions carried out for the purpose of protection against supposed dangers may become dangerous themselves, and thus a vicious circle may be created . . . The idea that forcing the gods to give protection may be dangerous, and that because of this danger one has to force the gods still more, is valid for any impulse-neurosis. In drug addiction, however, the idea that the protective measure may be dangerous is, for physiological reasons, a very real one. It *is* a danger.[121]

The same is true, to a lesser degree, in alcoholism. In this respect — the existence of a real danger — drug addiction, alcoholism, and snake-handling are identical. Snake-handling is gambling with Fate, dealing with a potentially dangerous and punitive thing.* Here again we may see a distinction between the true psychopath, who needs no such masochistic bargain with life, and the psychopathic character, who is a gambler. Indeed, in snake-handling, Barefoot is much like the gambler:

Gambling, in its essence, is a provocation of fate, which is forced to make its decision for or against the individual [Barefoot's supernatural "gifts" versus "I may be killed first"]. Luck means a promise of protection † (of narcissistic supplies) in future instinctual acts. But what is more important is that the typical gambler consciously or unconsciously believes in his right to ask for special protection by fate. His gambling is an attempt to compel fate in a magical way to do its "duty"; however, gambling is a *fight* with fate. The gambler threatens to "kill" fate if it refuses the necessary supplies and is ready, for this purpose, to run the risk of being killed. Actually the

---

* In the adolescent game of Russian roulette of a few years back, this same psychopathic element is present. In this game, the cylinder of a revolver, containing only one bullet, is spun around and then, without inspection, the gun is pressed to the temple and fired. The odds are one to five that the gamble will end in death. In milder, and in classically urethral flippant form, there is also the goldfish-swallowing by college students already noted, which also has its psychopathic symbolism. The game of "chicken" is still another case in point: racing stolen cars toward a cliff and hoping to jump out alive at the last possible moment; another version is to speed toward one another from opposite directions, forcing one driver to "chicken," or swerve at the last minute, sooner than the other. Contemporary hotrodding and drag racing contain similar psychopathic elements.

† Protection is explicitly promised to the snake-handlers in a hitherto uncited text: "Behold, I have given you authority to tread upon serpents and scorpions, and over all the power of the enemy: and nothing shall in any wise hurt you" (Luke x, 19).

unconscious "masturbatory fantasies" of gambling often center on parricide.[122]

Fenichel describes a gambler who had been greatly spoiled in his first three years, then suddenly deprived of his privileges by his father; thereafter throughout his life he asked for compensation. In Barefoot's case, the tacitly promised but undelivered narcissistic supplies of love were his mother's, but otherwise the father is still involved. The deprivation of the mother is blamed upon the father: hence Barefoot's later provocation of the police, the endless "testing" of the paternal emotional weather in snake-handling, while at the same time demanding of protection *by* the father (through the appropriated power or "spirit"), or, through luck, *from* the father's wrath (danger of death in the snake). Snake-handling magically compels or dares God to protect or to punish the communicant. Barefoot is well aware of the contingencies: in symbolic masturbatory handling of the snake he may get greater magic gifts and miracles — or he may be killed. Thus Barefoot's sexuality, in the technical analytic sense, is of a fearful "phallic"-masturbatory kind that fears external punishment for pleasure; it is not a secure, self-possessed, mature "genital" sexuality.

It is perhaps an obscure awareness of Barefoot's taunting of God that makes for his rejection by the larger society of his region. Roman Catholics, to be sure, may confidently expect miracles; but in the severely Protestant ethos of the rural South, God's grace must be earned. Salvation must be won by disciplined moral behavior. The ascetic Protestant ethos is also fundamentally against gambling, for this offers the promise of an unearned something for nothing.*

* I question, however, Dr. Thorner's position that the ethos of Judaism is not incompatible with gambling. For the mana in the Ark of the Covenant *automatically* punished and killed the servant of the Lord who, in all reverence and good will, tried to keep the Ark of the Covenant from sliding off the wagon; and the Old Testament Jahweh allowed no trifling, even with his Name.

However, New Testament theology is centered on a miracle, and the Hellenistic ethos departed from the Hellenic spirit of the Ionian nature philosophers and the later classic Greek belief in impersonal *ananke* or Fate, which was even above Zeus. The problem is a complex one, for the Protestant

In our middle-class [Protestant] society gambling is a disreputable activity. In [Roman Catholic] Italy, as in many European countries, gambling is taken for granted, and the state promotes its own lotteries. Protestants tend to identify law and morality and therefore consider illegal acts as immoral. The Catholic church makes no such identification. Gambling is a temporal matter. The state has the right to forbid it, but the legal prohibition does not make it immoral. According to the church, gambling is immoral only when the gambler cheats, uses money which is not his own, or deprives his dependents of what is needed for their maintenance. Recognizing that it often involves such deprivation and that it tends to be associated with immoral activities, the church looks with suspicion upon gambling; but that is quite different from an outright moral ban.[123]

The rural Protestant South therefore rejects the ethos of snake-handling as an irreverent trifling with the Lord. Indeed, Barefoot is so disingenuous as to protest that this is *not* what he is doing — "tempting the Lord" — but we are not constrained, on the basis of his acts, to believe his over-protestation.

In strict fact, the psychopathic character seduces, cajoles, and attempts to cozen Fate as though it were a *person*. This explains the triumphant thrill of the daredevil who "defies Death" (and compare Barefoot's reiterated statements of the thrill he gets from the breakneck riding of his motorcycle). The psychopathic personality

ethic has been shown by Weber and Tawney to be closely related to the spirit of capitalism and its contingent gambling; and the Roman Church has been in constant historic retreat from its initial positions, e.g., of condemning the Jews for the sin of usury. And in modern times, the bingo morality of the television give-away shows is a trend toward the Roman Catholic expectation of miracles and away from the Protestant position of earned worthiness. One does not even need to have recondite, earned knowledge to win the prize on some shows; and in some the "miracle" of the right answer has been contrived by coaching beforehand. Perhaps it was only the obsolescent among American consciences that were shocked by disclosures that some shows were rigged.

Protestantism itself, of course, has long argued the pros and cons of faith versus works, and there is no single Protestant position on the matter. Likewise the "sincere" characters of Madison Avenue have long promised *their* communicants the "miracles of science" — which is a contradiction in terms. Indeed, the controversy between salvation by faith and salvation through works affords us an index of important diagnostic value in assessing the oedipal stage of religions as projective systems. To opt for faith and miracle is to remain pre-oedipal and magical in world-view: to opt for works is to become at least oedipal in one's expectancies.

operates at times *by attempting to outwit reality itself*. This fact
suggests that psychopathics, for all their excellent and even superior
orientation toward reality, sometimes border on the schizoid in
their psychic mechanisms. The schizophrenic is the one who, in
being rejected by the earliest and most important Other (Reality
or Not-Self), his mother, in turn makes no libidinal investment in
the real world (personal or otherwise) outside his own skin, but
instead retains his love for that only world which gives him pleasure
and gratifies his Pleasure Principle, his own narcissistic psyche.
The schizophrenic owes no allegiance to the Reality Principle. What
has it done libidinally for him?

This is not, however, true of our subject. Although Beauregard
later shows affect-hunger both for his mother's and for his father's
love and affection, he had, after all, been loved in the first two years
of his life well enough to accept the gratifying reality of the world.
It is only, rather, that he has some later traumatized grievance
against it. There are, to be sure, discernible differences between the
physical world and the moral world, but Barefoot at times seems to
confuse them. The less schizoid we are, the more we accept the
reality of the physical world apart from our will in a basic and ultimately emotional sense; the world frustrates, is separate from one's
own wish, and only sometimes gratifies, but it *is*. Likewise, the less
psychopathic we are, the more we are able automatically to accept
the moral world mediated to us by loving parents.

But there's the rub! No parent can ever love unambivalently.
And no parent can ever be as rigorously consistent about moral
concerns as reality is *unfailingly* consistent about *its* business. Parents, too, are ambivalent toward frustrating moralities; and parental love can never provide the same consistency and impregna-
bility and "omniscience" as does external physical reality. Fire
always burns, but father only punishes sometimes. Perhaps this is
well enough, for only in this context can we finally perceive the
mere humanity of our parents and achieve some resolution of the
Oedipus complex. But to project a lingering fantasy of the omnipotent father, as Barefoot does, is to frustrate the maturation. For

in this process Jehovah runs the risk of exploitation by a not wholly believing son.

In the formation of the psychopathic character there is another process that can commonly be observed clinically: the conflict between the parents. Szurek writes that

If a particular behavior of interpersonal significance and one satisfying a need or drive has thus been integrated with full conscious approval of the parent or his surrogates, the person will have no guilt or anxiety and show no lack of integration in this activity . . . Regularly the more important parent — usually the mother, although the father is always in some way involved — has been seen *unconsciously* to encourage the amoral or anti-social behavior of the child. The neurotic needs of the parent whether of excessively dominating, dependent or erotic character are unconsciously gratified by the behavior of the child, or in relation to the child. Such — neurotic — needs of the parent exist either because of some current inability to satisfy them in the world of adults, or because of the stunting experiences in the parent's own childhood — or more commonly, because of a combination of these factors.[124]

The source of this moral ambivalence (unconscious, to be sure) lies in the compulsive personality of Beauregard's father (and mother too?); one or both of the parents unconsciously wants and encourages naughtiness in the child. In this instance that parent was evidently the father; thus Beauregard was taught by and through his father that he could get by. In his essentially masculine identification Beaureguard is chiefly heterosexual. We can therefore believe that in this identification he has responded primarily to his father's passive sabotage, on several counts, of his mother's hysteric religiosity. The inevitable inadequacy of his mother's hysteric defenses will also have contributed secondarily to the same sabotage. Beauregard Barefoot is very much the son of his parents in Szurek's sense.

Possibly this is one of the less typical of the several alternative ways of creating a psychopath. As we have seen, the criminal psychopath — as opposed to our present religious psychopathic character — is one sufficiently grounded in reality by an adequately loving mother, but who has later suffered a pathology in superego growth because of his relations to a violent and punitive father. In many clinical cases we can observe that the very violence of the father's punishments of his son is a cover for the father's ambivalence toward his son's misdeeds. A delinquent son disturbs such a father's own inadequate repressions; and the less adequate the father's repressions, the more violently he must punish the threatening sin out of his sons.* But moral panic is no substitute for paternal love and acceptance. Only parents who basically respect themselves can properly love their children in this sense.

In this same family constellation we often observe a mother withdrawing and protecting her unjustly treated son from the violent bully-father's wrath, sometimes through compacts between mother and son to prevent the father from finding out about the son's misdeeds. If the child experiences the advantages and the success of this maneuver often enough, he is essentially learning the psychopathic dodge, namely, getting by with it. The mother's protective love teaches him that he is not wrong, or that anyway the prohibition does not apply to him. It is for this reason, perhaps, that we so commonly find a feminine streak in the criminal psychopath. For as he is a lone wolf against all other males, he hates and distrusts them as he did his own brutal father — and thus he has not achieved an adequate masculine identification with his father, nor an adequate moral identification with his father's principles. The presence of this parental constellation, in fainter form, may also explain why the normal American male, while he tends to acknowledge the rightness of the male moral law, nevertheless sometimes tries to get by with it, whereas the normal American female considers that the male law really doesn't apply to her.

Talcott Parsons, in a penetrating essay, believes that the direct and positive identification of the girl with her mother makes for the well-known earlier maturity of girls. But boys — especially in

* Is this an explanation of why contemporary newspapers in the rigidly Fundamentalist South are currently so obsessed with stories of parents' brutality and violence toward their children? From whatever source, these are picked up off the news wires and published endlessly. Are these stories vehicles for projection and identification in the uneasy and insecure conscience of the South?

[152

a transitional or a matrist society, one would add—have a much more stormy time of it.

The boy on the one hand has a tendency to form a direct feminine identification, since his mother is the model most readily available and significant to him. But he is not destined to become an adult woman. Moreover he soon discovers that in certain vital respects women are considered inferior to men, that it would hence be shameful for him to grow up to be like a woman. Hence when boys emerge into what Freudians call the "latency period," their behavior tends to be marked by a kind of "compulsive masculinity." They refuse to have anything to do with girls. "Sissy" becomes the worst of all insults. They get interested in athletics and physical prowess, in the things in which men have the most primitive and obvious advantage over women. Furthermore they become allergic to all expression of tender emotion; they must be "tough." This universal pattern bears all the earmarks of a "reaction formation." It is so conspicuous, not because it is simply "masculine nature" but because it is a defense against a feminine identification. The commonness with which "mother fixation" is involved in all types of neurotic and psychotic disorders of Western men strongly confirms this. It may be inferred also that the ambivalence involved is an important source of anxiety—lest one not be able to prove his masculinity—and that aggression toward women who "after all are to blame," is an essential concomitant.

One particular aspect of this situation is worthy of special attention. In addition to the mother's being the object of love and identification, she is to the young boy the principal agent of socially significant disciplines. Not only does she administer the discipline which makes him a tolerable citizen of the family group, but she stimulates him to give a good account of himself outside the home and makes known her disappointment and disapproval if he fails to measure up to her expectations. She, above all, focuses in herself the symbols of what is "good" behavior, of conformity with the expectations of the respectable adult world. When he revolts against identification with mother in the name of masculinity, it is not surprising that a boy unconsciously identifies "goodness" with femininity and that being a "bad boy" becomes a positive goal. It seems that the association of goodness and femininity, and therewith much of our Western ambivalence toward ethical values, has its roots in this situation. At any rate there is a strong tendency for boyish behavior to run in anti-social if not directly destructive directions, in striking contrast to that of postadolescent girls.

As would be expected if such a situation is deepseated and has continued for several generations, it becomes imbedded in the psychology of adults as well as children. The mother therefore secretly — usually unconsciously — admires such behavior and, particularly when it is combined with winning qualities in other respects, rewards it with her love — so the "bad" boy is enabled to have the best of both worlds. She may quite frequently treat such a "bad" son as her favorite as compared with a "sissy" brother who conforms with all her overt expectations much better.[125]

But Parsons is writing of a contemporary matrist world, in which the emancipated mother has emulated the father even in his essentially masculine job of mediating the culture of the male society to his sons. Do primitives do better in leaving to the biologically stronger males the moral job of rescuing their sons from familial infancy and ritually initiating males into the male society?

But neither of these — the bully-father or the bully-mother — is quite true of Beauregard Barefoot's transitional family, which, half a century ago in a rural region of cultural lag, was still essentially a patrist society, an agricultural order in which the father was daily and constantly present as a model for his son (unlike the modern matrist urban or suburban family which is more nearly like what Parsons is describing). Furthermore, Beauregard's father was demanding, but not ultimately prohibitive or brutal; he was just, if not omniscient. Nor was he ultimately prohibitive sexually either; he somehow managed to teach his son not to take seriously hysteria and its protestations in females.

Nevertheless, wherever Barefoot turned, to father and to mother alike, he found the same walls of compulsive demand for performance and for renunciation — hard work demanded by his father, strict and prohibitive morality demanded by his mother. Thus, again, he is not a bland textbook psychopath who has officially settled matters by a patently spurious and dishonest Nazi-Soviet peace pact with his parents; rather, he is an oedipally confused and divided Underground persistently sabotaging both oppressive tyrannies. As Fenichel writes,

Certain impulsive characters by their unconscious behavior protest against the intense pressure they feel from their very strict superego [e.g., Beauregard's getting up to work after influenza, and his own mode of circumventing the overly strict demands of conscience or of his father; compare, too, his father-aided circumvention of the overly strict prohibitions of his mother]. In a less obvious manner, this may be the unconscious meaning of certain compulsive symptoms, the significance of which is a rebellion against the superego and the acquisition of proofs of innocence [e.g., in snake-handling]. Also, impulsive psychopaths, who often are considered to have no superego at all, reveal in analysis that they have temporarily isolated the demands of their superego, so that the demands are not operative when the "psychopath" gives in to his impulses.[126]

Barefoot has enough neurotic guilt to have some fear of the father-figure. He does not reject paternal and moral authority entirely, as the pure psychopath does. But he does remain thoroughly ambivalent toward the father, and insecure in his identification. Furthermore, with him it is not the mother protecting the psychopath against the classic brutal father. It is rather that the less stern, less categorical morality of the father undercuts the sterner morality of the mother. For him, the father is *not* the normally ultimate and obdurate sanctioning power: God is partly the ally of his id wishes. Thus, as with Beauregard, the psychopathic character may alternate between an insecure compulsiveness or seeming-so and an impure guilt-tinged psychopathy. As I have said elsewhere,

the compulsive is never able to push in the clutch pedal to disengage action and conscience; the psychopath "throws out" the clutch characteristically and careens along by free-wheeling. The normal person is sufficiently compulsive to have the clutch engaged in straight-away driving, though in going around corners he can ease his vehicle by a temporary free-wheeling drift [but always with one foot on the brake!]. Are there not certain cases, ordinarily classed as "compulsives" who from time to time "slip their clutch" to perform the overt psychopathic act, if only to enable the compulsive crime-and-punishment game to go on? That is, they "ride the clutch," depending upon current superego-id tonuses.[127]

This ethical tonus of the psychopathic character does not wholly escape registering on the feelings of normally moral people in the society. Thus the worthy and adequately religious Southern towns-folk feel uneasily that the snake cult is a somehow meretricious religiosity, and not a bona fide religion which secures a comfortable assent to the reigning mores. But they are caught on the horns of a dilemma: on the one hand, they must (mistakenly) identify Barefoot with their own sincere religiousness and hence uneasily defend him; on the other hand, his perceived treachery to values touches their own ambivalences, and they then just as violently denounce him as a fraud. In the first alternative, the baiting of the helpless and often foolish-looking police, and the cold manipulation of legalistic appeals to the Constitution in the courts, are highly available to the cultist putting up a smoke screen for his retreat. But his reiterated piety has a hollow and histrionic ring, and the basic reaction of people in the larger society is the second alternative — rejection. And perhaps understandably so. Barefoot, after all, has no great concern for the actual immoral behavior, in particular the sexual misbehavior, of his communicants (e.g., of the prostitutes who come to his meetings), but is solely preoccupied with the psychopathic game of dangerously baiting God in a half-magic kind of reality-testing.

The snake is an ignorant and instinctual organism, like the id itself, and sometimes does not punish its sinful handling. But we nevertheless feel that the psychopathic is here again close to the borderline of a schizoid indiscrimination between the escapable moral world and the inescapable physical world. Fire always burns, but father sometimes doesn't know and punish. True, the snake, like man, is an organism, and does not always act the same at all times. Still, most of us would prefer to treat it as one more example of the automatically operating and punitively dangerous physical world. The question is, why should a snake be made the judge of one's moral guilt or innocence? And, at bottom, is there a possible psychic dividend in his biting or not biting?

Only if the snake is a libidinized symbol of something else. For his own unrealistic reasons, the psychopathic character takes (no, *needs*) the gamble. Having learned that he may sometimes get by with his defiance and hoodwinking of his parental moral world, he quite dangerously attempts to apply the same rationale to his dealings with the natural world. But can centrifugal force and a tree at a curve in the road be outwitted as parents can? And can one dominate motorcycles and sexuality and snakes all with the same confidence? Do they really all belong in the same single category in nature? Are snakes and motorcycles really a part of the body ego in the same sense that sexuality is in the adult? Or is this possible only if all are functionally or symbolically equated, only if they wander in this obscure twilight zone at the ego boundaries of an immature personality — in a night where not only are all cats gray but where a cat can't be told from a hippogryph? Why erotize danger? Why try to cozen snakes? These symbols hide displaced identities!

Luck, for such gamblers as Beauregard, is a half-personified element in the physical world. Lady Luck sometimes smiles and then, fickle, sometimes withdraws her love — in a contest for the symbolic potency of other men, money. Can luck always be trusted to take over the self-judgment responsibilities of the shaky ego and the job of protecting and loving oneself? Here again Barefoot's psychopathy is somewhat delimited, however. He will take in his father's "spirit" but he will not drink poisons, and he knows that blowtorches burn. He stays within the symbolism of the erotized snake. Drinking and smoking are both officially evil according to his mother's prohibitive Baptist code, but he is able to accept both of these, as we have seen, with the tacit consent of his permissive father. Oral mastery and indulgence are not his basic problem. For these he has adequate defenses, and reaction-formations of a kind.

The ambivalence arises mainly in the area of sexuality. Barefoot did manage to find and marry a hysteroid and denying woman, but the evil serpent of Adam and Eve nevertheless comes back into his life. He is no subjugated ascetic. He is able to get his sexual gratifications elsewhere, though his wife distrusts him, in an atmosphere which is overtly orgiastic, frankly for enjoyment ("we come to church for a good time"), unrestrainedly emotional, and discreetly sexual. The joyfully guilty masturbatory handling of the phallic snake takes place freely in a cult asserting the power of mind over matter, and the same onanism is induced in his female communicants. In contravening the hysteric repression of sexuality in his female parishioners, Barefoot paradigmatically triumphs contemptuously over his mother and flouts her secretly ridiculed morality. And in the whole dangerous process he is the daring psychopathic gambler, largely convinced unconsciously of his final success in the "miracle" — but not without fear at times of guilty disaster.

The psychopathic character, then, has an appetite for "testing the limits" of physical reality, as if reality were as unsure and ambivalent as his parents were. He must know where he can get by, but must always skirt the possibility that a fast motorcycle may collide with an all too obdurately real tree.* Sexuality and danger are inextricably mixed for the phallic character, and the thrill is to triumph in having the pleasure without paying the price. Where father is not permissive, he can be outwitted. There is an all-powerful and all-good God, Beauregard reiterates — and then masters Him. God's values will finally prevail — if not now. God permits gratifying experiences of quaking, dancing, going into a trance (possessed by the Spirit), and handling snakes. In this there is a happiness, a vocation, and a pleasure, as well as a sense of the power of God in His servant. The only danger is that God may catch up with him some day and see through his "honesty." The fondled and taunted, kissed and teased Power may one day punish like lightning! Is this an adult male's confident possession of his own sexuality, or is it sexuality fixated at a phallic level of castration-anxiety? Is death the price of sexuality (and of what kind of sexuality)? Evidently so, in the fantasies both of the phallic-fixated psychopathic character and of the phallic-level hysteric.

Unfortunately — but inevitably, since he chose her — Barefoot's wife repeats the forbidding pattern of the mother: a "good" woman is either hysterically unapproachable or oedipally forbidden, though he may discard the rigidly anti-sexual maternal standards with respect to divorce (one snake-handling minister, we remember, argued for his right to marry himself on occasion) and to allow known streetwalkers, or otherwise vulnerable women, to attend his

* This specific tragedy overtook another psychopathic character, the exhibitionistic-shy Colonel T. E. Lawrence, the tortured and gifted "Lawrence of Arabia," alias "Aircraftsman Shaw."

services. It is here that we see the social relevance of the psychopathic character. Freud wrote that hysteria is the negative of the perversion: the repression of the wish is the opposite of acting it out. This is Barefoot's usefulness to hysteric women communicants, since the psychopath and the hysteric are the obverse of one another. In a dim, half-trance state, under the influence of induced excitement, the followers can abdicate their ego controls and hand over direction to the leader, secure in the expectation that a psychopathic and seductive personality will satisfy their forbidden desires for them. All mobs forget their inhibitions, their critical judgment, and their superego controls, and borrow for a time in moral holiday the superego of the leader.[128] (This is the reason, as Devereux [129] has pointed out, why charismatic political leaders like Hitler and certain figures in the French Revolutionary Terror — and certain intellectual leaders as well, like Rousseau — are so commonly psychopathic in the clinical sense.) The psychopath here himself performs the functions of the Snake in the Garden of Eden and seduces the hysteric from her repressions. For a hysterically repressed woman, conversely, there can be no more appetizing leader than the guilt-free and ego-mobile psychopath. And from such a leader's point of view, what better clientele can there be for his ministrations than hysterics who want to be seduced? Trilby and Svengali are fated for one another.

It is here worth remarking, further, that the psychic symbiosis of hysteric and psychopathic character join in still another respect. In the hysteric's denial of unacceptable wishes, there is typically a projection of her sexuality outside herself onto the phobic figure (the classic burglar under the bed — it is he who has the filthy lusts, certainly not she). Likewise, for the psychopathic character operating in this context and with his specific personality there is also a quasi-projection of sexuality outside into the phobic figure, the snake. Projection, of course, is also the typical mechanism of paranoia, and it is easy to see how, in other snake-handling ministers and in male communicants perhaps, the serpent might be a symbol in the service of the paranoid mechanism. True, in his theology, the snake is the Evil One; and there are, as we have seen, some secondary paranoid elements in Beauregard Barefoot's mildly persecutory personality. Nevertheless, the caution of phrasing the mechanism as a "quasi-projection" of sexuality in Barefoot's case is necessary in the interest of correct dynamic statement. With him, the fact that the sexuality is still half outside is as much the result of incomplete introjection as it is of later projection — just as the conscience (the snake) is ambiguously outside the body-image, again because of incomplete introjection of the paternal conscience. It is important to note, however, in a larger sense, that not only is projection onto things (the snake, for example) often utilized, but that in many social phenomena we also use persons projectively. This principle may serve partly to explain middleclass indignation against the snake-handlers, the clichéd attitudes of the North toward the South, and the like.

Barefoot's, then, is a socially adapted though somewhat mutilated solution of the oedipal problem, in counterfoil to a hysteric mother, and a solution possible, perhaps, only in a pathological subculture that uses predominantly the simple hysteroid mechanism of denial. In defining the problems of sexuality, as in others, there is a "cultural lag" in his geographical region. Indeed, the cultural discrepancies in time may help us to see him more clearly and sympathetically, since his problems are not quite like our own. Freud, in fact, predicted the decrease if not the disappearance of classical hysteria as time went on, owing to the spread of lay psychological insight into the shallow defense mechanism of mere denial characteristic of hysteria. Statistically, this is evidently true in the urbanized, sophisticated North. But what constantly surprises city-trained Northern psychiatrists is that the South still has such "old-fashioned" neuroses. As Ferenczi writes, "in our day it is becoming much more rare for people to produce obvious hysterias such as, only a few decades ago, were described as comparatively widespread. It seems as if, with the advance of civilization, even the neuroses have become more civilized and adult." [130]

Perhaps this is part of a larger social-psychiatric problem. Certainly the more sophisticated and urbanized sections of the South, whether Chattanooga or Durham or Tallahassee, firmly reject the implications and the ethos of the snake-handling cult; and upper-class folk are entirely correct in identifying it with a poor-white and lately rural population. But in all social classes, nevertheless, naïve hysteric *denial* still remains, since the Civil War at least, the prime defense mechanism of the South — we did not lose the War and we have no racial problem (except as it is fomented by alien agitators),* women are still Ladies, sexuality is sin, evolution is not true, we have no labor problems, and so on. But just as snake cultists are a rejected minority in the South, so also the South sometimes feels itself a rejected minority in the nation. Meanwhile, it is not entirely beyond the realm of possibility that the North uses the South as the scapegoat of its own conscience, as the projected phobic figure, the Devil. In this case, projection as a defense mechanism becomes less hysteric than paranoid.

The South as a whole is still today closer to the old frontier individualism and rural ethos than the rest of the nation. It has states rights in politics (when it can), local option in its morals, and extreme local autonomy of its conscience in its unreconstructedly and fundamentally Protestant sects. But the wounded regional ego cannot cast off an accusing superego, except at the peril of conscience's seeming an alien outside thing. There is a shameful pride still in being the Rebel, though with ever-increasing guilt and inwardly divided protest. But who can hate the South for yearning to become respectable in its own eyes? Thus, to the outsider, the South presents a picture of pseudo-psychopathic rebellion against the claims of a regionally external conscience, or self-protective reaction with a persecutory-paranoid defense; like other rejected subgroups, and like the snake-handlers themselves, it therefore seems to be delinquent. But the South does have a conscience, and a tender one at that, which is why its masculine protest is so loud. And of course Southerners understand the economic and social issues — which is

* The South has the same reaction to an alien intruder, John Kaspar, who came down to *preach segregation*! Even conscientious and liberal Southerners are nettled at the supposition that the South needs a regionally external conscience. For them, all such "foreigners" still seem like moral carpetbaggers of whom they have no need. But at the same time, in the centennial years, the South relives the Civil War (will it end differently this time?) even in its comic strips — and revives that epic of hysteria, *Gone With the Wind*.

why, with such justice, they are able so effectively to use the *tu quoque* argument in reply.

If all Southern classes are perhaps alike in their fixed and vehement insistence on local autonomy, in other ways they are very different. In the past, the South has commonly been interpreted on the basis of the classic plantation culture — as if this had been the background of most, or even a majority, of whites, and as if it were typical of all southern regions. It is certainly true that a great many Southerners would like to believe in or pretend to a plantation background for themselves. And because only the plantation class had both the literacy and the leisure to produce Southern literature, stereotypes of the South in other parts of the country have been largely based on the romantic past of the plantation culture, even into recent times when its decadence has been exploited by Southern writers themselves.

The plantation was characteristic, however, only of the Coastal Plain, not usual in the Piedmont, and non-existent in the Appalachian Highlands. In fact, for ethnic reasons, some whole states like North Carolina and Florida had very little plantationism indeed. If we are properly to understand the adaptation of Beauregard Barefoot as an individual personality to his cultural environment, it is necessary to turn attention to the southern poor white. Snake cultists are recruited almost entirely from the cracker, the redneck, and the wool hatter, newly emergent from the culturally archaic mountain fastnesses of the Appalachians and the piney woods of the Piedmont into the newly industrialized Piedmont and Coastal Plain, and not in any sense ever a part culturally or historically of plantationism, except as the old feudal class has to a degree become the new class of industrial entrepreneurs. The poor white, possessed of the divinely ordained superiority of a white skin, is puzzled at being nevertheless Negroid in economic status. Frustrated in acquiring the prerogatives of his white status, and hounded by his cultural incompetence into economic slavery in his new setting, he is loved only of God.

CHAPTER 12

Barefoot and the Poor Whites

THOUGH Barefoot and his parishioners draw upon an older background of rural fundamentalist religion, the modern snake-handling cult is also, in important ways, a phenomenon of acculturation and a reaction to a new cultural and economic setting. Much of the Old Testament can be understood as an ancient protest of rural folk against the iniquities of urban life, and as such it comes close to the feelings of poor whites, until recently rural, now drawn into the industrial towns and cities of the new South. This change of locale is sometimes highly significant; for example, in many mountain counties Negroes are rare or non-existent and therefore constitute no problem. The poor whites in these areas did not have the racial stereotypes of Coastal Plain plantationism. Only thus can we understand the presence of Negroes, another dispossessed class with which poor whites can in part identify, in the snake-handling cults of such places as Piedmont Durham. Such a racially mixed situation as the Durham cult would of course be unthinkable in Coastal Plain South Carolina or Tidewater Virginia.

Widely differing subregional ecology in various parts of the South has produced differing economic and class attitudes — sometimes even within the same state. Poor whites and plantation whites are as far apart in ethos as Roundheads and Cavaliers, who, indeed, sometimes constituted their respective historic ancestors. For one matter, Cavalier plantation culture was fully in touch with the fashionable wider world, at least that of the manorial class. By contrast, one must emphasize the cultural isolation of the new industrial proletariat in, say, the modern mill village * which, at best, is scarcely less than the isolation of the poor whites' earlier regions and, at worst, is laden with the frustrations of a tantalizing new awareness of invidious cultural and economic advantages which they cannot have. The older religion emphasized repression; only new repression can maintain the unstable new situation.

Economically marginal men, mill workers in all their institutions preach acquiescence and repression of feelings. The poor-white mill worker is not adventurous. Nor is he progressive, as union organizers are quick to discover. He is suspicious of all change and novelty. Selective migration of rebellious personalities may even increase the habits of repression, submissiveness, and homogeneity in the geographic relicts — an economic necessity all the more painful because of older rural habits of independent choice and autonomy. The authoritarian habits of an older élite shaped with reference to the Negroes, are carried over in the new élite with reference to the poor whites, who soon find out what is expected of them.

Mill workers lead routinized, monotonous lives. They hold low-paying jobs in a paternalistic environment and can never aspire to be more than semi-skilled laborers.† The bobbin-tender and the

* Snake-handlers represent many occupations among the laboring class, from the sharecroppers and sawmill workers in rural regions to the tobacco-factory and cotton-mill workers of industrial towns and villages. Although the mill workers taken here as an illustrative sample may represent an extreme case of culture shock, it is probable that they are in general typical of a Piedmont population from North Carolina to Georgia, and perhaps also of the large newly electrified and industrialized Tennessee Valley. In Florida, of course, the situation is further complicated by the immigration of large numbers of moneyed people from the urban North. But the cultural contrasts, in varying degree, are typical of all; and envy of power is psychologically central in the personalities of poor white snake-handlers.

† Observing the differences in education, for example, the poor white might be expected to discern schooling as an easy ladder up and out of his class. But this is less true of the poor white than, for less reason, of the Negro. The suspicious rural mind of the poor white makes him an automatic "mucker" on more than Fundamentalist religious grounds. What the race-proud poor white hates, and with permanent injured unforgiveness, in his upperclass white brother, is not being accorded full *class* status (for the mountain frontier society is democratic and classless) along with the expected, and accorded, *caste* status. He cannot admire or empathize with these unfamiliar cultural class skills from not having enjoyed them himself, and

weaver, having acquired skills easily learned in at most a few weeks and with no increment of additional rewarded skill as time goes on, must maintain a constant alertness to machine stoppage. Machines must not be idle, for if they are the worker is subjected to the criticism both of management and of other workers whom this stoppage affects. In the piece-rate system, which is universal in the South, a worker is paid for his output; and at the time of greatest machine failure and therefore most frantic work he is unpaid. As mill workers say, at these times they work harder and are paid less.

The constant compulsive stress under which mill workers operate is in other ways at great variance with their former agrarian tempo of work, though in habits of emotional repression it is identical. If the machines and the laborers work well, then in the as yet largely non-unionized South they must fear the stretch-out and the tending of still more machines. Efficiency is thus penalized, and there is a reverse reward for good work. Wage policy is not always geared to economics in the great cotton mills, but rather to labor-management tensions. The mill workers lives in a factory environment of high humidity, constant noise, and, in summer, heat often above a hundred degrees, commonly working six days a week, unless times are poor. Brief stoppages are ambivalently welcomed, for they allow one to go fishing or hunting — but without wages. Workers are separated from one another by the noise of clattering machines and by their own constant busyness. The individual worker has no immediate teammate, though he is dependent upon the efficiency of others for his piece-work wage. He works, therefore, in social isolation, often without even speaking to anyone for eight hours, standing on his feet, with no rest period and no lunch period, eating on the fly at some interruption of the smooth working of the machines, a sandwich in one hand while the other hand tends the racing machinery.

Commonly, to make ends meet, the wife of the mill worker also works, often on another shift. With equal wages, the mill girl is

he sees them only as traits to identify, and to hate in, his class enemies. From some years as a teacher in the South it is my impression that it is the very rare poor white who changes his social status through education. Also, the poor white–middleclass barriers appear even harder for the individual to cross than the middleclass-upperclass barriers are, and these are difficult enough.

often "uppity" in terms of the male dominance expected in the older patriarchal culture; she may manifest a marital independence; and since both parents work they at times present to middleclass folk an appearance of familial irresponsibility. Job tensions, hours, and anxieties are often translated into marital and familial problems. In the typical mill village, the houses, stores, and mills are all owned by the feudal class. Buying on time is widely prevalent, with deductions sometimes automatically made from wages. Mill hands have no backlog of savings and are easy prey to loan sharks, whose interest rates are twenty per cent per annum and upwards, and buying goods on time always brings with it threat of repossession. Thus economic tensions come to full strength again in the family.

Impartial students of mill villages maintain that the ruling class of the village controls, through its predominant economic power, the churches and the philanthropic agencies, the city council and other political agencies like the police, and even the schools. But most damaging of all to the individual personality, perhaps, is the mill hand's almost total deprivation of decision-making, in the mill or in the village, and his almost total dependence on and subservience to his economic master. There is indeed much buried resentment, but both religion and the family reinforce habits of conformity. For example, if one member of a family loses his job in the mill, the whole family may have to move out of its company-owned house. Physical punishment is easily and promptly meted out to children, often intensified by the strain of resentments the parents feel and displace but cannot otherwise express. Religion preaches a total submitting to the will of God. In psychiatric clinics these people are found, with monotonous frequency, to be passive-aggressive personalities.

Everywhere, blind obedience and strict conformity are inculcated by the mill worker's institutions. His cultural precepts teach him to fear Negroes (employed only in menial "outdoor" jobs so as to protect white women workers), as well as strangers, outsiders, and anything new. He is taught to *avoid* new experience.* In the church,

* In a small movie house on Main Street, during a revival of Walt Disney's *Fantasia*, I watched a group of mill workers grow increasingly restive at this

salvation is the central doctrine. More immediate social issues, such as those presented by trade unions, race relations, and economics, must be avoided by the preachers, under penalty of disapproval by their own parishioners. A life of poverty under a personal God of stern rewards and punishments is the religious conformity taught, and dissenters of all kinds risk hellfire. These are authoritarian personalities in classic form. Obedience is imperative to earn one the rewards of the afterlife, and for rules one must depend utterly, unquestioningly, upon the Holy Bible. Goaded by godly as well as by secular standards, the mill worker is puritanical, fanatic, narrow, and fundamentalist. Fate seems to have preordained him to be a textile worker. Even when he migrates from the South, he is lost, helpless, and without resources; when he goes to southern Michigan and Ohio industrial towns, he turns them into Southern places with his intransigent ethos. In *any* new situation, without adaptive resilience, he is functionally very much like the immigrant from a foreign country; and even in a Southern town he seems a rural primitive tribesman, with rigidly tribal values.

Trying to survive without the experience of choosing for himself or knowing a larger world and its alternatives, he characteristically falls back upon explosive Southern personal violence,* not the

strange experience; finally, after whispered consultations, they marched out in a body, indignant because this was not the usual cowboy picture. This same movie house — playing foreign movies to a college clientele and girly-girly sex-and-sin movies of the twenties to mill workers and tobacco farmers during market season — so confused both clienteles that it failed. The building was given a new false-stone front and is now a Holiness Gospel tabernacle. Similarly, after a public meeting of the city council, at which they had been addressed by doctors, dentists, and an internationally famous biochemist on the water-fluoridation issue, many people departed untouched by explicit scientific evidence and maintained a stubbornly paranoid belief in "poisoning," vast complotting economic interests, and so on. The panel of experts, which included my own very conservative dentist, was even accused of Communism. And to complete the picture, the town capitalist, an old man worth perhaps a hundred million dollars, also disapproved of fluoridation in large halfpage newspaper ads!

* The woodlands- and barn-burning Snopeses have often been taken by outlanders as creations of the febrile imaginations of decadent Southern writers, just as *Tobacco Road*, *Baby Doll*, and *The Ponder Heart* have been assumed to be picaresque caricatures. One should not make the other error of thinking them typical of all the South — for otherwise where did the moral sophistication of these writers come from? — but these writers, in my opinion,

derived aggressiveness of the tongue or the printed word. Largely unschooled, the mill worker finds these verbal modalities of social change unavailable to him; and, reciprocally, scientific knowledge or booklearning or even superior journalism has almost no effect on him whatever. He reads the local newspaper and comic books, sees by choice only movies that are streamlined fantasies, and is largely insulated from any thought-provoking presentation of real issues. He is easily led to accept the Cinderella fantasies of the cheap movies — for is not favoritism rampant in God's casting white men in such widely varied roles in town? Is not favoritism a constant threat in the mills, where strawbosses must be placated lest one be assigned to broken-down machines, and where women must solicit some notorious bosses with sexual favors? There is no pension system, only the bingo-morality of the television shows to support fantasy or thinking about the future. The tragedy is that, in his limited and violent world, the poor white has little experience or knowledge of *why* his betters might be his betters, and he maintains toward them only ignorant and irascible petulance, not even informed envy. Nor does age automatically dignify him. Obsolescent at forty or forty-five and likely to be laid off in favor of younger men, he has no habits that would give even his leisure some dignity. His only advantage in old age is that he is willingly absorbed into the extended family, for he now has his Social Security pension coming in regularly. As for social freedoms, these are mostly channeled into the old cry that Southerners must be free — to oppress the Negro. Intellectually, he suspects and fears all differences,

know exactly what they are talking about. For example, my country fishing pond was once dynamited by one of these denizens of the backwoods who also left other social commentaries on the premises. And a nationally known author, walking up the branch that feeds this pond, had shots ring out over her head from the whiskey still of this same dynamiter. A neighbor up the road says this man "would burn up your house and you in it if he thought he'd get away with it." Informed and responsible Southerners like Jonathan Daniels fear and despair more of the poor white trash in the future of the South than they do of the Negro. And, indeed, acculturation embitters these rigid rural types, so that they mistake surreptitious destructiveness for moral action, scatologic acts for independence of mind, sly animal cunning for intelligence, brutality and murder for manliness, and violence for wit. But, again, these are not the only poor whites by any means, but only the poor white trash.

because he does not know what else than like himself people can be. His only social and personal outlet, his only means of emotional expression and release, is his church, if only by phatic sabotage of what the church stands for: repression.

The workers in the great mechanized tobacco factories, and in the other growing industries of the South, are drawn from this rural proletariat. It is specifically this poor-white class to which the snake-handling cult primarily appeals. It is within this class that we must view Beauregard Barefoot's socially successful though perhaps unfortunate solution of the oedipal problem. The background ethos of all — leader and led alike — is repressive and compulsive, joyless and denying, economically as well as libidinally. But in the snake-handling cult they find miracle and mastery, and a full expression of their feelings. The communicant is granted emotional salvation and rescue from the deprivation and the dourness of his economic and general cultural lot. In the cult he can find proof that God, at least, loves him. For Barefoot, as an individual, there is a complementary emotional solution for his problems, too. Women forbid sexuality, but men are more permissive, and a phallic-manipulative enjoyment of male power is the denouement. How innocent are we, when, full of the spirit and of faith in the father, with the borrowed symbolic phallus we seduce our female communicants! What exhibitionistic enjoyment of urethral control-uncontrol! We do indeed dominate the serpent!

But is this really true? Are real problems being handled realistically? To this we must answer no; they are handled only symbolically and reactively, not abreactively — though we must be mindful ever of the great potency of symbolic dreams in giving men a false peace of mind, and realize meanwhile that this is precisely what projective systems are for. Nevertheless, the whole snake-handling cult in fact expresses an *un*-mastery of sexuality on the phallic level: it is an intense and repeated group attempt to abreact traumatic repressions and deprivations that never comes off because it is indulgence rather than therapy. It is not conscious, unfearful, self-possessed, or genital. Sexuality, carnal desire, snakes, the phallus — these are not really claimed in a confident and secure body-image. On the contrary, they are discrete, projected, separate, and dangerous. The snake is the Devil, evil incarnate and death-dealing. But the Devil fascinates: is he not one's own projected, hysterically unacknowledged, and unadmissible desires? The ego's integration has surely cracked when the ego cannot maturely and confidently meet the demands of the id that are prohibited by an intransigent superego. The evil, phallic part of oneself is projected as the separate and discrete serpent — and it can be mastered only through an *equally external* "power of God."

The evil and the good both seem to the cultist to be outside himself; but they are really both inside. The helpless ego tries to preserve itself by externalizing the struggle; the stupid and "external" instinctual danger, the snake (id), can be mastered only through the borrowing of a rather ambivalent God's power (the superego); and the snake as judging superego is highly unpredictable into the bargain. The snake cultist's God allows a handling and public preoccupation with the serpent, however, only so long as the communicant is "sincere" — which he knows he is not. But evidently the psychopath's and the hysterics' God, like the father, does not really know everything and is not aware of every secret sin. We must be loud in our faith to divert Him. Still, there remains the ever-present danger of His finding out. The fatal flaw in the adaptation is this: the tortured, twisting ego can never satisfy the demands of a superego that is itself culturally pathological.

But can a society never modify the cultural superego, the Sacred Past? Not so long as it insists that salvation comes only through allegiance to the sacred past! Cultural compulsions constrain societies as firmly as compulsive systems bind the individual neurotic. New times, new gratifications, and new responsibilities press upon them both, causing a crisis of adaptation. Snake-handling is a crisis cult of the acculturating poor whites, to use Devereux's term:

A crisis comes into being through the following process: In a situation of stress, which elicits *fear*, time-tested and traditional mechanisms of action no longer produce the expected results. This leads to a schizophrenia-like disorientation and to catastrophic behavior. *Fear*, which is an objective appraisal of the magnitude of a real danger, is replaced by *anxiety*, which is a sense of the inadequacy of one's resources in the face of stress. Since anxiety is harder to endure than fear, society rapidly becomes more preoccupied with alleviating its state of anxiety than its fear, and practically ceases to do anything about the danger which elicited fear in the first place.

Figuratively speaking, a society in crisis clamors for "cultural bromides" rather than for tools and weapons. This means that an autistically evolved intrapsychic "*threat*" replaces the objective "*danger*," and comes to occupy the center of the psychological field. Society then attempts to bring into being in reality — to "materialize" — precisely the kind of objective danger which corresponds to the initially intrapsychic threat [sexuality: the snake]. And it does so "accidentally on purpose" — in the manner of a "self-fulfilling prophecy" — for example, by behaving in such a manner as to encite "encirclement" or so as to force some of its members to become "traitors" or "spies." From then on the society fights the phantoms — the Frankenstein's monsters — which, in compliance with its needs to project its intrapsychic *threats* into the outer world, it brought into being, and therefore ceases to fight the initial, objectively real, danger.

In brief, crisis behavior is characterized by the presence of self-defeating mechanisms, leading to a downward spiralling, ever expanding, vicious circle, where the very attempts to cope with the problem on hand only exacerbate the stress and create new difficulties. We therefore feel that whereas "stress" is the result of the real impact of objective forces upon a society, *"crisis" is the result of a pathological response to stress.*[131]

The recently rural poor whites of the South are not handling their real social and economic problems through the snake-handling cult, nor their real problems of acculturation, nor their real intrapsychic stresses. Nor can Barefoot finally resolve his own psychological problems through this pseudo-therapy. First it is necessary to return to the scene of the initial psychological trauma — for him the shock to his infantile narcissism; for the narcissistically tribal society, the shock of acculturation. He keeps his hold on the emotional franchise of his communicants and keeps up his own narcissistic supplies ("everybody wants me to stay") only by means of a meretricious solution to his society's problems. But as the interviewer goes on to comment:

Even so, Barefoot's ingroup support is not an adequate defense mechanism. His inner conflicts are so great that he must utilize the outgroup, society, as a final layer of protection. The approval that he has received from his own group has not satisfied him and he seeks to gain further recognition from a larger group of people. However, because he realizes that he is unable to obtain this recognition, society at large becomes his persecutor (conscience or superego). The weaker his other defenses become, the greater does he feel the persecution from society. In fact, in his attempt to get publicity is seen his need for persecution and recognition (or disapproval) from society.

We can see that his snake-handling cult is headed for historical disaster — to the degree that he is not able to outwit, cozen, and "master" the greater society of the "educated people" he admits he is unable to understand. In this connection, it is interesting to recall the remarks of the Reverend Oscar Hutton of Virginia when police raided a cult meeting, and of the Reverend Colonel Hartman Bunn of North Carolina, who sought approval and justice in municipal, state, and Supreme courts, and would carry his seeking even up to Eisenhower himself. Evidently even to have God on one's side is not enough emotionally, so long as one's own conscience dimly perceives one's insincerity.

In his spurious solution, Barefoot is unstably provocative and ambivalently fearful of authority in the form of the police and of the state. He seems almost to seek their aggression at times and this, coupled with his mildly paranoid distrust of other men, is the source of a real problem for him. He can deny aggressive wishes (he is "changed" and his religion "takes the place" of these feelings for him — as indeed it does); he can masculine-protest his wishes to be in the armed forces (nobody enjoys a fight better than he does, but his religion is against these things); or he can be seductively and surreptitiously aggressive in baiting the police. But the external omnipotent power of the community and of the state of Florida may nevertheless overwhelm and destroy his psychopathic adaptation. In the long run neither his Father nor his cultural siblings can approve of his doings. Will the snake? And for how long?

Traumatized in his dependency needs, Beauregard Barefoot's is a sensitive, demanding ego, much hurt by any rejection, constantly requiring narcissistic supports and reassurances. His oral-omnipotent techniques of control, in preaching and in verbally managing his little cult world, could be called successful, were it not that he needs more. The phallic-omnipotent gambit is hardly more successful, with all its strenuous exhibitionism and dangerous phallic reality-testing — because he has replaced the intrapsychic anxiety (sexuality) with a real external danger (the snake). There is little straightforward and unfearful genital masculinity here, though there is sufficient masculine phallic identification to seize such gratification, in illicit or rationalized or secondarily symbolized contexts. But the snake as *fetish* is a de-fusion, technically, and psychiatrically perverse, i.e., psychopathic.

Beauregard was not able to identify adequately with either parent, and much of his security must remain in the phallic-narcissistic self. His maternal values he rejects intellectually, though he exploits them professionally. His father aids him in bypassing them; and then he must bypass his father. Like Jesus he has Jesus's gifts from the Father. But borrowed phallic male power is also somewhat dangerous. He can exploit these gradually received gifts and he may receive more — "if I'm not killed first." Outwitting God is a dangerous game. Likewise, overly provocative relationships with human authorities may bring about the confiscation of his snakes. The police will steal and take away his snakes, even the biggest ones. Our carpenter is not Jesus, and his Jesus is not God. He dare not be: for religion brings feminine identification for him (the lost snake again). Though his phallic identification is dangerous, ambivalent, and unsure, it is at least masculine. But with no *Book of Discipline*, this Ranter has only an undependable Inner Light.

Drawing from rural and consolidated traditional sources, Barefoot was initially successful in constituting his cult locally and establishing his congregation — indeed, building the snake-handling aspects of his cult upon an earlier Pentecostal religion already in existence. But the entrepreneurial class in the South (with a surprisingly small circulation of the élite, incidentally) has meanwhile moved from plantationism to industrialism, and Barefoot's world is changing. The increasing forces of urbanization in the South, especially in Florida, and the rise of a more powerful and sophisticated urban middleclass society, both bid fair finally to destroy his ministry, as has already happened to numerous other snake-handling congregations elsewhere. The love goddesses of Hollywood are spreading a new culture in the movie houses of the smallest towns. Television creeps ever farther out from the metropolitan centers of the South. And power over lives and motives has already moved from Wall Street to Madison Avenue.

In this latter-day Ranter we have the poignant, perhaps even pathetic, picture of a man who sought to solve his personal problems by externalizing them into a cult, but whose cult will probably be destroyed in time by the vast anonymous drift of cultural change. Truly, as Marian Anderson [132] says of music, religion also is "the beauty of men reaching out to comfort each other as they struggle against a common fate." It is true that we attempt to heal our individual sicknesses through emotional communication with our fellows. But is there poetic justice in the probable fate of Barefoot's cult? Without love, we become as sounding brass and tinkling cymbal. Is Barefoot's relation to his communicants genuine brotherly love, or is it exploitative psychopathy?

It is better to let his communicants answer this large cultural question: they love him. For to these poor whites — with their pinched and restricted economic background, their narrow rural horizons, and their dour and joyless culture — their church is the only place where they can freely and spontaneously *feel* and act out their feelings. "I believe that in the long run people are going to act on their inner feelings," says Beauregard Barefoot. And he is right.

Further, who can say that he has not done these people a service in helping them to move from an outmoded culture into a new one? There are many therapeutic communications in the human world besides those transacted in the office of the psychiatrist. If we are truly on the side of love and for the brotherhood of men, can we afford to protest the imperfect forms in which we find these things? Our own sense of power that comes from insights into these psychiatrically dubious goings-on should not blind us to the possibility that this psychopathic character — and a society, after all, has the rebels and the misfits it deserves, and has made, and can use for its own correction — this man who, for his own reasons, breaks through punitive cultural fictions and leads his people, however stumblingly, away from them, may be rendering his parishioners a therapeutic service all unofficially.

Everyone must have satisfactions, though for some these are reduced to the passive voyeuristic fantasies of movies and television. But the general culture of these poor whites is repressive; even if the church should grow more permissive, opportunities for entertainment in some rural areas in the South are still somewhat limited. We might put it this way: if you can't have it on Saturday night — which is the traditional time for secular fun — then what is the harm if you have it on Sunday night? For this purpose the poor whites need their minor Moses. What distresses us is the pathetically primitive forms the fun takes psychosexually. But what more indeed can be said of many of the other institutionalized forms of fantasy in our mass culture? What does it matter that there is a discrepancy between what the snake cultists are doing and what they say they are doing? Is this not our common human lot? Are other more respectable institutions wholly free of this? But is it not a waste of human energy to maintain irrational and useless prohibitions, and then have to spend institutions on unconsciously contriving the "return of the repressed" to allow for life to continue? And at what price in irrational guilt? Could we not thoughtfully and consciously contrive to remove all frustration and repressions save those necessary to get the work of civilization done? The painful thing to us, who are accustomed to a higher degree of sophisticated self-awareness, is that because of the pressures of their sadly neurotic and archaic and unhappy culture, these people have to have what satisfactions they can without any psychological self-possession, without any knowledge of who they are, and what they are like, and what they are really doing. But when men will not examine their sacred culture critically, is this not true of every civilization and its discontents?

} ACKNOWLEDGMENTS

Acknowledgments

T HIS study attempts to recount with the utmost possible descriptive accuracy a psychological phenomenon in the changing American South of our day. It is based upon a number of eye-witness reports and interviews, including those of Mrs. Henry Lehrberger and Dr. Jack Conrad, both former graduate students of mine. The photographs were taken by Mr. H. F. Pickett of the Medical Illustration Department of the Duke University Medical School. In the historical sections, all names and places are given exactly. But in the psychiatric sections, where such data are privileged communications, I have disguised in immaterial ways the names of persons and places.

Materials on the origins of the cult are owed to a brochure by Mr. J. B. Collins, entitled *Tennessee Snake Handlers*. This brochure contains no date, but from internal evidence I believe it to have been published shortly after August 24, 1947, and before the developments in Durham, North Carolina, in 1948, of which it makes no mention. For the latter events I have drawn upon a series of excellent newspaper accounts in the local press. For happenings in other states, I have cited accounts from several national newspaper services which, when carefully criticized and checked from my own knowledge, I believe to be of a high order of accuracy. In both the ethnographic and the classic historical sections I have carefully cited the scholarly sources.

The manuscript of this book had the benefit of the readings and criticisms of Mrs. Lehrberger and of all my colleagues on the senior staff of the Department of Psychiatry at the University of North Carolina Medical School in Chapel Hill. Dr. John Gillin, Dean of the Division of the Social Sciences, University of Pittsburgh, also kindly read the manuscript and criticized it from the viewpoint of his large and detailed research knowledge of southern regions. But the anthropological and psychiatric interpretations in the latter portion of the study are entirely my own, and any errors of mine can in no way reflect upon the judgment of my colleagues in the medical schools of Duke and North Carolina. To all my sources and generous readers I offer grateful acknowledgment.

} *NOTES AND INDEX*

Notes

[1] After this book was written I encountered an excellent article on snake-handling by Schwarz, who writes, "When the brothers and sisters arrive, they go among the congregation and onlookers to greet fellow-members cordially. At times the saints, who are always males, hug and kiss each other with the greeting, 'How are you, Honey?'" (Berthold Schwarz, M.D., "Ordeal by Serpents, Fire and Strychnine," *Psychiatric Quarterly,* 34 [1960] 405–429, p. 408).

[2] Keith Kerman, "Rattlesnake Religion," in Lealon N. Jones (ed.), *Eve's Stepchildren: A Collection of Folk Americana,* Caldwell, Idaho, 1942, pp. 93–102. In September 1940, D. Whitehead's "Handling Rattlesnakes to Demonstrate One's Faith" was syndicated by the Associated Press. Jean Thomas (*Blue Ridge Country,* New York, 1942, pp. 164f) has some data on the cult; see also E. Baird, "They Shall Take Up Serpents," *Woman,* 17, no. 2 (1946), pp. 36–39; R. W. Barbour, "The Reptiles of Big Black Mountain, Harlan, Kentucky," *Copeia,* no. 2 (1950) pp. 100–107; B. C. Clough, *The American Imagination at Work: Tall Tales and Folk Tales,* New York, 1947, p. 156; and N. Callahan, *Smoky Mountain Country,* New York and Boston, 1952, p. 91. L. M. Klauber's splendid monograph on *Rattlesnakes* (2 vols., Berkeley and Los Angeles, 1956, 2:945–947) also briefly describes the snake-handling cult. William Sargant, a British psychiatrist who visited Duke University in 1948, observed snake-handling meetings in Durham and devoted a few brief paragraphs to them in his article on "Some Cultural Group Abreactive Techniques and Their Relation to Modern Treatments," *Proceedings of the Royal Society of Medicine,* xlii, no. 5 (May 1949) 367–374. The bibliographic items listed in these first two notes, together with J. B. Collins's *Tennessee Snake Handlers,* mentioned in the Acknowledgments, nearly exhaust the available firsthand accounts of modern snake-handling.

[3] Kerman, *op. cit.,* p. 99.

[4] The Biblical texts suggesting this behavior are Isaiah XLIII, 2, and Daniel III, 25. Schwarz, *op. cit.,* writes (p. 415), "In one instance, the most faithful saint smeared fuel oil over hands and feet, and then proceeded to hold them in the midst of the flames for more than 10 seconds. Although there was some thick white smoke, the fuel oil on the skin did not burn. . . . The saint then cupped the palm of his hand and tried to ignite the little pool of fuel

oil in it with the blazing torch, but it only flickered a few times. As controls, an iron poker and a wooden dowel, that had fuel oil sprinkled on the surfaces, quickly burst into flames when in contact with the torch." The physicist will be unawed by this experiment: the white smoke is evidence of vaporization of the kerosene, which would in itself absorb many calories of vaporization. At the same time, the blood's circulation would keep a pool of kerosene cupped in the hands below the flash point of combustion and until, by convection-diffusion, the *whole pool* reached this flash point, no flame would result. A dry hand held ten seconds in a flame would in fact be more endangered than a kerosene-wetted one. Furthermore, a pool of oil below flash-point temperature will not ignite without a wick, at the site of which the necessary temperature may be reached.

⁵ Colorful names for autonomous local churches are not uncommon in the South. For example, in the Negro section of Durham is a group entitled "The Church of God in Christ New Deal Incorporated." Likewise, the Church of God, founded in 1903 by a salesman of the American Bible Society named A. J. Tomlinson (after a visit to the Holiness Church at Camp Creek in Cherokee County, North Carolina) frequently has colorful names for local churches: the Outpouring of the Latter Day Rain in Los Angeles; the Jesus Only Church of Harlem, New York; the Remnant Church of God in Lansing, Michigan; the Non-Digressive Church of God, the Justified Church of God, the Glorified Church, etc. Tomlinson became "Bishop" of this millennarian sect and laid out, in huge white letters made of concrete, the Ten Commandments in the Fields of the Wood eighteen miles west of Murphy, North Carolina. Tomlinson figured in the snake-handling cult, and it is possible that the Outpouring of the Latter Day Rain included snake-handling with the Church of God branch taken to Los Angeles. After his death the sect suffered schism in the hands of his rival sons, and still a third branch was set up in Chattanooga. One son, Homer Tomlinson, head of the New York City branch, ran for President of the United States in 1951, chiefly by fasting. On October 15, 1959, an Associated Press story said that: "For the first time since 1776, a king has claimed the state of North Carolina. Bishop Homer A. Tomlinson of Queens Village, N.Y., bishop and general overseer of one branch of the Church of God, in Asheville on one of seven Southern stops of his current national tour, proclaimed himself 'King of North Carolina' Tuesday in a ceremony on the courthouse steps. In an interview afterward, the new 'king' advised reporters that he expected to win the U.S. presidential election in 1960, and to be made 'king of all the nations of men' in 1966." In the accompanying photograph, Bishop Tomlinson is shown wearing a voluminous embroidered white kimono-like garment with wide long sleeves; on his head is a zigzag-pointed gold paper crown like one used in a child's charade. Between his knees is a globe, homemade, about a yard in diameter; above this he holds a sign neatly printed "King of North Carolina" and below this is a separate smaller sign proclaiming him "King of the World." (An excellent and detailed account of the origins and spread of the Pentecostal Holiness "Outpouring of the Latter Day Rain" Church may be found in Elmer T. Clarke, *The Small Sects in America*, New York, 1949, pp. 100–102.)

⁶ In meetings Schwarz observed, the men sat on one side of the church, the women on the other (Schwarz, *op. cit.*, p. 408).

⁷ Inasmuch as this newspaper reporter is not a recognized Africanist, the

linguist is entitled to be skeptical of his statement. "Speaking in tongues" is done in a rapid, staccato, unintelligible monotone (itself surprising, since West Africa is a major area of pitch accent) which is stereotyped whatever "tongue" is being spoken, a matter which will further amaze linguistic scholars. Furthermore, speaking in tongues has been observed in this region to employ only the familiar phonemes of South Atlantic English, and hence in any case the tongues are being spoken with an American accent. I have heard neither the bilabial V of Ewe, nor the clicks of Bantu and Hottentot, nor the pitch accent of Jabbo to persuade me that I was hearing an authentic African dialect.

St. Paul, incidentally, found it necessary to advise restraint and moderation in speaking in tongues (I Corinthians XIV, 26; see also the article by E. K. Mitchell "Prophecy (Christian)" in the *Hastings Encyclopedia of Religion and Ethics* 10:382–383, p. 383). The French scholar Salomon Reinach (*Orpheus*, F. Simmonds [tr.], London, 1909, p. 251) writes as follows: "Among the faithful of the primitive churches there were, of course, a certain number of visionaries, and of idle and degraded persons. Many believe themselves to be gifted with prophetic powers and disturbed the meetings by fits of *glossolaly*, that is to say, an outburst of inarticulate sounds. It was this gift of 'speaking with tongues' which the Apostles were supposed to have received at Pentecost by the grace of the Holy Ghost; later, the double meaning of the word 'tongue' was played upon, and it was maintained that the Apostles had been endowed with the power of speaking the idioms of all the people to whom they were to preach the gospel. The manifestations of glossolaly were checked at an early state; St. Paul forbids it altogether for women." Since women more often speak in tongues than do men in the snake-handling cult, and since historical continuity with primitive Christianity can be established, it must be stated that this practice by women directly defies the Apostle to the Gentiles, who must have known best of all the proper use of the gift of tongues.

[8] Schwarz, *op. cit.*, pp. 410–411.

[9] The practice of drinking strychnine is sanctioned along with snake-handling in Mark XVI, 18: "And if they drink any deadly thing, it shall not hurt them." The text in Mark doubtless refers to a Greek practice. "Down into classical times bull's blood was a sacred thing which it was dangerous to touch and death to taste: to drink a cup of it was the most heroic form of suicide" (Gilbert Murray, *Five Stages of Greek Religion*, New York, 1951, p. 19, citing Aristophanes' *Equites*, 82–84). When the bull was sacrificed to Zeus, "The bull is Sosipolis, Saviour of the city, in the making . . . [and] when Themistocles (Plutarch, *Life of Themistocles*, xxxi sub fin.) drank bull's blood, he identified himself with Sosipolis in his bull-form" (Jane Ellen Harrison, *Themis*, Cambridge, 1927, p. 154, footnote 2). In the Hellenistic Mithraic and Dionysian bull-slaughter, the symbolism is dramatically reversed: bull's blood is drunk not to commit suicide but to become immortal. Despite the Eucharist in Christianity, which clearly descends from Greek and Hellenistic sources, there is certainly no historical continuity whatever between the Greeks' drinking of "poisonous" bull's blood in classic times and the snake-handlers' drinking of strychnine at their meetings. On the contrary, these extremely low-church Protestants had long since been in historic revolt against such poperies as the sacraments, and most especially the Eucharist. The direct Biblical source is plain enough

to account for strychnine-drinking, as Mark XVI, 18 is interpreted by snake-handlers; and beyond this the only similarity is in the oral-incorporation fantasies concerning a dangerous male power, ambiguously "sacred," death-dealing, and immortality-giving. There are some interesting psychological resemblances also between the bullfight and snake-handling, but again without any possibility of historical continuity. It is oedipal Homo sapiens, not direct culture-history, and not Jungian archetypes, which is involved here.

[10] The belief that snakes like milk and can feed on it is ubiquitous in ethnography. In Armenian folklore, for example, there is the belief in "an ancestor visiting the home in the form of a snake which has to be fed with milk" (M. H. Ananikian, "The Serpent in Armenian Folk-Lore," in L. H. Gray [ed.], *Mythology of All Races*, 13 vols., 1916–1932, 7:73, Boston, 1925). Such beliefs might be cited almost indefinitely in European folklore. In Ruthenia, for instance, milk is left in a saucer on the doorstep of a cottage to feed a snake, who brings bad luck if not so fed (W. D. Hambly, *Serpent Worship in Africa*, Field Museum of Natural History Publication 289, Anthropological Series, xxi, no. 1 [Chicago, 1931] p. 61). Psychologically interesting is the vision of Alberico, a boy of ten, who was conducted by St. Peter and two angels through hell where he saw "a fearful wood of gigantic trees, bristling with thorns, from whose sharp and spiny branches were hanging by their breasts those heartless women who had refused to nourish motherless babes with their own milk; to each breast clung a snake, sucking that which had been so cruelly denied" (Homer W. Smith, *Man and His Gods*, New York, 1952, p. 266).

But the belief is not merely European. In Africa, the Budu of Uganda daily fed the sacred python milk (mixed with white clay) from sacred cows; the spirit of the python sometimes possesses a priest "who wriggles on the floor like a snake, uttering strange sounds and talking in a language which has to be interpreted to his worshippers" (Hambly, *op. cit.*, pp. 19, 21, 50). Various snakes were commonly totem animals among the Hausa, though sometimes the snake is emblematic of the evil eye; eggs and milk are offered to them (Hambly, *op. cit.*, p. 28). The Masai offer milk to sacred snakes, especially to dead husbands who return as snakes to plague their wives; the Wakikuyu of East Africa offer milk and fat to the snake messengers of the deities (Hambly, *op. cit.*, p. 34). Milk is offered to snakes in many parts of India, e.g., among the Gammallas, a Telegu-speaking group, who offer milk to cobras (Hambly, *op. cit.*, p. 61).

But herpetological truth cannot be established by a mere *consensus gentium* in folklore. Dr. Joseph Bailey, of the Department of Zoology at Duke University, assures me that skepticism concerning snakes' drinking milk is well founded, and he himself is confident that the belief is mere folklore. Such experimental evidence as we have invites further unbelief; see note 78.

If the biological evidence be accepted, the ethnological problem still remains. How, on grounds either of diffusion or of independent parallelism, can we account for the ubiquity of a belief in snakes' drinking milk which has no foundation in biological fact? I consider the only adequate explanation a psychiatric one, as discussed on pages 86–89, 94–98.

[11] Schwarz, *op. cit.*, pp. 410–411. Schwarz elsewhere writes, "The saints reported one unusual and enigmatic situation where it was alleged that two particular sisters frequently handled rattlesnakes that died (of fright?) during the ordeal. It is plausible then to conjecture that the rhythmic stimulation to

the serpent, combined with its possible terror during the experience, might produce, in the snake, reactions varying from relative inertia and drowsiness to cataplexy and even death." (*Op. cit.*, pp. 412–413.) That those causing snake cataplexy are invariably women suggests psychiatric explanations of the stories. Are there species-specific cataplexies different for Kentucky-Tennessee timber rattlesnakes and Carolina lowlands diamondbacks? But Carolinians find in their state, and use, both Appalachian timber rattlers and Coastal Plain diamondbacks alike, so that this is no explanation either. Snakes are surprisingly fragile, and may rather easily be injured seriously enough to cause death later; and yet they are also notably tenacious of life and can scarcely be supposed to die on the spot of heart failure or the like during meetings. Their occasional, but unaccountably rare, cataplexia is folk-interpreted as evidence of the holy spirit's visiting men and "dominating" the evil serpent. And, finally, it is doubtful that snakes are neurologically complex enough to "die of fright" but only, later, of physical injuries sustained during handling — which is never, however, intentionally rough! For me, the disturbed-reflexes hypothesis continues to be the most plausible explanation, unproved though it is.

[12] Quoted by Collins, *op. cit.*, p. 35. *Time*, March 10, 1947, reported briefly on the Tennessee anti-snake-handling law, stating that in the past two ministers of the cult had died. This is inaccurate. Tom Harden, a preacher, recovered completely and was repeatedly bitten, non-fatally, in later meetings. Garland Defriese, who also recovered, was not a preacher. Lewis F. Ford, who was bitten in a Dolley Pond meeting in September 1945, was a son of Walter Ford, a deacon of the church. And Hensley, a preacher, was not fatally bitten until the end of July 1955, and hence could not have figured in the 1947 news article. The second *victim*, Clint Jackson, was not even a member of the cult, much less a minister in it. Jackson, a man in his early forties, worked in a Chattanooga plant to support his wife and three children. He was injured while working there in July 1946 and released for medical treatment. He refused to see a doctor but went instead to a tent meeting of snake-handlers for their "healing prayers." Though a believer, Jackson was not a member of the Dolley Pond Church. During the meeting he took up a large rattlesnake captured only the day before by "sinner-men" on Signal Mountain, ten miles west of Daisy, and sold to a cultist for a dollar and a half. The snake bit Jackson on the hand and he died in a violent spasm forty-five minutes later while members prayed frantically over the visitor to their revival meeting.

[13] Collins, *op. cit.*, pp. 26–27.

[14] James Stalker, "Revivals of Religion," *Hastings Encyclopedia of Religion and Ethics*, 10:753–757, p. 756. The article referred to is "Bodily Effects of Religious Excitement," in *Princeton Theological Essays, 1st Series*, New York, 1846, and Edinburgh, 1856.

[15] Rufus M. Jones, "Ranters," *Hastings Encyclopedia of Religion and Ethics*, 10:578–580.

[16] George A. Barton, "Possession (Semitic and Christian)," in *Hastings Encyclopedia of Religion and Ethics*, 10:133–139, p. 138. For the famous "Kentucky Revival," see F. M. Davenport, *Primitive Traits in Religious Revivals*, New York, 1905, ch. IX. For a more popular account, see Archie Robertson, *That Old-Time Religion*, Boston, 1950.

[17] Sir James George Frazer, *The Golden Bough*, 1-vol. ed., New York, 1930, pp. 519–520.

[18] H. L. Friess and H. W. Schneider, *Religion in Various Cultures*, New York, 1932, p. 451.

[19] *Durham Morning Herald*, May 22, 1948. I am indebted to the editor, Mr. Steed Rollins, for permission to quote from this source.

[20] *Durham Morning Herald*, October 7, 1948.

[21] *Durham Evening Sun*, October 7, 1948; *Durham Morning Herald*, October 15, 1948.

[22] *Durham Morning Herald*, October 18, 1948.

[23] *Durham Evening Sun*, December 14, 1948.

[24] *Durham Morning Herald*, May 22, 1949.

[25] United Press dispatch from Huntsville, Alabama, July 17, 1951.

[26] Schwarz writes: "Although the author personally observed more than 200 instances of serpent handling, he has not witnessed a bite. Many of the saints have been bitten. Two, in particular, claim to have been bitten more than 50 times, and two others, more than 30 times each. One claims to have handled serpents more than 2,000 times in his career without once being bitten. When a Holiness member is bitten, medical treatment is refused. The saints use no definitive treatment and rely solely on their 'faith in the Lord' for a cure. Four saints knew, among them, of only 18 Holiness people who had died of snake bites in 31 years. They cited examples of men and women in their 70's and 80's who survived bites. Although there are instances of children as young as four years of age handling the serpents at the services, and also other instances where infants inadvertently handled serpents in private homes, no member of the Holiness Church knew of any case when a child was bitten." (Schwarz, *op. cit.*, p. 411.) There is a widespread belief in the United States that the rattlesnake will not bite a child; one must suppose that rattlesnake and copperhead venom, adapted as they are to paralyzing small vertebrates which are the snakes' food, are less fatal to larger animals than has previously been believed.

[27] Robertson, *op. cit.*, p. 170. Robertson writes that a son of George Hensley died of snakebite. "A husky young man who worked in a plant near Chattanooga, he had preached the faith to his fellow workers. The men in the plant had warned him of danger; once he had replied, 'I may be bitten some day to prove to unbelievers that the serpents will kill, and that we can only handle 'em when God anoints us to handle 'em.' After his death from a snake bite, which he received at a brush-arbor service, two thousand persons attended his funeral at Dolley Pond; at the climax of the service, six large struggling snakes, including the killer, were thrown into his coffin." (p. 172.) I believe that Robertson has confused Lewis Ford and Clint Jackson with Hensley's son — an opinion which numerous small inaccuracies in Robertson's brief account of snake-handling tend to confirm.

[28] *Durham Morning Herald*, August 14, 1954. See also article by Margaret Shannon, *Atlanta Journal*, c. August 15, 1954.

[29] *Durham Morning Herald*, August 22, 1955. See note 26 for Schwarz's figures. The numbers confirm each other: 14 up to August 1955, and 18 up to July 1960, maintaining about the same rate of one per year.

[30] *Durham Morning Herald*, August 31, 1955.

[31] *Durham Morning Herald*, July 28, 1955.

[32] Sir James George Frazer, *Folklore in the Old Testament*, 3 vols., London, 1919. 1:45–77. All data in the next five paragraphs are summarized from this source.

[188

[33] It is on such grounds as his "death" and "resurrection" that the obviously phallic Hermes has sometimes been accounted, of all things, a lunar deity (E. Siecke, *Hermes der Mondgott*, Jena, 1908–1909). As we shall later see, the death and resurrection of the phallus has, possibly, more proximate meanings. Moreover, it is not so much that Hermes (the chthonic snake messenger to the underworld of spirits) is a moon god, as that (successful) activity of the phallus affects menses. Nevertheless, there are, understandably, repeated, and obviously independent, associations of the "male" snake and the "female" moon in folklore. For example, note the curious case of the Brazilian Negro who was bitten by a rattlesnake and had recurring symptoms at certain phases of the moon (H. Koster, *Travels in Brazil*, 2 vols., 2nd ed., London, 1817, 2:56; in Klauber, 2:824 and 2:844). This may be the survival in Brazil of an ancient European belief (Pliny, bk. XXIX, ch. 22; see also E. Topsell, *The Historie of Serpents, Or, The Second Book of Living Creatures*, London, 1608, p. 33). Compare also the quite independent southwestern Indian association of snakes and menses. For example, the Yuki figurative name for the rattlesnake indicates that to them the source of the rattlesnake's danger lies in menstrual blood, which they consider the deadliest of all poisons (G. M. Foster, *A Summary of Yuki Culture*, University of California Anthropological Records, v, no. 3 [1944] 155–214, p. 214). Compare also the belief of the Hopi and other Pueblo tribes that the smell of a menstruous woman was so highly offensive to a rattlesnake that it angered him so that he would bite her (A. M. Stephen, *Hopi Journal*, 2 vols., New York, 1936, pp. 709, 756, 766; E. C. Parsons, *Pueblo Indian Religion*, 2 vols., Chicago, 1939, p. 1056).

[34] Hambly, *op. cit.*, p. 16.

[35] Hambly, *op. cit.*, p. 18.

[36] Hambly, *op. cit.*, p. 55; cf. also p. 38.

[37] Hambly, *op. cit.*, p. 9.

[38] Hambly, *op. cit.*, pp. 14, 16, 22. For the European and Semitic parallels see, in addition to Jane Ellen Harrison, *Prolegomena to the Study of Greek Religion*, Cambridge, 1908, the abundant evidence in that other classically rich source, R. B. Onians, *The Origins of European Thought*, Cambridge, 1954.

[39] Hambly, *op. cit.*, pp. 41, 42.

[40] Murray, *op. cit.*, p. 13.

[41] M. E. Opler, *Myths and Legends of the Lipan Apache Indians*, Memoirs of the American Folklore Society, 36:1–296, p. 275.

[42] W. Madsen, "Hot and Cold in the Universe of the San Francisco Tecospa, Valley of Mexico," *Journal of American Folklore*, 68 [268] 123–129. William Byrd, in 1728, was told of an even more authentic New World Medusa, an underworld judge of evildoers with tresses of writhing rattlesnakes (D. L. Rights, *The American Indian in North Carolina*, Durham, 1947, p. 96; in Klauber, *op. cit.*, 2:1094).

[43] D. G. Brinton, *Myths of the New World*, 3rd ed., Philadelphia, 1896, p. 142. Klauber (*op. cit.*, 2:1086) has some question about this practice and belief, lacking in Peruvian Indians today; the myth may be, at least in part, of European origin.

[44] P. Dudley, "An Account of the Rattlesnake," *Transactions* [of the Royal Society of London], 32 [#376] 292–295, Philadelphia, 1723, p. 294. R. P. Bieber and A. B. Bender, *Exploring Southwestern Trails*, Southwest Historical

Series (vol. 7, Diaries of Francis Xavier Aubry, 1853–1854), Glendale, California, 1938, p. 360.

[45] V. Randolph, *We Always Lie to Strangers: Tall Tales from the Ozarks*, New York, 1951, p. 140; *idem, Ozark Superstitions*, New York, 1947, p. 256; Klauber, *op. cit.*, 2:1235.

[46] Hambly, *op. cit.*, p. 40.

[47] E. Westermarck, *Origin and Development of the Moral Ideas*, 2 vols., 2nd ed., London, 1924 and 1926, 2:420.

[48] Klauber, *op. cit.*, 1:464.

[49] Hambly, *op. cit.*, p. 42.

[50] Hambly, *op. cit.*, p. 23. The correctness of Hambly's statement has been attested in the remarkable recent field work of H. Cory described in "The Buswezi, Initiation into a Secret Society in Tanganyika," *American Anthropologist*, 57 (1955) 923–952. This is a spectacular pseudo-blood-kin society which employs actual coitus as part of the ritual: no Tantrik "cult of the left hand" in India could be more specifically sexual than this Tanganyika rite. The Buyeye is a secret society of snake charmers in Sukumaland, Tanganyika, whose purpose is to give members knowledge of snakes, how to catch them, and how to cure bites. The initiation rites last a week; but, even so, these do not teach all the *expertise* ultimately needed and learned. Many powerful attributes are ascribed to the snake-spirit Ibambangalu (also known in Nyamwezi), one being that if he enters a house he immediately fills it by swelling up! He is a famous rain-maker, and holds a magic calabash containing rain in one hand and a magic wand in the other. In the *tambiko* worship of ancestors, a hole is dug and a pestle put in it, the participants holding the pestle with both hands for some time and bending over the hole (H. Cory, *Wall-Paintings by Snake Charmers in Tanganyika*, London, 1953, pp. 11–12, 42, 44; cf. also 46, 52, 60 and 62). It is evident on the basis of the above data that these Tanganyika tribes not only have a rich and re-duplicated phallic symbolism but also, perhaps, even have a conscious aware-ness of these symbolic meanings. The *tambiko* cult, incidentally, is an exact institutionalization of the classic magical "schizophrenic influencing machine" by which the individual psychotic mimics parental coitus.

[51] Hambly, *op. cit.*, pp. 30, 34.

[52] Hambly, *op. cit.*, pp. 23, 35–36, 70–71, 75.

[53] Dagny Carter, *The Symbol of the Beast*, New York, 1957, pp. 13, 16.

[54] Hambly, *op. cit.*, p. 66; for the modern belief, see p. 65.

[55] *Hastings Encyclopedia of Religion and Ethics*, 11:412, citing G. Watt, *Dictionary of the Economic Products of India*, London and Calcutta, 1889–1893, 6 vols., i, 429; see also J. Frayer, *The Thanatophidia of India*, London, 1874.

[56] Harrison, *Themis*, p. 267.

[57] Harrison, *Themis*, pp. 271, 265. In this quotation, as elsewhere, I have transliterated Miss Harrison's Greek.

[58] Harrison, *Themis*, p. 458.

[59] Klauber, *op. cit.*, 2:846.

[60] Charles Selten, *The Twelve Olympians and Their Visitors*, London, 1955, p. 180. This is an ex post facto myth, for Asklepios was originally a snake before he was a man. "On the snake-aspect of Asklepios [writes Jane Harrison] it is needless to dwell, it is manifest" (*Prolegomena*, p. 342).

[61] Herbert Maryon and H. J. Plenderleith, "Fine Metal-Work," in C. Singer

Notes

et al., A History of Technology, 5 vols., Cambridge, 1958, 1:621–662, p. 662.

⁶² Sir James George Frazer, *Spirits of the Corn and of the Wild*, 2 vols., London, 1912, 2:17f.

⁶³ Harrison, *Themis*, p. 297.

⁶⁴ Arnobius, v. 19, from Harrison, *Prolegomena*, p. 484. Clement of Alexandria (*Protrepticus*, III, 4) knew of a Dionysos in Chios called Omadius, the Raw One, with human sacrifice in his cult (as to the Cretan bull-god, the Minotaur). The Zeus-Zagreus-Dionysus "Orphic" cult of bull-slaughter and raw flesh-eating is at once the initial Titan totemism of the earliest Greek times in Hesiod, and the latest Hellenistic Mystery that led into Christianity and the Eucharist.

⁶⁵ Harrison, *Themis*, p. 266. The custom has survived into modern European times.

⁶⁶ Harrison, *Themis*, p. 265.

⁶⁷ E. R. Dodds, *The Greeks and the Irrational*, Berkeley, 1951, p. 275 (which contains copious references to the classical sources on snake-handling rites in ancient Mediterranean times).

⁶⁸ Harrison, *Themis*, p. 270. In his edition of Pausanius, commenting on IV, 14, 7, and also in his *Adonis, Attis, Osiris*, 2:70, Frazer collected a number of instances of fatherhood by snakes.

⁶⁹ J. A. MacCulloch, "Serpent-worship (Introductory and Primitive)," *Hastings Encyclopedia of Religion and Ethics*, 11:399–411, p. 406. MacCulloch cites profusely such authorities as Clement of Alexandria, Arnobius, Firmicus Maternus, Justin Martyr, and Plutarch for classic sources, and Anson, Jane Harrison, Dieterich, and others for modern. I have transliterated and translated several passages in Greek in MacCulloch which were unseemly in naked English in Edwardian times, but are not now.

⁷⁰ Gilbert Murray, *Five Stages*, p. 13.

⁷¹ J. J. M. de Groot, *The Religious System of China*, 4 vols., Leyden, 1901, 4:283–286; also Sir James George Frazer, *Baldur the Beautiful*, 2 vols., London, 1913, 2:44n. For the reasons for regarding the snake as a phallic symbol in Japan, see Weston La Barre, *The Human Animal*, Chicago, 1954, pp. 352–353.

⁷² Typical versions of the story of the rattlesnake and his detachable poison glands may be found in A. Dugés, "Apuntes para la Monografía de los Crotalos de México," *Naturaleza*, 4 (1877) 1–29, and 33–34, p. 17; H. G. Dulog, "The Angel of the Guard," *Forest and Stream*, 49, no. 11 (1897) no. 12, pp. 222–224; E. B. Kincaid, "The New Mexican Pastor," *Publications of the Texas Folk-lore Society*, 9 (1931) 63–68, p. 67; L. Pound, "Nebraska Snake Lore," *Southern Folklore Quarterly*, 10 (1946) 163–176, p. 175; and V. Randolph, *Ozark Superstitions*, New York, 1947, p. 254. However, the portion of the legend stating that when venomous snakes drink, they temporarily remove their venom, venom glands, or fangs (to avoid poisoning themselves) is very old. A. Calmet (*A Great Dictionary of the Holy Bible*, 4 vols., Charleston, 1812–1814) and A. E. Rendell ([tr.] *Physiologus, A Metrical Bestiary of Twelve Chapters by Bishop Theobald, Printed in Cologne, 1492*, London, 1928, p. 12) both attribute it to the *Physiologus* book of animal allegories which first appeared in the second century A.D. See also C. Owen, *An Essay Toward the Natural History of Serpents*, London, 1742, p. 173; and Lynn Thorndike, *A History of Magic and Experimen-*

191]

tal Science, 6 vols., New York, 1923–1941, 2:483 (Klauber, *op. cit.*, 2: 1216).

[73] J. Ferguson, *Tree Worship*, 2nd ed., p. 259, cited in the *Hastings Encyclopedia of Religion and Ethics*, 11:412, which source also cites Sir Edward B. Tylor, *Primitive Culture*, 2 vols., 2nd ed., New York, 1874, 2:123ff. The classic sources on snakes' immortality through shedding of the skin are, of course, Aristotle, Theobald's *Physiologus* (A.D. 2nd century), and Epiphanius's *Physiologus* (A.D. 4th century); this is also an old Hindu belief — although it is held far more widely than the Indoeuropean sphere, e.g., in Melanesia and in the Americas.

[74] Plutarch, *De Iside et Osiride*, 74, is the Greek locus classicus. The snake's cast skin and its association with a supposed immortality is exhaustively treated in Frazer's *Folklore in the Old Testament*, 1:66–77; see also Frazer's *The Belief in Immortality*, 3 vols., London, 1913–1924, i:70. The same symbolism and interpretation of the snake's renewing its life through casting its skin are found outside Europe in New Britain, the Bismarck Archipelago, Annam, Borneo, and among the Arawak of Amazonia and the Tamanachiers of the Orinoco (*Hastings Encyclopedia of Religion and Ethics*, 11:408). This is related to beliefs among Palaeosiberians like the Ainu and the Yukaghir (Leo Simmons, *The Role of the Aged in Primitive Society*, New Haven, 1945, pp. 218–219). In Melanesia, this belief in the immortality of the skin-sloughing snake became of central importance in the dogma of several cargo cults, in particular of the Mansren cult whose founder-prophet reputedly sloughed his skin like a snake and learned thus about immortality. See Peter Worsley, *The Trumpet Shall Sound*, London, 1957, for the cargo and other cults.

[75] G. A. Barton, "Stones (Semitic)," in *Hastings Encyclopedia of Religion and Ethics*, 11:876–877, p. 876.

[76] Enid Welsford, "Serpent Worship (Teutonic and Balto-Slavic)," in *Hastings Encyclopedia of Religion and Ethics*, 11:419–423, p. 422, citing Fabricius and Paul Einhorn, "Ein christlicher Unterricht," *Scriptones Rerorum Livonorum*, 2:624. "Puke" is clearly the north European wealth-guarding dragon version of the widespread Indoeuropean snake deity who appears as the *genius lectualis* of the Romans and the *genius loci* in India and other Indoeuropean regions.

[77] For a classical psychiatric instance of symbolizing the phallus as a snake, see Karl Abraham, "A Complicated Ceremonial Found in Neurotic Women," *Selected Papers on Psychoanalysis*, London, 1927, pp. 157–163. He summarizes (p. 161): "A snake is able to kill by means of its poisonous bite, hence as a symbol it can give expression both to coitus and to death phantasies." See also Ernest Jones, *Essays in Applied Psychoanalysis*, London, 1923 (pp. 141, 312, 323, 327, 334, and 349), Jones's *Papers on Psychoanalysis*, 5th ed., Baltimore, 1948 (pp. 101, 123, 127–128), and especially Jones's famous essay on "The Theory of Symbolism" (Jones, *Papers*, pp. 87–144). See also Jones's "Snake Symbolism in Dreams," *Psyche*, 6, no. 4 (April 1926) 87–89. For ethnographic instances of snake symbolism in addition to Hambly's and Klauber's, see R. F. Fortune, "The Symbolism of the Serpent," *International Journal of Psycho-Analysis*, 7 (1926) 237–243; J. C. Hassall, "The Serpent as a Symbol," *Psychoanalytic Review*, 4 (1919) 296–305; R. Reed, "The Serpent as a Phallic Symbol," *Psychoanalytic Review*, 9 (1922) 91–92; C. S. Wake, *Serpent Worship*, London, 1888; and E. M. Cesaresco,

Notes

The Place of Animals in Human Thought, London, 1909, pp. 1–136, especially p. 111. Cesaresco, who has most abundantly surveyed the entire field, states that snake worship is, beyond question, the greatest of all animal cults.

[78] "Milk is not a natural food of these reptiles, and stories of their fondness for it are imaginary" (Klauber, *op. cit.*, 2:1225). In 1950, E. R. Allen and W. T. Neill found that snakes refused milk even when denied water. "Once I poured two ounces of milk down the throat of a snake. When I placed it on the ground, the milk ran out of its mouth, for the snake, although able to expand its body to accommodate the liquid, was unable to retain it." (C. B. Perkins, "Snake Myths Smashed by Science," in Brandt Aymar [ed.], *Treasury of Snake Lore*, New York, 1956, 99–103, pp. 101–102.)

[79] *Folk Lore Journal*, 1 (1883) p. 256; W. Bennett and R. M. Zingg, *The Tarahumara*, Chicago, 1935, p. 128.

[80] Theophilus Hahn, *Tsuni-Goam, the Supreme Being of the Khoi-Khoi*, London, 1881, p. 81.

[81] Carl Lumholtz, *Unknown Mexico*, 2 vols., London, 1903, 2:352. "It may be added [says Lumholtz, 1:245] that the Huichols see serpents in their own floating hair, [and] in one organ of the body." Which organ this is may be surmised; but, failing that, it may still be inferred from the quotation in the text (though in this there are both displacement and over-determination). The Sonorans therefore also have the full oedipal body-image in their symbolisms.

[82] E. Owen, *Welsh Folk-Lore*, Oswestry, 1896, p. 349.

[83] Klauber, *op. cit.*, 2:1217–1218.

[84] R. J. E. Mauyduyt, "Sur Quelques Objets de Regne Animal, Apportés de la Louisiane," *Observations sur la Physique*, Paris, 1774, vol. 4, pp. 384–397, 388; Klauber, *op. cit.*, 2:1240.

[85] Klauber, *op. cit.*, 2:1253–1254.

[86] Smith, *op. cit.*, p. 266.

[87] J. A. MacCulloch, "Serpent-Worship, Introductory and Primitive," *Hastings Encyclopedia of Religion and Ethics*, 11:399–411, p. 410.

[88] T. R. Garth, *Atsugewi Ethnography*, University of California Anthropological Records, 14 (1953) 129–212, p. 190; in Klauber, *op. cit.*, 2:1156. The Kiliwa shaman story in the footnote is from P. Meigs, "The Kiliwa Indians of Lower California," University of California *Ibero-Americana*, 15 (1939) 1–88, p. 63; in Klauber, *op. cit.*, 2:1156. The Ute and Paiute data of the footnote are from O. C. Stewart, "Culture Element Distributions XVIII, Ute–Southern Paiute," *University of California Anthropological Records*, 6 (1942) 231–356, p. 317, in Klauber, *op. cit.*, 2:1149.

[89] *Hastings Encyclopedia of Religion and Ethics*, 11:59–60, p. 60: William Crooke, "Saints and Martyrs (Indian, Buddhist, Jain, and Hindu Saints)."

[90] Klauber, *op. cit.*, 2:1227.

[91] P. I. Nixon, *The Medical History of Early Texas*, San Antonio, 1946, p. 19; D. J. Baylor, "Folklore from Socorro, New Mexico," *Hoosier Folklore*, 6 (1947) 91–100 and 138–150, p. 150; Klauber, *op. cit.*, 2:876, 1138. The same method was long used in Zacatecas, according to Arlegui (José Arlegui, *Chronica de la Provincia . . . de Zacatecas*, Mexico, 1937 [1851 ed., p. 183]), and among the Tarahumara (Bennett and Zingg, *op. cit.*, p. 128). The Havasupai have a modified procedure: one who is bitten by a snake must catch it, and, grasping each jaw, endeavor to tear it lengthwise into two strips; if he splits it to the tail, he will recover, otherwise he must die (L. Spier, *Havasupai Ethnography*, Anthropological Papers of the American Museum

THEY SHALL TAKE UP SERPENTS

of Natural History, 29 [1928] 81–392, p. 283) – an extremely interesting symbolism. The Navaho followed the same method when a girl was bitten, although she herself was not required to tear the snake (G. A. Reichard, *Social Life of the Navaho Indians*, Columbia University Contributions to Anthropology, 7 [1928] 245, in Klauber, *op. cit.*, 2:1138).

[92] Klauber, *op. cit.*, 1:264.

[93] A. W. Rolker, "The Story of the Snake," *McClure's Magazine*, XXI, no. 3 (1903), 280–290, p. 283.

[94] D. G. Brinton, *Myths of the New World*, 3rd ed., Philadelphia, 1896, p. 136; L. Spence, *Myths of Mexico and Peru*, New York, 1913, pp. 74, 76; Brinton, *op. cit.*, p. 201; R. M. Dorman, *The Origin of Primitive Superstitions*, Philadelphia, 1881, p. 264; J. B. Webber, "Snake Facts and Fiction," *Texas Game and Fish*, 9 (1951), 12–13, 30, p. 30; Dorman, *op. cit.*, p. 264; and W. H. Hudson, "The Serpent's Strangeness," *Fortnightly Review*, 55 (1894), 528–537. All the references in this and the next two paragraphs are from Klauber, *op. cit.*, 2:1091–1093.

[95] J. Mooney, *Myths of the Cherokee*, Annual Report of the Bureau of American Ethnology, 19 (1900) 3–548, p. 294; W. H. Gilbert, *The Eastern Cherokees*, Bulletin of the Bureau of American Ethnology, 133 (1943) 169–413, p. 183; W. J. McGee, "Serpent Charm," *Popular Science Monthly*, 15 (1897), p. 180; H. H. Turney-High, *The Flathead Indians of Montana*, Memoirs of the American Anthropological Association, 48 (1937) 1–161, p. 27; E. C. Parsons, *Isleta, New Mexico*, Annual Report of the Bureau of American Ethnology, 47 (1932) 193–466, p. 277; *idem, Pueblo Indian Religion*, 2 vols., Chicago, 1939, p. 927; L. W. Simmons (ed.), *Sun Chief: The Autobiography of a Hopi Indian*, New Haven, 1942, pp. 17, 21, 42; W. Matthews, "Serpent Worship Among the Navahos," *Land of Sunshine*, 9 (1898) 228–235, pp. 230, 233; W. Morgan, "Navaho Treatment of Sickness: Diagnosticians," *American Anthropologist*, 33 (1931) 390–402, p. 401; J. G. Bourke, "Notes on the Cosmogony and Theogony of the Mojave Indians of the Rio Colorado, Arizona," *Journal of American Folklore*, 2 (1889) 169–189, p. 186; A. L. Kroeber, *Ethnography of the Cahuilla Indians*, University of California Publications in American Archaeology and Ethnology, 8 (1908), p. 315; L. Spier, *Klamath Ethnography*, University of California Publications in American Archaeology and Ethnology, 30 (1930) 1–338, p. 119; A. H. Gayton, *Yokuts and Western Mono Ethnography*, University of California Anthropological Records, 10 (1948) 1–302, p. 198; *Rudo Ensayo* [1763], 1894 ed., p. 192; Carl Lumholtz, *Symbolism of the Huichol Indians*, Memoirs of the American Museum of Natural History, 3 (1900) 1–228, p. 20; *idem, Unknown Mexico*, New York, 1902, 2 vols., 2:202; Dorman, *op. cit.*, p. 264; J. E. Thompson, *Mexico Before Cortez*, New York, 1933, p. 140 – cited from Klauber, *op. cit.*, 2:1091–1092. See also Ananda Coomaraswamy, *Rajput Painting*, 2 vols., Oxford, 1916, vol. 2, plate XXIV. Compare the modern American folk belief that to bring rain one should hang a dead snake belly-up on a fence (Klauber, *op. cit.*, 2:1257).

[96] H. K. Haeberlin, *The Idea of Fertilization in the Culture of the Pueblo Indians*, Memoirs of the American Anthropological Association, 3 (1916), p. 37; see also W. Fewkes, "Mamzrauti," *American Anthropologist*, O.S. 5:238–239.

[97] Bennett and Zingg, *op. cit.*, p. 128. For references in the footnote, see Klauber, *op. cit.*, 2:867, 1217, 1249–1251, and 1:464.

[98] Klauber, *op. cit.*, 1:443f, 2:1199, 1201, 845.

[99] Klauber, *op. cit.*, 2:1148 (Isleta); 2:1157 (Muskito and Sumo).

[100] Klauber, *op. cit.*, 2:1219–1220.

[101] Klauber, *op. cit.*, 2:1218, 1240.

[102] G. M. Foster, *A Summary of Yuki Culture*, University of California Anthropological Records, 5 (1944) 155–215, p. 214; Stephen, *op. cit.*, pp. 709, 756, 766; Parsons, *Pueblo Indian Religion*, p. 1056; for California Indians, see sources cited in Klauber, *op. cit.*, 2:1104. The Sumu have a counter-remedy; they spit on the snake's head to stupefy it with the hempweed they chew (*idem, loc. cit.*). For the alleged smell of rattlesnakes, see Klauber, *op. cit.*, 2:1237, 1239. The snake that kills by touch (Klauber, *op. cit.*, 2:1134) is to be compared with the timber rattlesnake that can allegedly kill with its breath (Klauber, *op. cit.*, 2:1195–1196).

The question of snake-smells and snake-smelling is doubtless to be regarded as belonging to the "anal" sphere of symbolizing — though sometimes over-determined by genital symbolisms of the snake as well — as is surely the use of various kinds of animal excrement to cure snakebites. Pliny lists a number of cures of snakebites with feces (Pliny, xxviii, ch. 42; xxix, ch. 15); they are mentioned in some of the earliest accounts of the rattlesnake (F. Hernández, *Quatro Libros de la Naturaleza, y Virtudes de las Plantas, y Animales que Estan Recividos en el Uso de Medicina en la Nueva España*, Mexico, 1615, fol. 192ᵛ; J. E. Nieremberg, *Historia Naturae*, Antwerp, 1635, p. 269) and in current folk cures in America (Klauber, *op. cit.*, 2:879). The use of mud, and the burial of a victim up to his neck in a manure pile, are probably related (Klauber, 2:893–894). It is difficult for me to see how even the most obtuse can fail to recognize the use of feces as *anal magic*, that is, the anthropomorphic imputation to or projection onto snake-poisons of a human horror of feces; or, even more simply, the use of symbolic poison as an antidote to real poison—apotropaic (Harrison), talion (Freud), sympathetic (Frazer) magic! —all resting on a logic of the anal phase, with its feeble ego-boundaries and imperfect discrimination of self/not-self. Possibly the idea of poison against poison (or medicine power against medicine power) is behind the use of tobacco both by the Abipones of Paraguay and by other Americans (Klauber, 2:884); the same would appear to be true of the widespread use of alcohol as a snakebite remedy (Klauber, 2:885–889); or of kerosene (Klauber, 2:889–890). Salt has been a cure for snakebite since the days of ancient Rome (J. Bostock and H. T. Riley [eds.], *Pliny's Natural History*, 6 vols., London, 1855–1857, 5:497, 509 [= bk. xxxi, chs. 33, 45]) and recalls the famous essay by Ernest Jones (*Essays*, pp. 112–203) on the symbolic significance of salt in folklore; gunpowder, used either with salt or alone, is related in symbolism.

[103] The extensive folklore on this remedy is summarized in Klauber, *op. cit.*, 2:877–878.

[104] Klauber, *op. cit.*, 2:1218.

[105] Abundant references are found in Klauber, *op. cit.*: the accident in the buckboard (2:1253), disturbing a mating pair (2:1259), the vengeful mate (2:1244), Cherokee voyeurism and dreams (2:1161), "fascination" (2:1222), Maidu incest-punishment (2:1107), Cora charm and aphrodisiac (2:1106), Maya dream symbolism (2:1103), New England and Cherokee beliefs (2:1186). The Pacific king snake is the "rattlesnake pilot" — oddly, in view of its occasionally eating young rattlers — which commands and governs the rattlesnake and strikes it dead with a bone in its tail; this sounds a little

like a termagant wife. The pilot snake also warns of danger and guides the rattlesnake to its prey, which they then share; this legend fails to show how this sharing is possible for creatures that swallow their prey whole (2:1243).

[106] Hambly, *op. cit.*, p. 72.

[107] R. F. Fortune, *Omaha Secret Societies*, Columbia University Contributions to Anthropology, 14 (1932) 1–193, p. 137; M. E. Opler, "Japanese Folk Belief Concerning the Snake," *Southwestern Journal of Anthropology*, 1 (1945) 249–259. Opler actually tried to argue in this article that the snake is specifically not a phallic symbol in Japan! On this and other Japanese snake phallisms, see Weston La Barre, *The Human Animal*, Chicago, 1954, pp. 352–353 (Phoenix Books, 1960, pp. 365–366).

[108] Sandor Ferenczi, "The Adaptation of the Family to the Child," in *Final Contributions to the Problems and Methods of Psychoanalysis* [= *Selected Papers*, vol. III], New York, 61–76, pp. 70–71.

[109] Sandor Ferenczi, "The Problem of the Termination of the Analysis," *Further Contributions*, 77–86, p. 80.

[110] In the classification of these related types, the work of Dr. Richard L. Jenkins is of great value. See his papers on "The Psychopathic or Antisocial Personality," *Journal of Nervous and Mental Disease*, 131 (October 1960) 318–334; "The Psychopathic Delinquent," *Social Work in the Current Scene*, New York, 1950, 292–301; "Patterns of Maladjustment in Children" (with Maurice Lorr), *Journal of Clinical Psychology*, 9 (1953) 16–19; "Patterns of Personality Organization Among Delinquents" (with Sylvia Glickman), *The Nervous Child*, 6 (1947) 329–339; and "A Psychiatric View of Personality Structure in Children," *Delinquency and the Community in Wartime*, pp. 199–217 (1943 Yearbook, National Probation Association, New York). In the categories set up in this last paper, the snake cult would be classified as Dr. Jenkins's "pseudosocial" Type III, in which there is group conflict only with the larger outgroup society.

[111] Ernest Jones, *The Life and Work of Sigmund Freud*, 3 vols., New York, 1955, 2:371–372.

[112] William and Joan McCord, *Psychopathy and Delinquency*, New York, 1956, as cited in Jenkins's 1960 paper, p. 322.

[113] David M. Levy, "The Deprived and the Indulged Forms of Psychopathic Personality," *American Journal of Orthopsychiatry*, 21 (1951) 250–254, p. 252. Jenkins's characterizations are taken from his cited 1960 paper, pp. 319, 324. L. H. Bartemeier, "The Neurotic Character as a Psychoanalytic Concept," *American Journal of Orthopsychiatry*, 1 (1931) 512–520. In this vexed area of psychiatric taxonomy, I have found of great value a review of the concepts by H. F. Darling, "Definition of Psychopathic Personality," *Journal of Nervous and Mental Disease*, 101 (1945) 212–226; for a study of the psychopath in a wider, specialized setting, see W. H. Dunn, "The Psychopath in the Armed Forces," *Psychiatry*, 4 (1941) 251–259. Dr. Leo Kanner has offered a famous definition: "A psychopath is somebody you don't like" (R. L. Jenkins, "The Psychopathic or Antisocial Personality," *Journal of Nervous and Mental Disease*, 131 [October 1960] 318–334, p. 319). For persons professing to be unable to identify clinically the syndrome "psychopathy" the substitution of the new term "sociopath" is of no great help, and only a further ambiguity — for the schizophrenic (whom all can recognize) is also a "sociopath" in a basic sense, as are all psychotics and neurotics as well, in other senses. For this and other reasons I eschew the recent official

neologism in this study. The least we should expect of a new term is that it not further confuse the issues. I agree with Jenkins who states his "belief . . . that the term [psychopath] will survive. It has the important virtue that, as a result of long usage and much observation and argument it is now a realistically descriptive term based on experience, rather than a theoretical term based on a deduction from preconceived premises . . . Whether we retain the name or not, the concept of the psychopathic personality will remain with us, for it is founded in experience, and we need it." (Pp. 318–319.)

[114] Walter Bromberg, "The Psychopathic Personality Concept Re-Evaluated," *Archives of Criminal Psychodynamics*, Special Psychopathy Issue, 1961, 435–442, p. 438.

[115] Bromberg, *op. cit.*, p. 441.

[116] Carlos J. Dalmau, "Psychopathy and Psychopathic Behavior: A Psychoanalytic Approach," *Archives of Criminal Psychodynamics*, Special Psychopathy Issue, 1961, 443–455, pp. 444–447, 452–453.

[117] Dalmau, *op. cit.*, p. 448.

[118] Dalmau, *op. cit.*, pp. 447, 454.

[119] J. J. Michaels, *Disorders of Character*, Springfield, Illinois, 1955.

[120] For the classic studies of the urethral personality, see Karl Abraham, "Ejaculatio Praecox," *Selected Papers*, London, 1927, pp. 280–298; I. H. Coriat, "The Character Traits of Urethral Erotism," *Psychoanalytic Review*, 11 (1924) 426–434; Sigmund Freud, "Libidinal Types," *Collected Papers*, 5:247, and "The Acquisition of Fire," *Psychoanalytic Quarterly*, 1 (1932) 210; H. Flournoy, "Dreams and the Symbolism of Water and Fire," *International Journal of Psychoanalysis*, 1 (1920) 245–255; and J. Sadger, "Über Urethral-Erotik," *Jahrbuch für psychoanalytische und psychopathologische Forschungen*, 2 (1910) 409. J. J. Michaels is the foremost exponent today of this neglected area of research.

[121] Otto Fenichel, *The Psychoanalytic Theory of Neuroses*, New York, 1945, p. 378.

[122] Fenichel, *op. cit.*, p. 372.

[123] William F. Whyte, *Street Corner Society*, Chicago, 1943, p. 140, cited in I. Thorner, "Ascetic Protestantism, Gambling and the One-Price System," *American Journal of Economics and Sociology*, 15 (1956) 161–172.

[124] S. A. Szurek, "Notes on the Genesis of Psychopathic Personality Trends," *Psychiatry*, 5 (1942) 1–6.

[125] Talcott Parsons, "Certain Primary Sources and Patterns of Aggression in the Social Structure of the Western World," *Psychiatry*, 10 (1947) 167–181, pp. 171–172.

[126] Fenichel, *op. cit.*, p. 166.

[127] Weston La Barre, quoted in Michaels, *op. cit.*, p. 97.

[128] Sigmund Freud, *Group Psychology and the Analysis of the Ego*, London, 1922.

[129] George Devereux, "Charismatic Leadership and Crisis," *Psychoanalysis and the Social Sciences*, 4 (1955) 145–157.

[130] Sandor Ferenczi, *Final Contributions*, p. 141. See also Frieda Fromm-Reichmann, "Psychoanalytic Psychotherapy With Psychotics," *Psychiatry*, 6 (1943) 277–279, p. 278; and Albert Lynch, "The Influence of Certain Cultural Factors in a Segment of the Patient Population of the University of North Carolina Memorial Hospital Psychiatric Center," paper delivered at

the 33rd Annual Meeting, American Orthopsychiatric Association, Chicago, March 13, 1957.

[131] Devereux, *op. cit.*, pp. 147–148. The process Devereux describes is analogous to the decompensation under stress which Selye has described in physiological terms.

[132] Marian Anderson, *Saturday Review*, March 24, 1956, p. 29.

Index

Aaron as snake shaman, 59, 82n, 97

Abraham, Karl, quoted on snake symbolism, 192

Adam and Eve, 55, 76–78, 84, 139

Africa, immortality legends in, 54

African snake symbolism, 63–64

Alabama, cult meetings in, 44, 46

Alcoholism, 147

Alexander, fathered by snake, 72

Amos v, 19, cited, 84

Anal symbolism and snakes, 195

Ananikian, M. H., quoted on feeding milk to snake-ancestor, 186

Anderson, Marian, quoted on music, 174

Aphrodisiacs, use of rattles and venom by Cora Indians, 104

Arnobius, quoted on phallic images in Arretophoria, 71

Arrow as phallic symbol, 76

Asklepios as snake, 70, 190

Associated Press: first publicity by, 13; at Dolley Pond meeting, 26–27; quoted on "King of North Carolina," 184

Bacchanalian rites, 71–73

Baptists, Southern Missionary: Barefoot's mother member of, 114–115; Barefoot breaks away from, 118; Barefoot destined to be minister of, 126; in Barefoot's family, 128

Bartemeier, Leo, quoted on psychopathy, 142

Barton, G. A., quoted on Kentucky revival, 30; quoted on Stone Age circumsion, 81

Bennett, W., quoted on Tarahumara snakes milking cows, 95; quoted on Tarahumara snake beliefs, 101

Bible, 9, 37; no text on neckties, 16; on wickedness in cities, 16; does not mention Coca-Cola, 17

Blood, menstrual, irritates snakes, 102–103

Blowtorch: in Tennessee, 14; in Kentucky meetings, 47; not necessarily dangerous, 183–184

Body as phallus, 75–76

Body-image symbolizing, 62, 75–76; snake and, 89–109; among Huichol, 193

Book of Discipline, 30, 173

Bosman, quoted on Dahomeyan snake god, 60

Brazen serpent, 83

Brinton, D. G., quoted on Algonkian immortal lightning-rain snake, 98

Bristol (Tenn.-Va.) *Herald and Courier*, quoted on Virginia cultists, 45

Bromberg, Walter, quoted on psychopathy, 143–144

Browning, J. D., re-introduces snake-handling at Pine Mountain, 12

Bruton, Wade, assistant attorney general of N.C., quoted on Bunn trial, 41, 43

Budge, E. A. W., quoted on Babylonian caduceus, 82n

Bullfight, 68, 186

Bull god, 68; in Greece and Asia Minor, 60n; rain giver in Egypt, Mesopotamia, and India, 67; and Mosaic Jahweh, 82n; eating and immortality, 89; Greek drinking blood of, 185; slaughtered in Zeus-Zagreus-Dionysus Orphic cults, 191

Bunn, Rev. Colonel Hartman: indicted under ordinance against snake-handling, 34; announces interstate conference to Durham press, 35; on coming services, 35; on interstate conference, 35; on MacArthur, 38; on mocking the law, 39; on resisting police, 39–40; argues own case in N.C. state supreme court, 41; escapes police, 41; on regulating snake-handling, 41, 42–43; on snakebites, 41–42; on snake-handling doctrine, 41–42; quoted on city council, 42n; on money, 43; on sinner-men, 43; sentence executed, 43; reappears in Durham after serving sentence, 44; police-baiting on radio program, 123n; thinks minister can perform own marriages, 135; litigation in N.C. courts, 172

Burnett, Hamilton S., judge of Tenn. court of appeals, quoted on insurance death, 26

California: as a center of cults, 31; aged woman bitten in Long Beach meeting, 46; snake dances among Indian tribes of, 107n

Cataplexia of snakes, 19–20, 23, 186–187

Cavaliers, 163

Chapel Hill, N.C.: hill woman in, 17; Scotch-Irish intellectual traditions in, 36n

Charming of snakes, 14n, 21, 83, 106, 190

Chattanooga: first publicity in newspapers of, 24; meetings and legal difficulties of cult in, 24–25; visitors at Dolley Pond meetings from, 26–27; plainclothesmen from, 28; first cult evangelism in, 33

Cherokee: not source of cult, 31–32; rainsnake of, 99; seer of rattlesnake

and photophobia or death among, 104; snake-eating by ball players among, 104; snake dances of, 107n; Barefoot allegedly speaks in, 120

Children: care of, 18; rattlesnakes do not bite, 103

Christmas neurosis, 119, 127

Church: buildings, 12, 16; names, 15, 25, 49, 50, 184

Church of God: Hensley takes cult to Pine Mountain, 12; origin of, 184

Circumcision and snake symbolism, 78–84; Hebrew, 107

Cobra, venom-spitting by, 104

Coca-Cola schism, 17

Coitus in Tanganyika snake cult, 190

Coitus-death fantasy, 62, 79–80, 101n

Collins, J. B., quoted on Harden and Chattanooga visitors, 26–27

Color change by snakes, legends of, 93, 101–102

Constitution of the U.S., 133, 134, 135

Copperhead, danger of, 14n

I Corinthians: x, 9, quoted on tempting Christ, 11n; xiv, 26, cited, 185

II Corinthians xi, 3, cited, 84

Cory, H., quoted on Tanganyika phallic snake cult, 190

Covington, Mansel, recovers from snakebite, 48

Craig, Mrs. Ruth, dies of rattlesnake bite, 44–45

Cretan snake-goddess, 94–95

Crooke, William, quoted on St. Gugga or Zahir Pir, 97

Dalmau, C. J., quoted on psychopathy, 144–145, 146

Dance: with snakes in cult meetings, 9; of two snakes, 71n; with snakes, among American Indians, 106–107n

Daniel iii, 25, cited, 183

Davis, Ernest, dies from drinking salvation cocktail, 28–29

Day, John, brings suit against cultists, 13

Death from poison-drinking, 28–29, 45, 185

Death from snakebite: rarity of, 13n, 20, 188; of Ford, 23–24, 25–26; of Jackson, 25; of Alabama man, 46;

of Ramsey, 46; of Valentine, 47; of Yost, 48; of Hensley, 48–49; of Hall, 49; of Elkins, 50

Defries, Garland, bitten in meeting but recovers, 12, 15, 187

de Groot, J. J. M., quoted on Chinese snake stories, 74

Desegregation in N.C., 36n

Deuteronomy: VIII, 15, cited, 59n; XXXII, 24, cited, 84

Devereux, George: cited, 159; quoted on crisis cults, 170–171

Diffusion of snake-handling: in Chattanooga, 25–28; begins in Southeast, 28; from Tennessee to Florida, 32–33; from Tennessee and Alabama to Georgia, 46–47

Dionysian mysteries, 68, 72, 73–74, 89, 185, 191

Dionysus: and snakes, 70, 72; and immortality, 86

Divine king, 66. *See also* Rain king

Dodds, E. R., quoted on Greek snake-handling, 72, 72n

Dolley Pond Church of God With Signs Following: founded in *1943*, 15–16; meetings at, described, 17–24; communicants cited under Tenn. state law, 26–27; evangelizes Chattanooga, 33

Dragon: Lettish, 93; wealth-guarding, 192

Dreams of snakes, 63, 104, 192

Drinking, attitudes toward, 16–17

Duke Law School mock trial of snake-handlers, 39n

Duke University, desegregation of Graduate School, 36n

Durham, N.C.: tobacco-auction time in, 17; African dialect, 19; tobacco-barn radio singers, 19; snake-handling grafted onto earlier cult, 32; city ordinance against snake-handling, 34, 42, 42n; interstate conference in, 34ff; snake-handling comes to, 34; desegregation in, 36n

Ecclesiastes x, 10, quoted on snake-charming and speaking in tongues, 11n

Egypt: and snake symbolism, 64; as center of phallic snake symbolism, 66–67; reincarnation in, 67

Einhorn, Paul, quoted on Lettish house dragon, 93

Eleusinian mysteries and snakes, 73–74

Elkins, Mrs. Robert, fatally bitten in W.Va. meeting, 50

Estep, James, bitten in Ky. meeting 49

Eucharist, 68, 87, 185

Fabricius, quoted on Lettish house dragon, 93

Faith healing, 9–10, 13, 19, 39, 123

Faith Tabernacle, Lafollette, Tenn., offered cultists under Morris plan, 25

Fascination, in snakes, 104. *See also* Charming of snakes

Fatal Boot, legend of, 101n

Fatherhood by snakes, 72, 191

Feathers as snake attribute, 61–62

Fenichel, Otto: on gambling, 147–148. quoted on psychopathic superego. 154–155

Ferenczi, Sandor: cited on hypocrisy, 131–132; cited on lying and morality, 132; cited on autoplastic and allo-plastic distortions, 141; quoted on hysteria as archaic neurosis, 160

Ferguson, J., quoted on snakes' immortality, 78

Fiery serpent of Bible, 104

Fire: handling of, 14, 21–22, 35, 47, 101, 183–184; and urethral personality, 146

Fish as phallic symbol, 75

Florida: as a center of aberrant cults, 31; diffusion of cult to, 33; free laying on of hands in, 38n; meetings moved from Ga. to, 49; Barefoot grows up in, 113–114

Fluoridation, 167n

Flying snakes, 83, 95, 95n

Ford, Lewis F.: death from snakebite, 23, 187; first publicity to cult, 24; death held not accidental, 25–26; widow not entitled to double indemnity, 26

Fox, George, and Ranters, 30

Frazer, Sir James George: quoted on Cherokee attitudes toward snakes, 31–32; cited on sympathetic magic, 195

Freud, Sigmund: on Moses as an Egyptian, 82n; on man with sense of mission, 126; on Shakespeare's Richard III, 138; on unanalyzable types, 138; on hysteria as obverse of perversion, 159; on talion, 195; on libidinal types, 197

Friess, H. L., quoted on itinerant ministers of early Methodism, 32

Funeral services, 23, 47, 48–49

Gambling, 147–149; and psychopathy, 156–158

Garden of Eden legend, 55, 77–78, 139; as allegory on individual maturation, 86–87

Genesis as etiological myth of man, 86–87

Genesis: II, 16–17, on Adam and Eve, 77; II, 25–III, 5, Eve's temptation, 76; II, 14–15, serpent's punishment, 77; III, 19, Adam and Eve's punishment, 78; III, 22–23, expulsion from Eden, 85–86

Georgia: troubles of snake-handlers in, 5; cult meetings in, 28, 29n, 46; diffusion of cult to, 28, 33; bus segregation in, 36n; law against snake-handling, 46; meetings moved from, 49; birth of Barefoot in, 114; Barefoot preaches in towns of, 120–121

Grasshopper Valley, Tenn.: origin of cult in, 11–12, 32; snake-handling revived in, 15

Greek: snake deities, 69–74, 83; snakes as immortal, 78; gods and immorality, 88; drinking bull blood, 185; snake cults, 191

Haeberlin, H. K., quoted on Hopi snake-phallus-arrow-lightning symbolism, 100–101

Hair: as snake attribute, 61–62; growth stimulated by rattlesnake oil, 62

Hall, Mrs. Sally, fatally bitten in W.Va. meeting, 49

Hambly, W. D.: on snake worship in Africa, 59; on python worship and rainbow snakes, 60; on Abyssinian snake antidote, 62; on African snake beliefs, 63; on fertility and reincarnation concepts in Africa, 63; on snake beliefs of Ibo, 63; on venom-spitting by cobras, 104; on Budu snake priest, 186

Harden, Tom: bitten by snake, 15, 187; leader in 1940's, 15; arrested in Chattanooga, 24; frustrates reporters, 26–27; police-baiting by, 123

Harrison, Jane Ellen: on Crecrops as year daimon, 69; on mana of snake among Greeks, 69; on Hermes as phallus and snake, 70; on Greek bull sacrifice, 185; on Asklepios as snake, 190

Hays, Raymond: brings cult again to Grasshopper Valley, 15; handles two snakes at Dolley Pond, 21; uses blowtorch in meetings, 47

Hebrew snake symbolism, 76–83; cults, 107

Henotheism and snake god, 58–59, 60, 83, 85

Hensley, George Went: founds cult, 11–12; becomes pastor of East Pineville Church of God, 12; takes cult to Ky., 12; present at meeting, 14; keeps cult alive in Ky., 15; mode of handling snakes by, 21; arrested in Chattanooga, 24; appeals conviction, 25; cult prophet, 31; preaches from Tenn. to Fla., 32; legal troubles in Tenn. and diffusion of cult, 33; allegedly bitten four hundred times, 45–46; death of, 48–49, 187; widow of founder quoted, 49; teaches snake-handling to Barefoot's teacher, 121; historic background of his ministry, 291

Hermes: as snake, 70; as moon god, 189

High god as snake, 58–59, 60, 83, 85

Higher Criticism, 11

Hindu, rain serpent, 100. See also India

Holiness Church, offshoot of Methodism, 29, 32

Holy kiss, 13, 18, 136
Hopi: not source of cult, 31; rain snake as phallus, 92; snake-phallus-arrow-lightning symbolism, 100; snake dance of, 106n
Huichol: believe lightning and fire are snakes, 100; snake symbolism of, 106n; phallic symbolism of, 193
Hutton, Oscar: and diffusion of snake-handling, 32; at Durham conference, 35; preaches in Va. and Ky., 35; handles snakes in Durham, 36–37; describes persecution in Tenn. and N.C., 38, 172; criticizes fellow minister, 47
Hypocrisy: college student's sense of, 131n; Ferenczi on child's sense of, 131–132
Hysteria: denial as defense mechanism in, 65–66, 160–161

Immortality: man's loss of, 55, 78; and snakes, 77–85, 192; among Greeks, 88–89; and eating, 95n
India: snake gods, 61; snake symbolism, 64; as center of snake species, 68; snake as *genius loci*, 192
Interstate conference of snake-handling cult, 34ff
Isaiah: xiv, 29, quoted on Nehushtan's destruction, 83; cited, 59n; xxvii, 1, quoted on Leviathan, 83; xxx, 6, cited 59n, 89; xliii, 2 and lxv, 25, cited, 83

Jackson, Clint: dies of snakebite, 25, 187
James iii, 7–8, quoted on poison tongue, 84
Japanese: legend of vagina-seeking snake, 105; and Barefoot's brother, 117; snake symbolism, 196
Jenkins, R. L.: cited on psychopathy, 142, 143, 196; quoted on term psychopath, 197
Jeremiah: viii, 17, quoted on Lord's threat to punish with serpents, 83; xlvi, 22; cited, 84
Jesus: St. Paul on, 11; words at Pentecost, 11; no proof ever wore necktie, 16; arrested for preaching, 37;

advises disciples to be wise as serpents, 59n; quoted on generation of vipers, 84; his supernatural gifts, 173
John iii, 14–15, quoted on worship of serpent and of Jesus, 84
John the Baptist, bearded cultist in N.C., 38n
Jones, Ernest, quoted on unanalyzable types, 138
Joshua and origin of circumcision 80–81
Jung, C. G., cited, 54, 61, 76, 186

Kanner, Leo: quoted on psychopaths, 196
Kentucky: Hensley takes cult to 12; first legal action against cult in, 13; cult kept alive in, 15; more snake-handling in, 32; Hutton preaches in, 35; visiting cultists in Durham, 35; Fundamentalism and laying on of hands, 38n; state law against snake-handling, 42, 44, 47; meetings in, 47; belief rattles aid childbirth, 102
Kerman, Keith, quoted on bodily movements of cultists, 14
Kiss, Holy, 13, 18, 136
II Kings: xviii, 4, cited, 59n; xviii, 11, cited, 83
Klauber, L. M.: quoted on fatalities from snakebite, 14n; on curing snakebite by biting snake, 97; on originality of shamans, 97n; on saliva as snake poison, 98, 102; on rattlesnakes' not biting children, 103; on snakes and milk, 193
Knives as phallic symbols, 76
Knowledge, 86, 89
Krishna: bull god avatar of Vishnu, 68; exploits with snakes and other animals, 105

La Barre, Weston, quoted on psychopathy, 155
Lawrence, Col. T. E., 158n
Laws against snake-handling, 5, 9, 13, 24–25, 33, 34, 42, 44, 46
Lehrberger, Mrs. Henry, biographer of Beauregard Barefoot, 114n, 179
Lettish house dragon, 93, 101

Levy, David M., quoted on psychopathy, 142
Lightning and snakes, 98–101
Los Angeles, snake cult in, 31
Lucian, scholiast on, quoted on phallic images, 71
Luke: x, 18, quoted on power over serpents, 147n; xi, 11, cited, 84
Lumholtz, Carl: on Sonoran snake suckling, 95; on Huichol snake symbolisms, 193

MacArthur, General Douglas: assimilated to Rev. Colonel H. Bunn, 38
McCord, Joan and William, quoted on psychopathy, 141–142
MacCulloch, J. A., quoted on Dionysian and Eleusinian mysteries, 73–74; on snake suckling, 96
McGready, James, and Ky. revival, 30
Mark: xvi, 17, cited, 15; xvi, 17–18, quoted on Biblical basis of cult, 11; xvi, 18, cited, 17; xvi, 18, quoted, 185, cited, 186
Marriage, minister may perform own, 8, 53
Maryon, Herbert, quoted on Cretan snake goddess, 70
Massey, Benjamin R.: brings snake-handling to Durham, N.C., 34; convicted of snake-handling, 41; serves time on roads, 42n
Mating, disturbance of snakes in, brings death, 103
Matthew: vii, 9–10, cited, 84; x, 16, cited, 59; xxiii, 33, cited, 84
Medusa legends, 101, 189
Meetings, visiting at, 18
Meigs, P., quoted on Kiliwa shamans, 97n
Menses and snakes, 62, 102–103, 189
Methodism: American, 29; and circuit riders, 32
Micah vii, 17, cited, 84
Michaels, J. J., cited on psychopathy, 146
Milk: fed to snakes, 23; offered to Masai snake-husband, 63, 90; snakes as sucklings, 94–96; belief that snakes like, 186; not drunk by snakes, 193

Mill workers in South, 164–169
Miller, Gordon: cult leader in Ga., 28; is not Barefoot, 29n
Moccasin, danger of, 14n
Moon and snakes, 189. See also Menses and snakes
Morris, C. D., offers Faith Tabernacle to cultists, 25
Moses: snake shaman, 59, 82n, 83; and circumcision, 80–83; and serpent in wilderness, 84; staff paralleled in America, 97; Barefoot as modern, 175
Movies, 166–167n, 168, 174
Murray, Sir Gilbert: on Zeus as bearded snake, 61, 74; on Greek bull-blood drinking, 185
Music in meetings, 10, 13, 14, 18, 28, 122
Mysteries: Dionysian, 68, 72, 73–74, 89, 185, 191; Eleusinian, 73–74

Nashville, Tenn., Grand Ole Opry in, 19
Neanderthals and immortality, 79. See also Old Stone Age
Negro: present in meetings, 4, 40; in Durham conference, 36, 36n; belief rattles aid childbirth, 102; outdoor jobs of, 166; oppression of, 168; church names, 184. See also Desegregation
Neolithic rain bull, 68
New Testament snake symbolism, 84–87
New York as early center of aberrant cults, 31
North Carolina: troubles of snake-handlers in, 5; diffusion of cult to, 33; claims moral leadership in South, 36n; desegregation in, 36n; free laying on of hands in, 38n; Cherokee of, 120
Numbers: xxi, 8, cited, 59n; xxii, 6–9, quoted on fiery serpents and Nehushtan in wilderness, 82–83

Oak, its acorns as phallic symbols, 75
Odor, alleged, of snakes, 103
Oedipus, Krishna as, 105
Old Stone Age: time-depth of snake

symbolism, 67–68; hunting cults, 76; and circumcision, 83; snake god, 83

Old Testament: snake symbolism, 76–86; as protest of rural folk, 163

Olmsted, F. L., quoted on early American preaching, 6n

Ophites, Gnostic snake worshipers, 67

Oral-biting talion legends, 97–98, 193–194

Oral pregnancy legend, 97

Oral symbolism and snakes, 94–98

Origin of Death legends: African, 55–58; Semitic, 76–81

Orpheus, 68, 74, 191; decapitated head and snake head, 78n; and immortality, 86

Osiris as snake, 67

Parallel evolution in culture, 74–75

Paranoia, 172

Parsons, Talcott, quoted on masculine protest in American boys, 153–154

Pentecostal Church: offshoot of Methodism, 29, 173; snake-handling grafted onto, 32, 173

Perkins, C. B., quoted on inability of snakes to hold milk, 193

Phallic snake, 60, 60n, 63–64, 66, 192–193; cults, 63, 190; and fatherhood, 74. *See also* Mysteries; Snake

Phallic symbolism: of snake in Africa, 65, 190; from nature, 75–76; Huichol, 193

Phallus, Hermes as, 70–71

Pharaoh: as rain king, 59; asks miracles of Moses and Aaron, 81–82

Physiologus, 191

Pine Mountain Church, meetings at, publicized, 13

Pit vipers, heat sense of, 21, 106

Plantationism in South, 162

Plenderleith, H. J., quoted on Cretan snake goddess, 70

Poison-drinking, 22, 40, 98; death from, 28; in Tenn., 33; police chief says no ordinance against, 35–36; promised at Durham conference, 35; interpreted, 108; in classic times, 185

Police: arrest Harden, 24; baiting of, 26–27, 35, 38, 39, 40, 48, 156; in Tenn., 26f; relations with cultists, 26–28; act against Durham cultists, 34–37, 39–41; seize copperheads at Zion Tabernacle, 34; raid Zion Tabernacle, 36–37, 40–41; Bunn offers to kiss, 37; ignore snake-handling meetings, 39; search for Bunn, 40–41; arrest Ala. preacher, 46; arrest Rev. Vernon and discover hidden snake box, 47; arrest Covington, 48; raid Ky. meetings, 49

Preaching, 6n, 19, 30

Pregnancy and snakes, 102–103

Primal-scene fantasy, 93

Prohibitions among snake-handlers, 13, 16–17

Projection as defense mechanism, 169–170. *See also* Hysteria; Paranoia

Protestant ethic and gambling, 148n–149n, 149

Proverbs: xxiii, 31–33, xxx, 18–19, 84

Psalms: lviii, 4, cited, 14n; cxl, 3, cited, 84

Psychokinesis, 39n, 136

Psychopath, 137–139, 140ff

Quakers: in Piedmont, 29, 36; and Ranters, 30; and snake cultists, 31

Rain and snakes, 60n, 89–90, 98–101

Rain dances, 99–100

Rain king: Moses as, 59; in Africa, 60, 67, 82n

Rain snake: in Old and New Worlds, 60n; in America, 66, 98–101; symbolic meaning of, 89–90; in Africa, 190

Ramsey, Reece, fatally bitten in Ala. meeting, 46

Ranters: in England, 30, 31; in America, 174

Rattlesnake: diamondback, 13n–14n; god of American Indians, 61; legendary preferences of, in biting, 103

Reinach, Salomon, quoted on speaking in tongues, 185

Return of the repressed, 66, 175

Revelation: ix, 19, quoted on serpentlike angels, 85; xii, 9 and xx, 2, quoted on the Devil as a serpent, 84

Rhine, J. B., his investigators of PK

phenomenon visit snake-handling meetings, 39n

Richard III, Freud on Shakespeare's, 138

Robertson, Archie, quoted on death from snakebite, 188

Rolker, A. W., quoted on rattlesnake's alleged suicide, 98

Roman Catholicism and gambling, 148

Roman *genius lectualis* snakes, 192

Roundheads, 163

Russian roulette, 147n

St. Paul: quoted on tempting Christ, 11; his eschewing Gentile circumcision requires Christ, 80; cited, 84, 185

St. Peter, conducts Alberico through hell, 96, 186

Saints (snake-handling cultists), 13, 183, 186

Salt symbolism in folklore, 195

Samson and Delilah song, 8, 53

Schizophrenia, 140

Schizophrenic influencing machine, 190

Schneider, H. W., quoted on itinerant ministers in early Methodism, 32

Schwarz, Berthold, quoted on cataplexia, 20; on holy kiss, 183; on fire-handling, 183–184; on death of snakes, 186–187; on rarity of snakebite, 188

Scorpions and snakes, 62, 94, 147n

Scottish-Irish revival in Ky., 30

Selten, Charles, quoted on snakes' immortality by shedding skin, 70

Semitisms in Africa, 57, 59, 60, 64, 82n

Serpent, brazen, 59

Serpent, fiery, 82. *See also* Snake

Shiva, phallic god of India, 60, 68, 90

Shoupe, Preacher, holds services under Morris plan, 25

Singing by cultists, 14, 18–19, 46

Sinner-men, snakes caught by, 13, 23n, 187

Smith, Homer W., quoted on Alberico's visit to hell, 96, 186

Snake: symbolism in Old World, 54ff; as phallus, 54, 63–65, 103, 192–193; becomes immortal by eating fruit of Tree, 55; henotheized older god, 58–59; as high god, 58, 60, 85; as familiar of medicine men, 59, 83; as projection of body image, 108. *See also* Body-image symbolizing; Phallic snake; Snakes

Snake charming, 14n, 83, 106; in India and America, 21; in Africa, 190

Snake dances among American Indians, 106n–107n

Snake fatherhood, 63, 72, 74, 191

Snake gods: Greek, 58, 61, 69–74, 189, 190; Hebrew and others, 107

Snake-husband, 60, 63, 72, 90, 105, 186, 191

Snake-handlers: bodily movements of, 6–7, 8–10, 13, 14, 18, 20, 36, 37–38, 53; racial ideas of, 7; prohibitions among, 13, 17; dress of, 16

Snake-handling: laws against, 5, 9, 13, 24–25, 33, 34, 42, 44, 46; city ordinance against, 9; injunctions against ancient, 11n; origins of, 11ff; origin of, in Barefoot's church, 121

Snake-swallowing, 97

Snakebite: suffered fatally by individuals, 12, 13n–14n, 15, 23–24, 44–45, 45, 46, 47, 48, 48–49, 49, 50; danger of, minimized, 13–14n; rarity of, 20; deaths from, 23; number suffered by individuals, 40, 45–46, 188; salt as cure for, 195

Snakes: condition, 7, 14n; attitudes of cultists towards, 7–8, 19; caught by unbelievers, 13, 22, 23n; sickness in, 13; methods of handling, in meetings, 13, 19–21; deafness in, 14n; no "doctoring" of, 14n; taming of, 14n; fragility of, 14n, 78n, 187; handling disturbs reflexes of, 19, 20; cataplexia of, 19–20, 23, 186–187; care of, 22–23; milk and, 23, 94–96, 193; death of, in meetings, 23, 186–187; police killing of, 28; tumescence alleged of, 59, 60, 63, 90, 101–102, 106; scorpions and, 62, 94, 147n; dreams of, 63, 104, 192; dance of two, 71n; longevity of, 78n;

skin-casting and immortality, 78–80, 84, 98, 192; tenacity of life in, 78n; as wicked, 83–84; legends about swallowing young, 96n; urethral symbolism of, 98; lightning and, 98–101; as uncanny creatures, 105–106, 107; anal symbolism and, 195

South, local autonomy in, 25n

South Carolina, John Wesley leaves, 29

Southern writers, 167n–168n

Speaking in tongues, 7, 11n, 12–13, 38n, 39, 120, 123, 184–185, 186

Spence, L., quoted on American Indian snake symbolism, 98

Stalker, James, quoted on Ky. revival, 30

Strychnine-drinking, 22, 40, 185

Supreme Court of the U.S., refuses review of N.C. supreme court decision, 42

Symbolism, nature of, 66, 90–93

Szurek, S. A., quoted on unconscious parental encouragement of psychopathy, 151

Talayesva, D. C. (Sun Chief), quoted on Hopi snakes and water, 99

Tantalus and immortality by eating, 88–89

Tarahumara: snake symbolism of, 101, 106n; belief in poison-ejaculating snakes, 104

Tennessee: persecution of cultists in, 5, 25–28; Hensley leaves, after Defries' accident, 15; meeting near Daisy, 25, 26; state law against snake-handling, 26, 42, 44; origin of cult in, 31, 32; meeting in Kingsport, 33; cultists at Durham conference, 35; Fundamentalism and laying on of hands, 38n; lay preacher from, bitten fatally in Ga. meeting, 46; fatal snakebite in meeting, 48

Thumb as phallic symbol, 76

Titans, totemic ritual of, 191

Tobacco Road, 17

Tomlinson, A. J.: snake-handler in Cherokee, N.C., 31, 32; founder of the Church of God, 184

Tomlinson, Homer A., Bishop of Church of God and "King of North Carolina," 184

Totemism, 67, 186, 191

Tree of Knowledge, 86

Trophies, 88

Tumescence, alleged of snakes, 59, 60, 63, 101–102, 106

Unknown tongues. *See* Speaking in tongues

Urethral personality traits, 197

Urethral symbolism, 100; of snakes, 98

Vagina dentata legend, 101n

Valentine, Rev. Lee, fatally bitten in Ala. meeting, 47

Vernon, Rev. William, arrested in Ky., 47

Virginia: troubles of snake-handlers in, 5; John Wesley in, 29; diffusion of cult to, 33; Hutton preaches in, 35; cultists believe bites test power, 41; state law against snake-handling, 42, 44, 45

Wade, P. M., coroner of Hardin Co., Ky., quoted on Covington's arrest, 48

Watt, G., quoted on snake species in India, 68

Weber, Max, on Protestant ethic and gambling, 149n

Welsford, Enid, quoted on Lettish house dragon, 93

Wesley, John and Charles, spread Methodism in South, 29

West Virginia: visiting cultists at Durham conference, 35; state law against snake-handling proposed, 50

Whyte, W. F., quoted on Roman Catholic and Protestant gambling attitudes, 149

Wood, tumescent at snakebite, 102

Yost, Mrs. Anna Marie Covington, fatally bitten in Tenn. meeting, 48

Zeus: and chthonic snakes, 58; as Meilichios, 61; as snake, 73–75

Zingg, R. M.: quoted on Tarahumara snakes milking cows, 95; on Tarahumara snake beliefs, 101

Zion Tabernacle: meeting place of snake-handlers, 3; snake-handling comes to, 34; *Life* magazine at, 35; raided by police, 36–37, 40–41; newsreels taken at, 39; inadequately rural for news photographers, 40; Bunn reappears at, 44